THE P[illegible] TO DOCU[illegible]TARY EDITING

The Practical Guide to Documentary Editing sets out the techniques, the systems and the craft required to edit compelling professional documentary television and film. Working stage by stage through the postproduction process, author Sam Billinge explores project organisation, assembling rushes, sequence editing, story structure, music and sound design and the defining relationship between editor and director.

Written by a working documentary editor with over a decade's experience cutting films for major British and international broadcasters, *The Practical Guide to Documentary Editing* offers a unique introduction to the craft of documentary editing, and provides working and aspiring filmmakers with the tools to master the art.

Sam Billinge is a documentary editor with more than a decade's worth of experience editing prime-time documentaries for British and international television.

THE PRACTICAL GUIDE TO DOCUMENTARY EDITING

Techniques for TV & Film

SAM BILLINGE, GBFTE

Routledge
Taylor & Francis Group
NEW YORK AND LONDON

First published 2017
by Routledge
711 Third Avenue, New York, NY 10017

and by Routledge
2 Park Square, Milton Park, Abingdon, Oxon OX14 4RN

Routledge is an imprint of the Taylor & Francis Group, an informa business

Library of Congress Cataloging-in-Publication Data
Names: Billinge, Sam author.
Title: The practical guide to documentary editing : techniques for TV & film / Sam Billinge.
Description: New York : Routledge, 2017. | Includes bibliographical references and index.
Identifiers: LCCN 2016050964 (print) | LCCN 2017010112 (ebook) | ISBN 9781138292185 (hardback) | ISBN 9781138292192 (pbk.) | ISBN 9781315233123 (e-book)
Subjects: LCSH: Motion pictures—Editing. | Television programs—Editing. | Documentary films—Production and direction. | Documentary television programs—Production and direction.
Classification: LCC TR899 .B53 2017 (print) | LCC TR899 (ebook) | DDC 777/.55—dc23
LC record available at https://lccn.loc.gov/2016050964

ISBN: 978-1-138-29218-5 (hbk)
ISBN: 978-1-138-29219-2 (pbk)
ISBN: 978-1-315-23312-3 (ebk)

Typeset in Joanna MT
by Apex CoVantage, LLC

For my beautiful girls
Louise, Xanthe & Cora

CONTENTS

ACKNOWLEDGEMENTS

The creation of this book required the guidance, support and time of many people without whom it would not have been possible.

First, I would like to express my deepest gratitude to Dr. Catherine Elliott, Martin Johnson, Laura Kissel and Jason Osder for taking the time to read the manuscript and providing me with their expert feedback, as well as Simon Jacobs and John Makowski at Taylor & Francis Publishing.

In addition, I would like to thank Charles Miller, David Stewart and Matthew Cracknell for their friendship and counsel. Their thoughtful comments are greatly valued.

I would also like to thank Leon Ockenden and Vanessa Hehir for their friendship and help with the photographs.

Thanks also to John Lester for helping me to discover editing when I was fourteen years old and John Simpson CBE who helped me to find my first TV job.

I would like to give a special thanks to Penny Palmer and Peter Leonard. When I was a junior editor they gave me the chance to cut their films when they didn't have to.

Finally, I would like to thank my family for their support and love. In particular, my father Dr. Mark Billinge for his encouragement and assistance while writing the book, and for always helping me with my homework.

Above all, my wife Louise and our children Xanthe and Cora. I love you all.

INTRODUCTION

I was thirteen when I discovered skateboarding.

I spent every moment I could cruising the streets of Cambridge, in thrall to a counterculture that I had discovered by watching Californian VHS cassette tapes. The energy of these films, their beautiful pictures and soundtrack inspired me. I decided there and then that I wanted to make my own skateboard videos: a decision that soon led me to discover editing. I spent some years shooting and editing my own skateboard films and then selling the cassette tapes in local shops. I enjoyed all of the stages of production, but I knew immediately that I liked editing the most. For me, editing was the most critical aspect of the production process; the defining practice which gave films their feeling, energy and impact.

Eventually I found myself working as a runner for a television facility in West London. Whilst I had edited some basic films of my own, I lacked the experience and confidence to take editing to the next level. I had a clear idea of the kind of films I wanted to edit next, though I did not yet possess the skills to edit them effectively.

Nonetheless, I was keen to learn and set about reading and watching all I could. However, I was surprised to discover that there was almost nothing available that really explained and guided me through the editing process. There were a few books and videos that touched on aspects of the craft, though they tended to focus more on anecdotal tales rather than offering any real educational pathway. The most significant advances I made came from my own trial and error, and luckily, a great many hours spent interrogating experienced professional editors.

Once I grasped the basic principles of editing and, later, some of the more advanced practices, I was able to develop my own project frameworks and build up the confidence to find my own personal voice and style. I have spent the years since then editing a diverse range of prime-time television documentaries for large international broadcasters, and I have remained consistently employed as a documentary editor. Over time, I have honed my skills and made them a part of my daily practice, honing them to the point where they are wholly intuitive. Then—suddenly—something rather startling occurred to me.

I realised that many of the skills practised by the expert film editor are treated as rather closely guarded secrets, perhaps because many professionals simply do not want to spread the craft too widely and so encourage competition for themselves. Alternatively, many editors would maintain that editing cannot really be 'taught' at all, arguing that the skill can only be acquired through practical experience and, still more importantly, from basic intuition. I agree, of course, that—as with anything in life—experience is important. However, I also believe that many of the skills required are simply 'knacks' that can be taught and learned with relative ease. For this reason, I suggest that the *real secret* is practice, patience and an unwavering commitment to the task.

As a result, I have written this book to help those who find themselves where I was early in my career: hungry to learn the skills at the heart of documentary editing, yet unsure where to find them. *The Practical Guide to Documentary Editing* draws on everything I have learnt directly through my experience as a professional editor, as well as those aspects of the craft I have learnt through discussion with many other successful (and consistently employed!) documentary filmmakers. I will attempt to explain in simple, practical terms everything I have learnt, every mistake I have made, and every technique that has helped me to improve.

This book provides the reader with a comprehensive overview of the techniques, knowledge and logistical methods essential to the professional documentary editor. It will guide you through the essential steps of project organisation, selecting shots, ordering sequences, as well as working with sound effects (otherwise referred to as sound design) and music. Equally important, it will describe and help you to understand the nature of the close relationship that exists in the edit suite between the director and editor. It is my hope that, after reading this book and applying its principles through assiduous practice, you will be ready to face any project which comes your way: crafting compelling, cohesive and clear stories from disparate materials, whilst working harmoniously, to time and budget.

While I do not claim to have addressed every issue you are likely to encounter (and therefore to have provided *all* of the answers), I have produced this book with the intention of making it the most complete and comprehensive guide to documentary film editing yet written.

I hope this book will be of value to both the fledgling and the experienced film editor. Since editing is a core skill, I hope it will also be of use to practitioners in other areas of filmmaking—directors for example—not least by making them aware of the 'ingredients' which—properly assembled—make for a successful film; the challenges editors encounter; the decisions they face and the vital contribution they make during both the production and post-production phases of this enthralling and important enterprise.

PREFACE

Documentary is often used as a synonym for a particular visual style—usually hand-held and rough. However, documentary isn't defined solely by how it's photographed. It's much more about storytelling. So much so, that whilst there might only be one visual signature of the documentary genre, there is a whole range of narrative approaches one can take.

For example, observational documentaries typically focus on an aspect of ordinary life and circumstance, whilst presenter-led stories guide the audience through the perspective of an individual authorial voice. Drama documentaries mix real life events with dramatic reconstructions in order to tell their story. Further, documentary covers the whole gamut of human experience and accomplishment from science and the natural world to history and the arts. Documentary earns its name from this unique approach to story and storytelling.

While there are many genres of documentary, readers should know that in the course of this book I have focused primarily on the editing of commercial television documentary, since this form makes comprehensive use of *all* of the editing techniques and skills common to every other type of documentary. However, by extension, many of the practices described here will be of relevance to other genres of editing, including fictional narratives and adverts.

For the sake of brevity, I will sometimes refer to documentary films simply as *films*, since this terminology is common within the industry. In many instances I shall refer to editing as *cutting*. This is also an industry term, which originates from the days of physically cutting celluloid, prior to the introduction of digital editing; a *cut* being the point in a film where one shot instantaneously changes to another. Lastly, I shall at times refer to the human beings featured in documentary as *characters*, since again, this is an industry term.

I have designed this guide to be independent of any specific software package or tools. Indeed, the principles discussed within the book can be used alongside any editing software of your choice. As a result, I have chosen to exclude any information relating to the technical configuration or setup of the tools, as well as everything directly preceding the editing stage itself.

Most importantly, I have structured this book in a way which best explains and unpacks the many interconnected aspects of documentary film editing. I strongly recommend reading it to the end before beginning to apply this knowledge, as many points discussed later in the book are integral to earlier stages of the editing process. Thereafter, the book can be used as a reference resource and dipped into as and when appropriate.

Finally, I would like to emphasise that there are many ways to approach an editing project. This guide is based on a method that I have developed over many years through my own experience. I have, as far as possible, drawn on my wider experience of the professional community, to give the most appropriate context and clearest perspective on best working practices. Though this book remains necessarily subjective, I hope, at the very least, that my methods will serve as a guide and an inspiration, which you can adapt as required to suit your own personal working practices. Certainly, I have found that my methods have helped me to make good decisions and have consistently produced results which directors respect and the public finds appealing.

Thanks for picking up this book. I hope you enjoy it and profit from it and that it supports you in your pursuit of the art of film editing, which I believe to be one of the most powerful and rewarding contributions to filmmaking.

In setting out the ideas and techniques central to this book, I have tried to be as clear and unambiguous as possible. However, there is always room for improvement: so your thoughts and feedback will be gratefully received. I will endeavour to incorporate them into future editions of the book.

Sam Billinge, 17 August 2016
www.sambillinge.com

THE POWER OF DOCUMENTARY

"After nourishment, shelter and companionship, stories are the thing we need most in this world."

—Philip Pullman[1]

Documentary storytelling is arguably the most powerful change-creating art form available to us today. The power of documentary lies in its unmatched ability to inform and educate an audience in a manner that is both entertaining and authentic. The results can move people in astonishing ways.

Errol Morris's pursuit of truth in *The Thin Blue Line*[2] led to the reopening of a murder case and Randall Adams's eventual release from jail. Adam Curtis's *The Power of Nightmares*[3] changed the way in which those who watched it perceive the threat of Al-Qaida and challenged the way in which, as a society, we often accept uncritically received opinion.

A great documentary endeavours to convey the *whole* story in all its rich complexity by focusing on the people and actions that have shaped it: gathering, selecting and ordering the information into a thought-provoking yet entertaining package. Even though the recorded material and other elements that make up the documentary have been carefully chosen and arranged during the editing process, the events themselves are not fabricated. When we watch a documentary, we are watching a representation of real life, albeit through the lens of a camera.

This is where the power of documentary really lies, for if we are able to *engage* our audience, connect them to narratives with which they are unfamiliar and allow them to experience both the conflict and resolution such narratives engender, then we are in a privileged position to inspire and enlighten them. More ambitiously, we can help shape the debate and perhaps even improve the world in which we live. Such a position brings, of course, responsibility: not least the responsibility to tell the story appropriately and with integrity of both purpose and technique.

WHO ARE FILM EDITORS AND WHAT DO THEY DO?

> "The person who makes or breaks a film is not the scriptwriter or the director, but the film editor."
>
> —Alistair Cooke[4]

Whilst editing is not the only important contribution to the documentary production process, it is the stage of production where the film can be most radically shaped and, thereby, significantly defined or potentially destroyed. The editor works with footage gathered by the director, making selections and combining these shots, along with other elements, into sequences that ultimately constitute the finished film. The editor's job is both technical and creative: working with images, dialogue, graphics, music, sound effects and other elements to create a compelling and meaningful experience for the audience. The editor is the last person in the filmmaking assembly line and so is the ultimate determinant of what the audience will see in terms of both content and context.

Editing is highly idiosyncratic. The same material given to a different editor is likely to result in an entirely different film. Editing is not, as many industry outsiders might think, a job that simply consists of cutting out 'the bad bits.' In a world which at times seems predominantly left-brain orientated, editing is a remarkable antidote. It is both analytical and system-orientated (left-brained) and creative free-thinking (right-brained).

Almost all documentary films come together in the edit. Some films arrive in the cutting room with only the loosest of scripts and, ever more commonly, in the absence of directors who are still busy shooting the rest of the film. The editor is charged with finding the story within the material, clarifying the information, making selections, then structuring and presenting the story in the most effective way. Even films that arrive in the edit with a robust script often leave transformed, as story ideas evolve during the editing process. It is perhaps not too far-fetched to liken this to the process Michelangelo described in sculpting: finding the finished sculpture already contained within the stone.

However, editors do not usually work alone. Filmmaking is a collaborative art form. Editing is primarily a partnership between two people: the editor and the director. The director will have broadly conceived and shot the film, and then once in the edit, he or she will work with the editor to wrestle the narrative structure from the mass of materials. The director will generally have an interest in the aesthetics of the film, including the picture sequences and choice of music, but it is usually left to the film editor to first scope, appraise and craft the available resources.

As the editor, we do not have to handle all of the storytelling ourselves, though it is essential that we are confident storytellers, capable of spotting story gaps, creating connections and meaningful juxtapositions in narrative information. We must be capable of understanding and even doing much of the director's job in the cutting room so we can step in and assist when required to do so. We must also develop a keen sense of what the film requires in terms of audio/visual approach and design.

Two disciplines are, therefore, central to documentary editing: editorial composition and the crafting of pictures and sound. They will form the basis of this book.

It is worth remembering at the outset that editors can only work with the materials they have at their disposal. As editors, we are often fixing or working around other people's mistakes to make the best of everybody else's contribution to the film and trying to make them look their best. A simple rule, quickly stated and often remembered is: *the less you notice the editor's work, the more successful they have been.*

It is for this reason perhaps that the role of the film editor is often misunderstood and even more often undervalued. Little is known about editing other than by editors themselves, and very few outside of the industry seem to care much about it. The only people who *really* know what goes on in the cutting room are the editor and the director.

Despite this lack of wider recognition, editing is hugely respected within the industry and rightly recognised as an absolutely critical aspect of film-making, not least because, for the audience viewing the finished work, it is the contribution with the most immediate, visceral and exciting impact. A film is made, but can just as easily be broken, in the edit suite.

Key Point

- The documentary editor's job is primarily based on the mastery of two storytelling skills: editorial composition and the crafting of pictures and sound.

NOTES

1 The Guardian Online, "Sustainable storytelling is a powerful tool that communicates vision". Accessed 19 October, 2016. www.theguardian.com/sustainable-business/blog/sustainable-stories-powerful-tool-communicates-vision

2 Errol Morris, *The Thin Blue Line* (Miramax Films/Umbrella Entertainment, 1988).

3 Adam Curtis, *The Power of Nightmares* (BBC, 2004).

4 Alistair Cooke, *Alistair Cooke at the Movies* (Penguin, 2011), "Coalmining in Hollywood—Longevity: Letter from America, BBC, 11 April, 2003".

1

THE FUNDAMENTALS

STORYTELLING 1.0

> "The shortest distance between truth and a human being is a story."
>
> —Anthony de Mello[1]

Storytelling is the most powerful and enduring means of communication. It has been fundamental to the development of society as far back as human history can be traced. As individuals too, many of our early learning experiences are likely to have involved stories through the spoken and written word, as well as through creative role-play. Even before we had the ability to articulate our thoughts and feelings in written form, we learned to make sense of the world through stories.

As a result of this early conditioning, it seems that we all have an in-built understanding of story. When we watch a film, it is the story that speaks to us most immediately, and so it follows that it is the story that is the single most important aspect of any film.

In order for a film to be great, it must have a compelling story to tell—and that story must be told in the most effective way possible. As editors, we cannot always choose the stories we are given, but we can help to shape them and thereby influence both their reception and impact. We can help structure and clarify the narrative through the arrangement of events and the careful inclusion and exclusion of content, and we can strengthen its impact through the imaginative use of pictures, sound and music. We can also regulate the ebb and flow of the story through our choice of pacing and rhythm.

Since the central narrative message is the key to all great documentary making, the editor's primary focus must be first to understand the story in all its depth (what is this film about?) and with all its nuances (what points of view can be brought to it?) and then decide how best to tell it. Every subsequent aspect of editing is built on this foundation.

Establishing the Story Foundations

> "Conflict is to storytelling what sound is to music"
>
> —Robert McKee[2]

Nearly all successful stories, from the earliest folk tales to the latest blockbuster films, appear to share a singular common feature: a narrative arc that begins with a conflict between people or situations and ends in a successful resolution. This 'formula' appears to satisfy some deep-seated human need to find order in disorder, harmony in discord and sense in confusion: a pathway through the woods, as it were, to the beckoning light of home. This desire, to be presented first with contradictions and then with reconciliation determines whether we find stories gripping and/or their conclusions satisfactory. Stories without conflict lack interest whilst conflicts without resolution leave us either disappointed or distressed. It follows then that conflict is the driving force of all good stories and that every story must involve conflict of some kind.

John Yorke, speaking primarily of cinema and theatre, describes this archetypal story form in the following way:

> A protagonist is introduced with a goal, a desire with which the audience can easily sympathize, and then an antagonist is introduced, as an individual or a representative of an opposing force, standing in his or her way. The movie becomes their conflict, and its sequences become the more or less linear escalation of that struggle, the cowboy with the gunfighter, the lovers with parents opposing. . . . This seamless conflict built to a third-act confrontation—the climax—and ended

> with a resolution that fit the mode, death in a tragedy and marriage, most typically, in a comedy.[3]

In documentary, this conflict usually comes between a character (the presenter, interview subject and/or other contributors to the film) and his or her physical or social world, within his or her personal relationships or within himself or herself. Since documentary is a highly visual and linear medium, we tend to focus on external conflict which we can readily see, that is, inter-personal conflict or conflict with the physical or social world.

In *Man on Wire*,[4] high-wire daredevil Philippe Petit (protagonist), hears about the planned construction of the World Trade Center and is seized by the idea of tightrope walking between the two towers (his goal). He plans the stunt for six years, away from the authorities who threaten to derail his plan (forces of antagonism). Philippe experiences many challenges in reaching his goal: how he will gain access to the building, scale his way to the top and get the heavy wire across the two buildings—as well as the various natural forces which threaten the success of the crossing itself (the escalation of the struggle). Despite these challenges, Philippe makes the crossing (the climax) and becomes something of a star, making history in the process (the resolution).

This notion of conflict inspires our journey through the film and stimulates our quest to resolve it. This search for resolution then determines the places we go, what our audience will see and what they will learn. Understanding this conflict takes us through time and eventually on to the finale, where the conflict is resolved, and where we, in turn, reach our conclusion. The journey will make our characters and our audience change the ways in which they see the world.

The path to resolution is rarely singular and never without alternatives: during the production process, and even more so at the start of the edit, there is usually a wide (sometimes bewildering) range of possibilities for the film.

The director is likely to have grappled already with this near infinite number of possibilities and, using both instinct and careful research, will have boiled things down to just a few. He or she will arrive at the edit with a fairly robust, yet broadly untested, idea of the direction in which they would like to take the story. This is where the editor's contribution usually begins.

The editor must help decide the direction in which to take the story from here on, choosing what to include, and crucially, what must be excluded to make the narrative clear and compelling. This can seem a daunting prospect at first. Fortunately, we can break down the decision-making process into a logical series of steps.

- **First ask, what is the film about?**
  We need to understand the nature of our story and the conflict within it. This is what our film is about. We should be able to describe this in a sentence or two. The result is referred to as the *central argument*. Every aspect of the film will hang from and depend upon this argument.

  Understanding our film's central argument at the beginning of the project, and keeping this in mind throughout the edit, will help keep our efforts focused and maintain clarity in our thinking. Every decision we make should be seen through this conceptual 'lens.'
- **Next ask, what are the scenes about?**
  Once we know what this conflict is, we must attempt to understand the various tests and experiences our characters will need to go through to resolve it. Each of these tests will form the basis of our scenes.

  I usually find that each scene tends to work best when it addresses just a single significant aspect of the film's central argument at a time: illustrating one part of the challenge faced by our characters, testing their ability to measure up to that challenge and, ultimately, motivating them to change their stance or understanding. This change makes them stronger, taking them (and the audience, too) from a place of relative ignorance to a position of knowledge. This new-found knowledge provides us with the 'piece of the puzzle' we need to move on to the next step of the journey—the next scene and then the next—incrementally building the wherewithal to resolve the central conflict and, in so doing, allowing protagonist and audience alike to reach a satisfying conclusion.

  This path through the film is often referred to as the *story arc*.

  Having said this, it is clear that the documentary editor cannot always be successful in giving the audience all of the answers. Often a superficially simple story can become more complex and irresolvable as it progresses. Indeed this discovered complexity may become the foundation of the whole story. For this reason, not all films can have a satisfying or unambiguous conclusion, since the events which may *eventually* lead to that conclusion may not yet have taken place. However, upon reaching their own—perhaps interim—conclusion, documentary editors can be said to have given the audience the wherewithal to form more informed and detailed views of the subject *for themselves*. This broader accomplishment can in turn provoke a new way of looking at the subject and ultimately our world.

Finally, there are instances where more than one aspect of the film's central argument may play out within a single scene. For example, in an observational documentary that follows the life of a character intimately, a scene of mother and daughter preparing an evening meal might, for instance, illustrate multiple aspects of their relationship—wealth, health-consciousness and any number of things.

It remains the case, however, that we are attempting as best we can to keep each scene as simple and connected to the broader story arc as possible.

- **Next we must consider, how does the film end?**

Logically, our film ends when we have successfully brought resolution to the conflict identified at its beginning. As filmmakers, we will have taken our audience on a journey from a place of relative confusion, uncertainty or ambiguity (conflict) to a place of relative certainty (resolution) by equipping them with the wherewithal to know how to resolve the conflict *in their own minds*. This may not take the form of a definitive answer arising inevitably from the story as told, but rather a clear suggestion of a direction toward which the audience might look to find the answer for themselves. When both are satisfied we have reached the end of our film.

However, it is not often clear at the beginning of the edit how the film will end. Documentary story is often shaped by unpredictable forces. The weather or other unforeseen events may determine what directors are able to shoot, adversely affecting the availability of on-screen contributors, or rendering inaccessible a required location. Each and any one of these may alter the intended narrative and compromise the materials available to the editor. As a result, documentaries are rarely scripted prior to the edit with any great precision. Only once the rushes are in the can and the edit begins, are we in a position to evaluate what we really have to work with and decide where to take the film.

However, once we are in the edit and we have established where the source of conflict in our story lies, we can begin to establish relatively quickly where the conclusion to this conflict is likely to be found. At this stage, there may still not be a *single* clear path to our much sought resolution: rather *several* possible routes. Even so, we must establish *some* notion of an ending, so that we can begin to track our path through the film to reach it.

- **Finally ask, who is the audience?**
  Is the film for a very general public, for science fiction fans, knowledgeable professionals, families, over-sixties, eight-year-olds? Ultimately we are making our film for an audience, and we must be clear who that audience is. Establishing this at the very outset is critical since it will determine every aspect of our storytelling, from our choice of words through to our chosen editing style and the music that underscores it. Understanding the age, likely level of prior knowledge, conceptual sophistication and attention spans of our intended audience will be key to how we choose to pitch and voice our film.

  As the film's editor, we are privileged to help decide what the audience will see—and the context in which it will see it. We determine what we might call the film's *tone*. In this sense, we are the supreme arbiters, holding a position of significant responsibility and demanding exacting discipline. We must resist, as far as we are able, imposing our own views or subjecting the audience to opinions derived only from our personal beliefs and prejudices. Ideally, the editor should seem to have no voice at all, the story being told only by the characters featured within it.

  In short: every decision we make must be made with the audience in mind.

We are sometimes left to wrestle with these big questions alone, at least at the start of the edit, and for this reason it is good to have a clear system in place. By doing so, we can quickly get to grips with the story and begin to break it down into something manageable.

Fortunately, more often than not, the director will accompany us early on in the edit. He or she will likely have developed a rudimentary script for the film and shot the scenes in anticipation of the edit and thus be able to help us establish the story structure. When the director is present, I would suggest making these questions a discussion point at the very start of the edit, before anything else. In this way, it is easier to make a common cause, to avoid critical misunderstanding and to work in tandem for the remainder of what may turn out to be a long and intense process!

In order to make the most of these early discussions, I like to arrive at each new edit with a fresh mind and as deliberate a naivety towards the subject matter as I can manage. For this reason, I prefer not to undertake much prior research or reading. I think of this as a sort of *constructive ignorance*, as my superficial lack of knowledge allows me to approach and clarify the story in my own mind in a manner similar to that which the viewer will adopt as he or she first encounters it. I am, in effect, playing the part of the audience. If I don't understand something, I just say so, and the director then needs to explain it to me in as plain and simple a form as possible. This genuine ignorance, together with the answers my questions elicit, allow us to better understand the materials and better craft them into something clear and compelling: something the audience is more likely to understand.

Key Points

- Conflict is the driving force of all stories.
- Every decision must be made with the audience in mind.
- Ask lots of questions at the start of your project and all the way through!
- No question is ever ridiculous. If something doesn't make sense, ask more questions until it does.

EDITING 1.0

As well as helping to guide the film's narrative, the editor is primarily responsible for its tone and feel (i.e., its style and craft). We take the specially shot camera footage, known as *rushes*, and combine them with other elements, such as stock footage, still images, graphics, music and sound effects, into sequences. These sequences ultimately constitute the finished film.

Before we can start editing though, we must first organise our project, and whilst I want this book to remain non-technological in approach, the following couple of sections are the unavoidable exceptions.

Setting Up the Edit

> "If I had eight hours to chop down a tree, I'd spend six sharpening my axe."
>
> —Abraham Lincoln[5]

Great organisation is essential for great editing. A large editing project will consist of thousands of individual clips, which unless rationalised, will quickly become unmanageable.

First, we must ensure that we have a simple, clear system in place to catalogue these many assets so we are able quickly to recall what we need, when we need it. Once we have this system in place, we can focus solely on the creative aspects of the edit, without logistical distraction. There is nothing more frustrating than having a moment of inspiration and then losing the magic of it in the search for the materials which weren't where you thought they were. It doesn't simply waste time, it drains energy!

The way you choose to set up your project is a matter of choice and should reflect the way you like to work. However, there are some basic steps that I would urge you to follow: they have certainly helped me keep very disparate materials under control and my sanity in check! Personally, I like to set up a new editing project by first creating a set of new folders (commonly referred to as *bins*), which will each contain the main groups of files with which I will be working with during the edit (see figure 1.1).

1. **CUTS**—My edited sequences will live in here.
2. **ASSEMBLIES**—The selections that I make from my rushes will live in here.
3. **RUSHES**—The original rushes clips will live in here.
4. **ARCHIVE**—Stock footage will live in here.

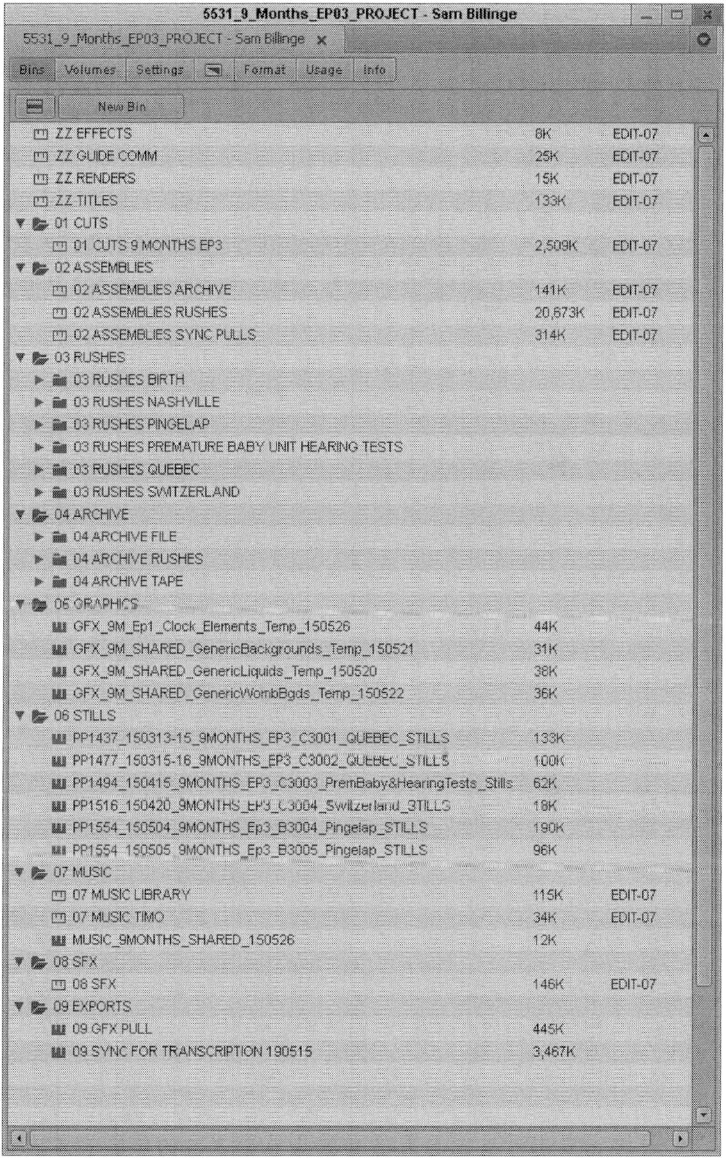

Figure 1.1 Project Layout

A screen shot of my project window. Here you can see the basic structure I like to use to organize the materials for each of my films.

5. **GRAPHICS**—Motion graphic elements live in here.
6. **STILLS**—Still images live in here.
7. **MUSIC**—Imported music lives in here.
8. **SOUND EFFECTS (SFX)**—Imported sound effects live in here.
9. **EXPORTS**—Duplicate sequences for play-out live in here.

I also keep these bins at the very top of my project for quick access:

- **GUIDE COMM**—Recorded voiceover narration, also known as *guide commentary*.
- **EFFECTS**—Any custom visual or audio effects that I have created and would like to reuse.
- **TITLES**—Title captions.
- **RENDERS**—Render files.

> Tip! Give each folder and bin an ascending number or letter before its name, such as *01 CUTS* and *02 ASSEMBLIES*, in order of their importance and your need to prioritize access to them. If you then sort your project alphabetically, they will always stay listed in order.

It may also be a good idea to mirror this folder structure on your media drives at a desktop level, before importing your files, so that you can easily trace back items to their source location if needed.

Once you have organised everything within your project, it's time to get your rushes laid out and to start viewing them.

Preparing to View Rushes

Rushes usually arrive in the edit as multiple individual clips. It is maddeningly easy to lose track of them, since there are so many and their file names, as created within the camera, are often a cryptic series of numbers.

Attempting to work directly from these master clips can be time consuming, inefficient and fiddly. As a result, making any worthwhile editing decisions based on working directly with these clips is usually highly impractical.

To make life easier, I like to first copy each folder of my rushes clips into new sequences within the project and then work from these sequences entirely. I do not touch my master clips again. By working from sequences, rather than the original master clips, all of my rushes remain in one consistent order, in one consistent place, which I can quickly access and use.

Remember that not all editing software packages work in exactly the same way, and so this is my method of working, based on the most common professional tool in use today.

The way I work is as follows:

1. **First, I order the rushes bin chronologically.**

   Initially, I want to view my rushes in the order in which they were originally shot. The rushes clip names will likely indicate this by way of ascending file numbers. Alternatively, you will usually be able to work this out from the clip's *timecode*.

   Timecode is the internal clock data from the camera itself. It is a twenty-four hour clock based on a number format as 00:00:00:00 (hours:minutes:seconds:frames). For example, 03:01:05:17 would be three hours, one minute, five seconds and seventeen frames.

   This timecode is recorded in camera along with the pictures and sound, and embedded within the clip. Timecode helps us in the edit by identifying every clip, and every frame within that clip, with its own unique reference.

   There are two kinds of timecode:

   - **Time of Day Timecode**

     This timecode records the actual time the clip was recorded. It is useful for live events and multi-camera shoots where shots taken from many cameras will need to be synchronised and it is necessary to established when each camera stopped and started rolling. The timecode data shared between the cameras allows us to group them together accurately and quickly.

   - **Record Run Timecode**

     The timecode for the clip is pre-set within the camera. This can be any number. Most camera operators begin their first camera roll (the source card on which the rushes media will be stored) with 01:00:00:00 for simplicity, and they identify each subsequent roll as 02, 03 etc. The timecode then only counts up when the camera is actually recording. As the camera stops and starts, the timecode will typically pause and resume with the next recorded clip.

You can find any clip's timecode from the timecode column in your rushes bin.

Whichever method you use, arrange your rushes clips so that they are listed chronologically in your bin, with the earliest clips at the top.

2. **Next, I create a new sequence within my *ASSEMBLIES* folder and drag the rushes clips into that sequence.**

Once I have created a new blank sequence, I drag all of the relevant rushes clips into that sequence. I then name the sequence after the scene or broader subject associated within the rushes contained in that folder.

This process creates a *timeline* (see figure 1.2). A timeline is a graphical depiction of the audio and video tracks, sequenced one next to the other. We will use a timeline to edit our film. We can use multiple timelines for different purposes; from simply viewing shots and listening to audio of a few seconds, to cutting entire programmes of an hour or more.

I repeat this process for all of the rushes clips in my film, putting them into sequences labelled by scene or subject.

Now, rather than having to click through hundreds of short clips every time I want to find a shot, I can simply refer to my tight group of 12–16 neatly labelled sequences which contain everything. With just a couple of clicks, I can scroll through these sequences in seconds to find the shot I want—and I never have to look at the master rushes clips again.

3. **Finally, if I have multiple cameras or master audio to sync, I do this next.**

Many cameras will only capture low quality guide audio that is embedded within the video clip. The high-fidelity master audio is recorded separately, usually on to a disk-based recorder. In this event, I locate the master audio and sync this up to my pictures within each assembly sequence.

Ensure you do this before editing any of the clips in your sequence. Attempting to sync up master audio to cut sequences later down the line is incredibly time consuming and unreliable. While I am always keen to get cutting, it's always worth getting the audio synced up first!

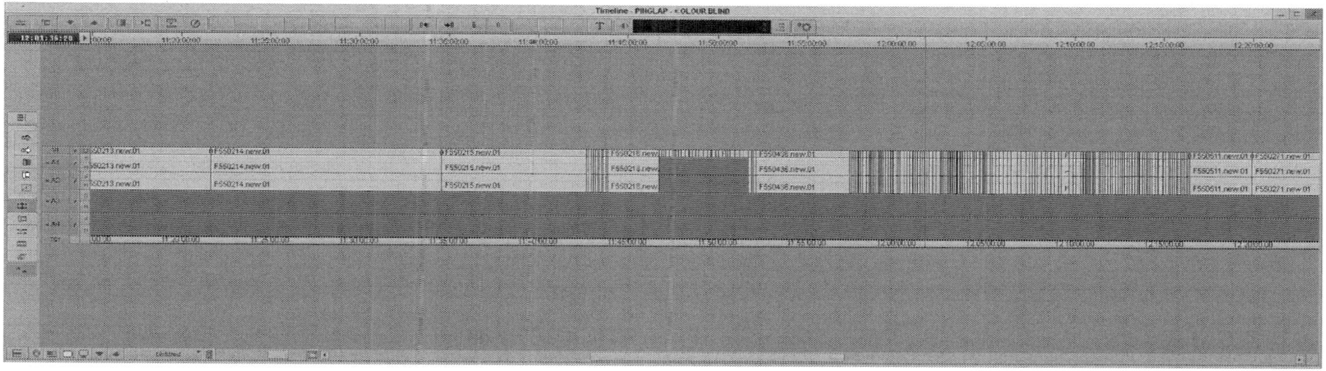

Figure 1.2 Rushes Timeline (pre-viewing)

A timeline with the rushes for a new scene.

An extra trick that I find useful before I begin viewing my rushes is to identify which clips consist of spoken material, known as *sync sound*, and which are not, and then I distinguish them. To do this, I skim through my rushes sequence, and when I find any shots that are *non-sync* (i.e., no spoken sound at all) I drop their audio tracks down to a lower track in the sequence timeline (see figure 1.3).

In this way, when I come to editing I can navigate through my sequences faster: just glancing at my timeline I can clearly see where the different components of my rushes are and jump straight to them.

Rushes are made up of many shot types and textures. I will go through how these work in more depth later on, but for now here are the basic groups we have to work with:

- **Interviews (IVs)**
  An interview setup is where a key person or persons with specialisms connected to the story is/are interviewed around a set of questions. They may have been a witness to a key event, or an expert in a relevant field. Often these interviews are conducted in a formal manner with the subject sitting down within a composed frame. In other instances, these interviews can be informal, with the subject walking around or casually taking part in another activity while being questioned.
- **Cutaways**
  These are shots that illustrate the environment outside of the interview setup and any other places of relevance to the film. They give the scene a sense of location, context and scale.

  As documentary editors, we rely on cutaways to tell our story. When they are used effectively, in combination, they will communicate much of the mood and feeling of the film and help to reinforce its narrative. These shots are also commonly known as *GVs* or *General Views*.
- **Actuality**
  These are sequences of shots that exist to illustrate and clarify a process or experiment related to the story happening in front of the camera. They will usually centre around a particular action, event or activity.
- **Pieces to Camera (PTCs)**
  In a presenter-led film we are also likely to have words spoken directly to the camera. These statements are designed to give the audience a key

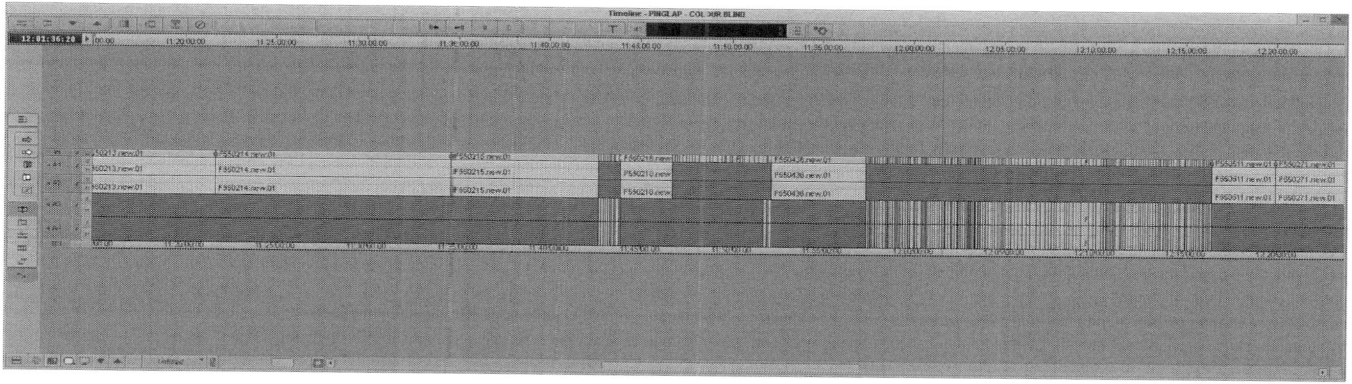

Figure 1.3 Rushes Timeline (sync 1&2, atmos 3&4)

A timeline with the rushes for a new scene ready to view. The sync sound (consisting of interview and actuality) are on channels A1&2 and I've moved the non-sync clips' audio down to A3&4.

piece of information in a direct and personal manner or to clarify and interpret something that has been said or illustrated previously.

Just before we start watching our rushes and getting down to the fun stuff, it's worth taking a moment to think about how we'll keep our sequence timelines organised.

Track Laying the Edit

Editing a documentary inevitably means we need to work with multiple tracks in our software timeline. Most of these timeline tracks will probably be audio; i.e., dialogue, voiceover, sound effects and music, though there will of course be a few picture tracks, too.

It is essential, as in any aspect of editing, that we are highly organised and systematic in the way we set out our timeline. By taking proper care and keeping things logically arranged, we can more easily navigate our sequences and locate whatever we need with ease. Having a clear system also makes it easier in the event anyone else should need to work our timeline, such as an edit assistant, audio mixer or colourists (who balance and enhance the colour and light levels of each shot for the finished film).

We should keep our timelines organised from the start of our edit to save any ugly unpicking later on, particularly as our timeline gets longer and more intricate.

There are many ways we could choose to organise our timeline. However, this is the way I like to set things out (see figure 1.4):

- **V1—This is my main picture track.** I keep all of my sequence shots here. This will be interview pictures as well as B-roll.
- **V2—Overspill.** I keep this free for any effects that require more than one video layer. I also keep any shots that require work or attention here.
- **V3—Titles.** Title captions live here.
- **A1/2—Sync sound.** All dialogue spoken on camera, such as interviews, actuality and pieces to camera live on these stereo tracks.
- **A3-A10—Sound effects.** All sound design is organised on these tracks.
- **A11/12—Music.**

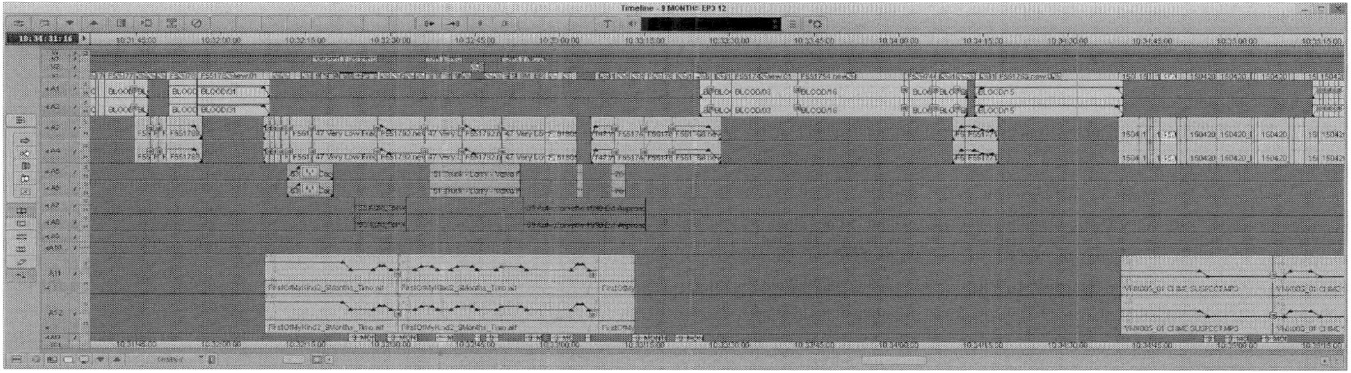

Figure 1.4 Track Layed Timeline

The neat track layed timeline I'm currently working on.

- **A13—Voiceover.** Note that I only keep one track for voiceover, as it is mono. I centre-pan the audio so that it plays as stereo across both speakers.

This is just a guide. Some projects require more sync tracks (depending how many microphones have been used). Some films will require more or less sound design and some films have no music or voiceover at all. The important thing is that each discrete group of materials has its own set of tracks so that we can navigate our sequence and locate whatever we need with ease.

Now that we have a good grasp of the technological systems necessary to edit our documentary, we can begin to view and work with our rushes, the primary building blocks of our film.

Viewing Rushes for the First Time

When we view our rushes for the first time, we are effectively deciding what will be in our film, and crucially, what will not. This is an important part of the editing process and so we need to be focused and diligent, as anything overlooked here may be *lost for good*.

I often find that the director is not present in the early stages of the edit; particularly during first appraisal of rushes and even the early cutting of sequences. They are often still shooting elements of the film or generally recovering from a busy few weeks and months leading to the edit. However, some directors are keen to be present throughout the edit and this is, of course, their prerogative. Whenever possible, however, I prefer to be alone during the early stages of the edit, since this allows me the space to settle into the project, to understand the rudiments of the story in my own way and at my own speed and to assess independently all the materials I have to work with.

Regardless of who is and is not present at this stage, we are watching our rushes in order to:

- Understand the extent, scope and complexity of the resources with which we have to work.
- Familiarise ourselves *completely* with them.
- Identify the material that best supports our narrative.

- Remove the material that does not support our narrative.
- Further organise our rushes in helpful ways.

I will typically have around sixty hours of raw rushes material at the start of an editing project. The completed film will usually be an hour long; a shooting ratio of 60:1. Shooting ratios can vary enormously. I recently cut a scene with twenty-five hours of rushes for a single six-minute scene. That's a shooting ratio of 250:1!

All films will be different, but the point is that most of the material you have at your disposal will never make the final cut. Therefore, we must discipline ourselves to select only the very best of our rushes. The rest is just noise. By focusing only on our best material and thereafter ignoring the discard pile, the editing process that follows will be quicker, easier and infinitely more efficient.

Remember that viewing rushes takes time: *real* time, so an hour of rushes takes about an hour to watch, depending how much is going on within them. This time is an essential (and unavoidable) part of the editing process. While the audience will be unaware of this huge investment of time when it watches the finished product, if we wish to get the very best out of our rushes we cannot skimp on this proper review of the materials: we must go through all of it patiently and with a keen eye to what is and is not likely to make it into the final film.

Unfortunately, it can be the case that there are circumstances that appear to act against us at this stage. The time it takes to view rushes is not always fully appreciated by the other creative forces outside of the edit—particularly executives and those who are not connected with the daily crafting of the documentary. Generally, they are keen to see a finished, working programme as early as possible, and there can be pressure to deliver the goods more quickly than we ourselves consider prudent.

An executive said once said to me, "We just don't have time to view these rushes as we really need to get this scene cut." My response was, "Right, so I'll just pick shots at random then, see how they go together, and fingers crossed it'll work?" "Oh no," she said, "I want it to work too." I said nothing more.

We must be realistic when appraising our rushes at the start in terms of the time it will take to watch—and ultimately cut them. The scene with twenty-five hours of rushes took nearly three working days to watch. Only then could I begin to cut them into a finished story.

There are three broad groups of rushes in documentary that we shall explore: interviews, actuality and cutaways.

Viewing Interviews

When viewing rushes, I usually like to listen to all of the spoken material first; primarily the interviews. This is because the interviews will form the spine of the film. The interview materials we have, the selections we make from them and the order in which we place them, will inform every other part of the edit. It is important that we get a complete overview of them first.

As far as possible, I will listen to interviews with the director present—as they are always keen to remain aware of (and usually involved in) editorial decisions about the film. In this regard, the interview material is key. Sometimes the director will even listen to the interviews outside the main edit and make a number of pre-selections; providing me with a short-list of what they consider to be the best bits. During that time, I can be watching more rushes or cutting other material. Personally, I like this approach as we can both be working on the film in tandem and increasing the rate of progress as we do so.

In the instances where I am listening to and selecting the interviews, I am looking for two things, in order of priority:

- Clips that reveal the interviewee's *character*. On a fundamental human level, we are all mostly interested in (and interpret what we hear from) a person on the basis of their personality.

  When listening to an interview, we are searching for statements which reveal the interviewee's character: their feeling for and contact with the events pertinent to the emerging theme of our film. Look out especially for anything funny, poignant, pithy or generally unexpected.

  Often the body language of an interviewee can be as telling as their words, so we should pay attention to the facial expressions and body movements as well as to the spoken content of the interview. We may, for instance, be able to tell when a contributor is being untruthful about something; saying one thing but appearing to be something else. This could be a perfect narrative 'hook' for us.

We will usually be picking the bits that the interviewer (usually the director) thinks are the best—and these are often interesting moments which haven't been foreseen.

- Second, we should be listening particularly carefully for statements from our interviewees that explain the *story* around the events which are germane to the theme of our film. This could be a description of how the events of our story unfolded from their perspective.

  I often find that interview contributors are not especially good at extended exposition—certainly anything more complicated than a simple statement. Placed in front of a camera, contributors tend to ramble: to over-elaborate, obscuring the main facts, in long-winded and invariably dull attempts to try to make (and remake) their point. As a result, we need to be highly selective of our interviews, choosing what is necessary to reveal what they were *really* trying to say. Ideally, we want to find and keep only those parts of the interview in which our contributors are able to express themselves clearly and concisely. However, even in a rambling interview, if you know you can get what you want by cutting it down later on, you will still pick it.

  It is worth remembering that we can usually fill in any gaps in their story later by use of voiceover narration, additional interviews or, in some instances, title captions.

I begin by watching an interview from the front of the first clip in my rushes sequence. When I hear something that satisfies the criteria outlined above, I keep it, and play on. When I come to something that does not, I place in and out marks around the 'offending' part of the clip and delete. I move on in this fashion until the end of the interview.

At the end of this whole process, I have a concise sequence of clips that contain the most useful spoken parts from the interview. This sequence of selections is called a *sync pull* (see figure 1.5) and we will soon use it to structure our new scene. I repeat this process for all of the interviews in my rushes sequences.

Figure 1.6 is a short extract from an interview. You can see the selections that I made from it underlined. The rest of the interview was cut out.

Transcripts, like the one in figure 1.6, are a useful time-saving device to have in the edit. If your film has time and budget to have them made, I suggest you

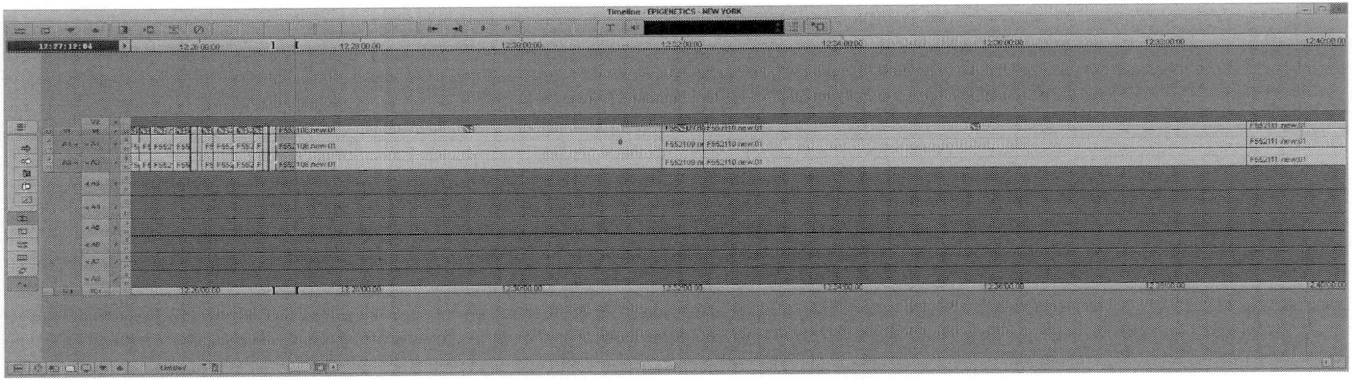

Figure 1.5 Sync Pull

Work in progress: pulling sync for a new scene.

Timecode	Interviewer
17:22:14:03	So Susie, tell me what is your eye condition?
	Susie
17:22:24:05	It's a rare condition called Leber congenital amaurosis. It affects the retina of my eyes. I was born with very poor eyesight and I have been nearly completely blind for most of my life.
	Interviewer
17:23:55:00	What are the challenges with living with your eyesight?
	Susie
17:24:05:13	A lot of things really. I struggle to cook for myself. I can't play a lot of sport. I have learnt to look after myself but I still find many tasks in life difficult.
	Interviewer
17:26:31:20	How were your reactions and feelings when you first met Simon?
	Susie
17:27:00:05	I fell in love with him the first time I met him. And we talked about it and agreed to it.
	Interviewer
17:27:15:03	Did you think that your condition would be an issue to him?
	Susie
17:28:22:05	Yes, at first I thought he wouldn't be interested in me. I didn't think that somebody normal would want to date a blind person.
	You know there are some things that I wasn't capable of doing, so that's when Simon can help me.
	Interviewer
17:29:40:15	Like what?
	Susie
17:29:42:09	You know like when I cook, I will need his help to chop the vegetables. I have to go to the hospital regularly. There are lots of things in everyday life that are challenging when you are blind.
	He has transformed my life in that way. My life has changed enormously since Simon came along.

Figure 1.6 A Transcript Extract

	Interviewer
17:30:55:10	So in your family, how many are blind and how many are not?
	Susie
17:31:15:20	Only my Dad.
	Interviewer
17:35:07:23	So Simon, how has your everyday life changed since you met Susie?
	Simon
17:35:42:11	Yes it has changed quite a lot. It took some getting used to in the beginning but I was immediately up for the challenge though. I love Susie and I can't imagine wanting to do anything else with my life.
	Interviewer
17:36:25:04	How do you feel about having kids one day?
	Susie
17:36:33:04	We have discussed it a lot. I think we would like to start a family together someday.
	Simon
17:36:45:04	We are concerned that our children could be born blind, but we will still love them just the same.
	As I explained to you earlier, life can be challenging and sometimes things get tough but we love each other a lot and are looking forward to the future together.

Figure 1.6 (*Continued*)

do so. Having a paper log of your interviews can save a lot of time, especially in films with a lot of interviews, as you do not have to watch through your entire interview in real time to locate the best bits.

I usually find that the director will take charge of the transcripts, skim reading them to find the sections of interview likely to be most useful to the edit. They highlight the key sections and hand them back to me, so that I can make a sync pull up using the rushes, which we can then further appraise and structure.

Of course, transcripts do not give us any indication of the body language, manner of delivery or technical quality of the shot, which will only come from watching the rushes themselves. So it is always worth viewing them before making any irrevocable editorial decisions.

Key Points

- Focus on the emotional content of interviews.
- Contributors are often poor at explaining concepts. Limit factual exposition from contributors to a minimum.
- It is always worth getting transcripts made whenever you have a lot of interview material. You will rely on these more as the edit goes on.

Viewing Actuality

Actuality is a term used in documentary to describe the coverage of real-life events, places and people—often where the subjects are seemingly unaware of the camera's presence. The action is not always pre-planned and can occur both spontaneously and unexpectedly, so the camera coverage is often less comprehensive than that of traditionally set up scenes.

Actuality rushes form the basis of many documentary genres, from observational films (such as Steve James's *Hoop Dreams*,[6] as well as the films of Louis Theroux and Michael Moore), to reality television (such as *Keeping Up with the Kardashians*[7]) and *Cinéma Vérité* (such as the Maysles brother's classic, *Salesman*[8]). While each uses actuality to a greater or lesser extent in their storytelling, their motives for doing so remain broadly the same: the audience is able to watch events unfold candidly, as though viewed by an invisible bystander.

The primary intention of actuality is to represent the truth of what is occurring in a chosen moment (as witnessed by the director) as objectively as possible. Actuality is also commonly used to show a process in action, as if playing out *in situ*.

When viewing actuality, I apply the same principles as if I were viewing a formal interview. I am primarily interested in the quality and relevance of the spoken material, keeping rambling exposition to a minimum, concentrating instead on those parts which reveal most about character and contain a high level of emotional content. I often find that the expositional bones of the scene are revealed quite clearly (and often with more depth and feel) through the actions and movements within frame, rather than explicit articulated explanation.

In addition to these two points, I am looking for the following:

- Shots that help me understand the context of the scene: actions that help explain the activity and the feelings of those involved in it. These could be facial expressions or other body language.
- Shots that help me to understand the geography of the location. This is especially important where the action within the scene (and the camera) is moving around a lot.

Actuality rushes can be very dense and detailed. There is usually a great deal of action within the frame and potentially many competing voices, combined with a freer and open approach to the photography. As a result, viewing actuality can take longer than interview and other rushes since we need to be alert and take care to select the most telling and appropriate details. For example, a small raise of an eyebrow could provide the critical signal in an actuality led scene, so we must remain vigilant and take our time to get the most out of this material.

For this reason, I do not usually ask for transcripts to be made of actuality. Since so much of what is worthwhile to the edit is in the expression itself and the *way* the words are said—rather than the words themselves—we really need to watch the rushes in order to be able to judge their worth.

I usually find that directors leave me to watch actuality alone, since viewing them requires more time, patience and focus than our combined efforts are worth. Later, when I have a cut down version of the actuality scene (containing the 'best bits'), we will work together to take it forward.

Actuality is as key and instrumental a storytelling device as interview material—indeed it is frequently even more so. Actuality has a unique ability to express the ineffable aspects of the story; revealing subtle emotional interplays between characters in a manner that is highly realistic and authentic. Interview material, by comparison, can often come across as much more constructed, manufactured and clinical. After all, interview is retrospective in tone, where as actuality is 'in the moment' and therefore more immediate in its impact.

Viewing B-Roll

Once I have created a sync pull for the interviews relevant to my new scene, I next view the cutaways and other supporting shots that surround them. These are referred to either as *GVs* (*General Views*) or as B-roll. The term 'B-roll' itself is quite loose and underwhelming (originating from the early days of celluloid-based editing) but these shots can cover a wide number of scenarios, such as:

- Supporting shots around an event, picking up details from within the story and the setup of the location.
- Actuality sequences covering live events, such as demos or interactions between people.
- Cutaway shots. On their most basic level, this could be a presenter's facial expressions (in response to an interview answer) or their hand gestures.

You could view your B-roll prior to viewing your interview and actuality material if you prefer, though I usually like to get a solid grip of the narrative first, through the spoken material which informs the way I understand and select the supporting rushes.

To begin the process, I play clips in real-time from the beginning of the rushes sequence so that I do not miss anything that could be useful.

I am looking for shots that:

- Illustrate my story by supplying context and clarity to the scene. I look particularly for shots that help establish location and geography.
- Illustrate and clarify any processes or experiments relevant to the story.
- Give depth to the portrayal of the people within the story. I am particularly interested in their faces and body language. Faces clearly help communicate to others our emotional state, revealing the state of mind of the person speaking. Eyes are particularly helpful in this regard and can say a great deal more than words alone.
- Have interesting movement. Shots with movement within the frame are more interesting and energising than more static and photo-like shots.

They add dynamism to a film and also cut much better. We will discuss this in detail later on.

As I watch through, I cut out everything that I do not feel contributes to these objectives. This includes anything which feels incongruous, tonally wrong, ugly, dull, hard to see or hear, or otherwise liable to require more effort to make effective than the content is worth. I place in and out marks around these 'offending' clips and delete them. When I come to a section with no significant content, I will skim through until the next point of interest, removing what has preceded and building up a selection of the best and most useful shots within my sequence.

Tip! When selecting shots, I test my decision making using the rationale that, if upon seeing or hearing something for the first time **I** am moved in a significant way, then it is likely to have the same impact on **other people**, i.e., the audience. As fellow humans, we generally exhibit, and respond to, the same emotional signals. By using a 'gut instinct' approach to shot selection, I am able to establish where the heart of the story lies with relative ease and a reasonable degree of confidence. In this way, I am also better able to identify and filter out the extraneous materials, i.e., the likely discard pile of shots that simply do not excite me.

I usually find that an hour of rushes will come down (without too much difficulty) to just a few minutes of usable material once I have finished watching through. At the end of this process you will be left with a concise high quality sequence of your best clips for a specific scene. You will have a neat run of interview highlights and a selection of the best shots that support them, ready to craft into a beautiful and effective story.

It is likely that you will also have these rushes pretty much committed to memory by now and will be thinking of neat ways in which the shots and sounds can go together to tell your story. This will help immeasurably during the next stage of the editing process when we begin to cut our sequences together (see figure 1.7).

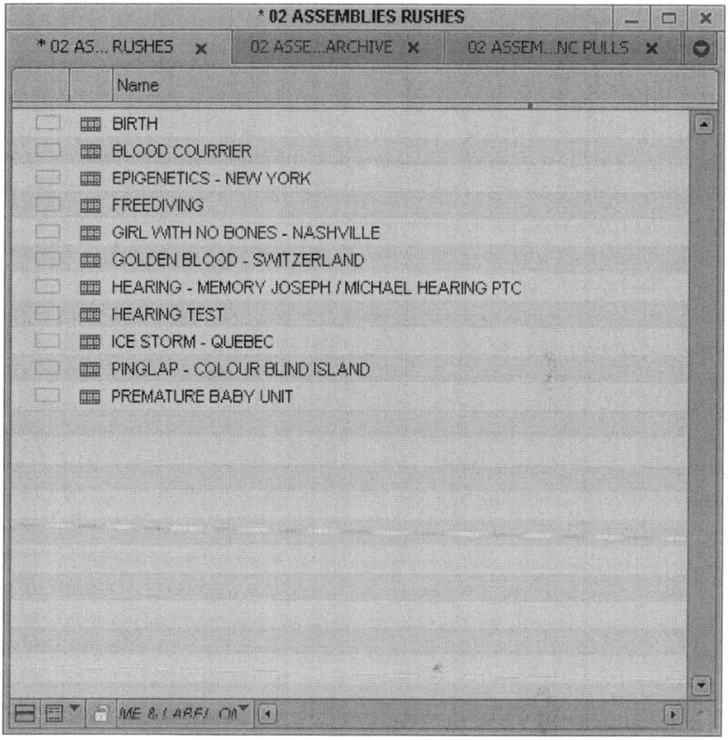

Figure 1.7 Rushes Assemblies Bin

A few thousand rushes clips have been grouped into eleven sequences, ready to edit.

> Tip! Try watching your cutaways with the sound muted. I often find this helps me focus on selecting the best pictures without becoming distracted by the background sounds outside of the frame, which will generally be of limited use anyway. Unless these shots have obviously distinctive and relevant sounds that will contribute to the storytelling, I generally assume that I will be sourcing alternative sound for these clips.

Key Points

- Remember what it is like to see and hear something for the first time.
- Your audience will probably only watch your film once.
- When you see or hear something that has an effect on you, it will also have an effect on your audience.
- Be strict when making selections. Your film will have to be a lot shorter than your rushes, and you do not have time for everything.

NOTES

1 www.goodreads.com. Accessed 19 October, 2016. www.goodreads.com/author/quotes/54195.Anthony_de_Mello

2 Robert McKee, *Story: Style, Substance, Structure and the Principles of Screenwriting* (Regan Books, NY: 2006), 211.

3 John Yorke, *Into the Woods: How Stories Work and Why We Tell Them* (Penguin, London: 2015), Kindle edition, 27.

4 James Marsh, *Man on Wire* (BBC Storyville/Discovery Films/Red Box Films/UK Film Council/Wall to Wall, 2008).

5 www.quotes.net. Accessed 23 October, 2016. www.quotes.net/quote/2442

6 Steve James, *Hoop Dreams* (Kartemquin Films/Fine Line Features, 2004).

7 *Keeping Up with the Kardashians* (Ryan Seacrest Productions/Bunim Murray Productions, 2007).

8 Albert Maysles/David Maysles/Charlotte Zwerin, *Salesman* (Maysles Films, 1969).

2

STARTING TO EDIT

UNDERSTANDING THE TASK AHEAD

> "It's as if somebody gave you all the pieces of a jigsaw puzzle and no picture of what the puzzle is supposed to look like. Maybe there's three or four jigsaw puzzles all mixed up. You've got to put all those pieces together and make a picture."
>
> —Geof Bartz[1]

Now that we have broken down our rushes into shorter manageable sequences, we are ready to start cutting. It's worth taking some time to think about how our edited sequences will fit together to make the finished film; laying out the pieces of the jigsaw so to speak, before putting the picture together.

Commercial television documentaries will usually begin with a short scene known as a *pre-title tease*. The pre-title is the 'sales pitch' for the film to follow. It is designed to convince an audience that they should stay to watch the whole film by taking the most enticing extracts from the body of the programme and cutting them together in a way that is exciting and dynamic. Pre-titles are usually short, trailer-like sequences, and while they are a part of the final broadcast film, they can be seen as a prelude to the main programme.

What follows the pre-title is often a more considered scene that sets out the main premise of the film. This is called the *post-title*. The post-title is there to outline in the simplest terms the conflict at the heart of our story: the reason we need to embark on a journey at all. We often use this scene to set out what the worst-case scenario might be, given the circumstance. This sequence informs our audience that the journey is going to be treacherous and difficult, but also intriguing and so worth sticking with. We want this conflict to feel genuine, significant, relevant and even daunting but not impossible to conquer.

The pre-title and post-title are often wrapped together into one single scene, in order to avoid potentially tedious repetition, and quickly lead the audience into the first in-depth scene of the film.

After the post-title we may then have two or three successive scenes, each exploring an individual aspect of the central narrative. Each of these scenes builds on the last to reach a conclusion, drawing their themes together. It is at this point that we can introduce an *act junction*. This is a scene designed to consolidate what we have learnt so far (and thus reassure the audience that they have 'got it'); it refreshes their knowledge and prepares them for the next stage of the narrative journey. The next run of scenes will focus on another aspect of the subject matter, often one that turns the ideas of the first act on their head by exploring the problem from a different perspective. The exposition of this perspective then leads to another, more nuanced and perhaps more challenging *but still interim* conclusion and, in turn, to another *act junction*.

This process will then repeat for a final time, with two or three further scenes, which aim to resolve the themes of the first two acts, leading to the film's ultimate conclusion and so to the end. This particular example of documentary is called a *three-act structure*, as it is designed to mimic in some ways the traditional narrative structure common in Hollywood films. (Incidentally, this structure is also the tried and tested formula of all eighteenth- and nineteenth-century theatre and opera which itself stands in a much longer theatrical tradition. So it might be said to have a proven 'form.') We will revisit this basic three-act structure later, exploring a number of important refinements which can be brought to it.

This is just one example of course. Documentaries come in many shapes and sizes and not all documentaries are designed with a television audience in mind. Many documentaries, for example Channel 4's *Welcome to Romford*[2] and Werner Herzog's *Grizzly Man*,[3] dispose of the pre-title altogether and simply begin with a strong first scene. I personally favour this approach where at all possible. Some films dispose of act junctions or summaries of any kind, and simply keep journeying forward through the scenes, though pursuit of a single uninterrupted linear narrative can bring problems of its own. Some documentaries eschew this common structure all together, such as *Zindane*,[4] which takes an entirely experimental approach to story structure. The film simply follows the eponymous Zinadine Zidane around a football pitch, until the last minutes of the game when he is sent off as a result of a brawl.

Your subject matter and target audience will determine the best structure for your particular documentary. The director whom you are working with will also usually have a preferred structure in mind by way of a script. The script will provide a provisional placement for each scene, and it is worth sticking with this structure—in the beginning at least.

DECIDING WHAT TO CUT FIRST

> "It is those who concentrate on but one thing at a time who advance in this world."
>
> —Og Mandino[5]

The beginning of the edit can be quite daunting. We have so much to achieve. We are at the foot of a mountain looking up. How do we climb to the top?

Well the answer is simple: one step at a time.

We cannot focus our energy on every scene and sequence in our film simultaneously, impatient as we might be to see the whole come together quickly. Our goal is to cut our film as perfectly as possible, and to do this we must concentrate our energy on getting one thing right at a time.

When we watch a well-crafted documentary, it flows from beginning to end as if it were one seamless whole and, in the best examples, with an inevitability that makes alternative narratives impossible to imagine. It is easy to forget that it is actually made of smaller successive blocks, each of which is the result of deliberate choices. Every one of these blocks, or *sequences*, was built independently.

So which sequence should we tackle first? I usually like to give the whole project impetus by dealing with something simple first; something short with fewer shots. This warms me up so I can be ready for the more difficult aspects later on, once I have begun to get a feel for the film and start properly to master its language. Look at your rushes assemblies' sequences and pick a scene.

When I began editing *Countdown to Life*[6] for the BBC, we had a number of intricately scientific and expositional scenes which, taken together, would explain what happens to a foetus during the last three months of pregnancy. In one scene we explained the role of osteoblasts, cells that change soft cartilage into hard bones. In another, we looked at epigenetics—changes in organisms caused by modifications of gene expressions. All interesting, yet rather heavy stuff. In order to break the ice, I first cut a scene of our presenter, Michael Mosley, playing with various noisy rattles and bells in front of an ultrasound scanner, to test whether a baby could hear them or not. A simple, straightforward little piece of the puzzle, after which I felt ready to take on something more substantial.

On the flip side, I would always avoid cutting the pre-title sequence until as late into the editing process as possible. While the pre-title may be the very first scene of the film, it is often an amalgamation of the film's other scenes, so it is much easier to have a good working version of those stories first, and then simply take the 'best bits' from those cut stories to create the pre-title. I remember an executive producer once saying early on into an edit; "Great news, we've got three days until the commissioner sees the film and they only want to see the pre-title and the first ten minutes!" Now, I'll paraphrase to avoid expletives, though the essence of what I said was along the lines of "Well, she'll just have to wait for that."

> Remember! You do not have to cut your scenes in chronological order, as they will appear in the final film. The order of your scenes may very well change later anyway. You can cut the blocks of your film in any order that feels right to you.

Key Points

- Our goal is to cut our film as perfectly as possible. To do that, we must focus only on getting one thing right at a time.
- A whole film is just a succession of smaller interconnecting blocks.
- Break the ice by starting with something simple.

APPRAISING A NEW SCENE

> "I believe an editor's prime roll is storytelling with as much clarity as his material will permit."
>
> —John Wilson[7]

Now we have chosen a scene to edit first, we must next decide how we are going to put it together. Each scene is going to tell its own mini story, which will connect to the over-arching storyline of the whole film. We want to explore this scene in the clearest, most cogent, interesting and compelling way possible.

The process of building a new scene is twofold:

1. First, we must select and structure the scene's spoken content. This is the skeleton upon which all else will depend.
2. Next, we must craft the aesthetic aspects of the scene: its pictures, sound and music. This is the flesh on the skeleton (though just as significant a contribution to the film's overall meaning and presentation).

At the start of a project, every scene has a huge range of storytelling possibilities, so it can be difficult to decide in which direction to go. In order to find a path and save myself from going crazy in the process, I have developed a system which allows me to determine the best direction to take, eliminating in the process less satisfactory alternatives.

1. **First, remember that each scene should focus primarily on one aspect of the film's broader story.**
   While the narrative arc of the documentary will tell a full and rich story, each individual scene should aim to cover just one facet of the

whole. This is not always easy, since there are instances where the complexity and overlap of the material across scenes is such that we cannot isolate one message from the next. In this sense, the scene can be seen as delivering more. However, is important to keep in mind the reason for aiming for this simplicity

Documentary is unlike other forms of storytelling we encounter in life, for example books, which are able to sustain a much more discursive narrative (to digress and add extra detail) without losing either their basic thrust or their audience. Documentary is by its very nature more linear and it becomes much harder for viewers to hold on to ideas in parallel, particularly if we attempt to move around too much.

So, before I begin to cut any new scene, I always make a deliberate point of asking the director "What is this scene about?" Asking this helps me to establish my hold on the scene and keep its purpose firmly in view. In this way, if other options present themselves as we work through the material, we can be quick to evaluate their merits and decide whether or not to pursue the avenues they open up.

Crucially, we must not cram too much in to any one scene.

> Tip! If you find the scene you are working on is too complicated to slim down in this way, then consider breaking it into two or more separate scenes, each concentrating on a single point.

2. Ask, is this scene essential to the story?

Every scene must have a purpose. That purpose is to maintain the film's dynamic, make a distinctive contribution towards its narrative arc and, by systematically exploring the aspect in question, enhance the audience's understanding of the films central argument. In this way, each individual block moves us progressively and inexorably towards the film's ultimate conclusion.

Two examples of how we can present the scene are:

- To set up a question at the start of the scene and answer it by the end. I cut a small scene for *Inside the Human Body*,[8] for example, in which we posed the question, "Why do we have a groove on our upper lip, just below our nose?" (This is called your *philtrum* as it happens.) Through the scene, which shows a scan of a developing embryo, we discover how our faces are assembled like a puzzle and come together in the middle of the top lip—creating the groove. The question posed at the beginning of the scene is answered definitively at the end.

Happily, the scene linked particularly well into the theme of the overall film, which was *Creation*.

- To set up a problem or conflict at the start of a scene and resolve it at the end.

  In *Countdown to Life*,[9] I cut a scene about a young girl born without the ability to make bones. As a foetus, her body was unable to produce a particular essential protein. Nobody, including her parents, thought she could live (the conflict). One day, her parents hear of a new drug being trialed that could help her. Little is known about it—and it may or not work—but there is no other option. She is put on the trial and after an agonising wait of several months, she is scanned. Amazingly her body has begun to develop bones. The drug has worked, and she is able live a long and happy life (the resolution).

  Again, this scene, as well as working effectively as a freestanding story, linked into the theme of the film, which was the final three months of a foetus's life in the womb.

  If the scene you are dealing with does not clearly link into the central argument of your film, no matter how pretty or entertaining it might be, you must either find a *legitimate* way to make it connect, or cut it out entirely.

  Further, you should ensure that the scene is not going to replicate any other scene in terms of the information it will communicate. If you have two scenes that are similar, choose one of them (usually the clearest, most energetic and best looking) and discard the other.

3. **Recognise that stories usually work best when they are told through people.**

We are all hardwired to recognise and connect with other people through our emotions. Emotions, their richness and spontaneity, are the most powerful tools we have at our disposal as filmmakers. Empathy, sympathy

> and commonality in our basic human response to stock situations are both a guide and a resource for us, and an intelligent understanding of how to 'exploit' these tools is key to successful documentary filmmaking.
>
> So, regardless of our film's subject matter, whether it's about karate or kittens, if we can focus our narrative around the lives and feelings of the characters featured in our story, we are already onto a winner. As an audience, we live vicariously through the experiences and feelings of the on-screen characters. We are more likely to care about the central argument of the film if we know why it is important to us and our own lives, and having an 'avatar' through which we can connect is key.
>
> Equally, when we are thinking of how to shape our scene, wherever possible we should focus on people either in interview or actuality or both. We must prioritise our character's emotional contact with the events of the story over their factual exposition of that story.

So, when taking on a new scene, first think how its story will connect with the central argument of your film. What unique information will it convey to your audience? Are you able to create a human-centric focus in telling this part of the story? How do you want the character to be perceived and how do you want the audience to feel when they watch them?

Key Points

- Each scene should aim to explain just one key aspect of the film's central argument. Ask: What is this scene really about?
- Ask: is this scene essential to the story? If not, cut it out!
- Wherever possible, tell your story through people.

STRUCTURING A NEW SCENE

Like complete films or acts, scenes have their own internal structure. Typically, they move from setup to confilict to crisis, before rebuilding to climax and resolution. In this sense, scenes have their own three-act structure, and mimic an archetypal story shape.

The scenes of nearly all commercial television documentaries are made up of interview clips, actuality and pieces to camera with voiceover in between to bridge the gaps. However, it is worth noting that not all documentary genres make use of all of these elements. For example, observational documentaries do not often use voiceover narration; relying instead on actuality and interview to tell their story. *CinémaVérité* documentaries are made of actuality alone.

Now that we understand the broad framework for the scene we can begin to structure it in our timeline. This process is known as *blocking out* the scene.

When we *block out* a scene, we are arranging all of the spoken components from our rushes, such as *interviews*, *actuality* and *pieces to camera* and, where needed, recording *voiceover narration* to produce an audio led structure for the story. I like to think of this stage as creating a sort of radio version of the scene that you could listen to with eyes closed and it would still make sense.

At this stage, we are not concerned with the 'look' or aesthetics of the scene (for example, its sequence of pictures or music). We are experimenting to establish a shape for the story and the broad components we will need to tell it. Once we have this foundation, all of the remaining picture and sound elements can be brought together with comparative ease.

When blocking out a scene I am mostly interested in two things:

1. **Story logic.** Presenting the information clearly, concisely and in a well-defined, dramatic order.
2. **Story rhetoric.** Deciding upon the character, manner and point of view from which the story is to be told.

Whenever possible, I will work closely with my director during this stage of the edit to ensure we are both in agreement regarding the way the scene is going to be shaped.

First I establish the spine of the scene, working with the interview clips that we watched earlier on by doing the following:

1. **First, I make a new sequence.**

   I put this sequence in my *CUTS* folder at the top of my project. I am going to use this sequence to block out and then edit the new scene.

2. **Alongside this sequence, I open my rushes assemblies' sequence.**
   This is the sequence I made when I first watched the rushes. It contains the sync pull for the scene I am going to block out.
3. **I copy the interview clips from my assembly sequence into my edit sequence.**
   I work from a copy of the interview sync pull as I want to keep the original as a backup should I need to refer back at any point.
4. **Working from my edit sequence, I cut down the sync pull further.**
   I want the finished scene to be as short as possible in order to keep it as impactful and entertaining as possible. I find that most scenes are between three and six minutes long once cut together, depending on their content. This duration will need to include any voiceover, music and spaces to let the pictures develop freely where needed.

   In order to meet this target duration, I usually have to cut down my sync assembly still further. I listen through it again and cut anything that isn't the very best of the best: excising any parts that are repetitive or any clips explaining process or offering factual exposition which can be much better explained using voiceover. We will discuss working with voiceover in the next section.
5. **Once slimmed down, I move the sync clips into order.**
   Remember, we are interested in telling the story in the clearest, most interesting and dramatic way possible. This is almost certainly not the order in which the interview was conducted.

Key Point

- Nearly all documentaries are made up of interview clips, actuality and pieces to camera with voiceover in between to bridge the gaps.

ORDERING INTERVIEW CLIPS

The order we choose for our interview clips will decide when and in what way the audience will learn of each part of our story. The order of our interview clips is, therefore, one of the key determinants of how the audience will experience our film. The same piece of information, or interview clip, revealed at a different point in the finished film, will have a dramatically different effect.

There is no right or wrong way of ordering clips. It is a matter of personal choice. However, by taking this matter seriously and properly questioning why we have made the choices we have, we can make an enormous difference to the narrative coherence and dramatic impact of our film.

Earlier on I pulled these clips from my interview rushes (see figure 2.1). Remember, this was just an extract and the full interview would have been several times longer, with many more clips to choose from.

Original Order of Clips as Shot	**Reorder of Clips**
I was born with very poor eyesight and I have been nearly completely blind for most of my life.	I fell in love with him the first time I met him.
I have learnt to look after myself but I still find many tasks in life difficult.	I didn't think that somebody normal would want to date a blind person.
I fell in love with him the first time I met him.	There are lots of things in everyday life that are challenging when you are blind. I struggle to cook for myself. I can't play a lot of sport.
I didn't think that somebody normal would want to date a blind person.	My life has changed enormously since Simon came along.
There are lots of things in everyday life that are challenging when you are blind.	It took some getting used to in the beginning but ~~I was immediately up for the challenge though.~~ I love Susie and I can't imagine wanting to do anything else with my life.
My life has changed enormously since Simon came along.	We would like to start a family together someday.
It took some getting used to in the beginning but I was immediately up for the challenge though. I love Susie and I can't imagine wanting to do anything else with my life.	We are concerned that our children could be born blind, but we will still love them just the same.
We would like to start a family together someday.	We ~~love each other a lot and~~ are looking forward to the future together.
We are concerned that our children could be born blind, but we will still love them just the same.	~~I was born with very poor eyesight and I have been nearly completely blind for most of my life.~~
We love each other a lot and are looking forward to the future together	~~I have learnt to look after myself but I still find many tasks in life difficult.~~

Figure 2.1 Transcript Extract, Re-Ordered

The transcript extract we visited in Chapter 1. On the left is the original sync pull and, on the right, my re-order of the same clips.

This is just one example of how we could begin to structure our scene. I have chosen to start with an emotional *hook* ("I fell in love with him the first time I met him") in order to prick the audience's curiosity. At this point, we haven't given anything away, just a sense that something interesting is going to develop. I then set about revealing the backstory: that the woman is blind and life is challenging. We are slowly building up a picture.

We could have started with the facts: "I was born with very poor eyesight and have been nearly completely blind for most of my life," though my instinct tells me that this might be a bit stark and cold, and less enticing for the audience. This might be an appropriate way to start for other scenes, though, in this instance, I feel that it is the romance in their relationship that is the key element rather than the problem with her eyesight. Coming to the matter of her eyesight later on may provide an element of surprise and an intriguing progression of the story.

In total, I usually only want four or five pieces of sync to make the spine of the scene. If I have multiple interviews to incorporate, I also copy them into my edit sequence and set about weaving them all together using this method.

Note! Do not edit directly from the rushes assemblies sequence. We want to preserve this sequence for future reference, in the event we will need to go back to recut the scene later on with more or different material.

Key Points

- We are aiming for our scenes to be as short as they can be and certainly no longer than they need to be.
- We want to tell the story in the clearest, most interesting and dramatic way possible. This is seldom achieved by sticking to the order in which the interview was conducted.

TRIMMING INTERVIEWS

Once we have cut down our interview clips to a usable length and placed them in some order, we will often need to tidy up some of the finer details of what they say. This is often where our interviewees "um" and "ah" a great deal whilst thinking between sentences, where they pause or falter, digress, or repeat phrases when no repetition is required.

These moments can undermine our confidence in what the interviewee is saying, making them appear inarticulate or simply impeding the delivery of the message, robbing the scene of energy in the process. As editors, our aim is to make our interview contributors look as good as possible, and so we should help them along with a trim or two where we can.

There are a few things to consider when trimming an interview:

- **Keep voices sounding natural.**
  Ensure that the reassembled clips join together in a way that sounds natural and true to a real-life conversation. Listen to their intonation and manner of delivery when matching clips up. The timing of the edit, as well as the energy of each adjoining clip is crucial here.
- **Cut as little as possible.**
  The more cuts we make, the harder it is to keep the natural sound of our contributor. Try and limit your cuts to key points that are interfering with the story's flow.

  Some editors—and some directors, too—do not like interviewees to "um" or "ah" at all and are quick to cut them all out, creating many tiny internal edits within an interview clip. Personally I think a few "ums" do no real harm; rather they reinforce the idea that this is a real person thinking and speaking their mind in a natural way. Furthermore, some hesitation on the part of the interviewee may be helpfully revealing: disclosing in a raw and honest way the emotional response a particularly difficult question may provoke.

  Above all, I want the audience to believe that this is an unmanipulated sequence that properly represents what the interviewee wanted to say. After all, we have a duty to the contributor who has given his or her time in good faith to represent them fairly. The more I can resist getting the scissors out and artfully manufacturing the interview, the better!

- **Establish where, if at all, to keep interviewees in vision.**
When we make cuts in the audio of an interview clip, it is inevitable that we will make cuts in the picture, too. These cuts, known as jump-cuts, can look ugly and distracting. So to smooth them out, we will overlay cutaway shots to conceal the edits. (I will say more about this later.)

While it is necessary to make some edits in our interviews, we should try to preserve as much of the original clip as we can. There are two reasons for this.

First, it is of general interest to the audience to be able to see the person who is speaking at certain points. This is particularly true when we first hear an interviewee speak: in order to put a face to a voice. It is also the case at moments when body language is a key component of the message; for example, when an interviewee laughs, cries or emphasises something with a hand or other physical gesture. At these moments, seeing the interviewee can tell the story far more effectively than the words alone.

Second, once we do see the interviewee in vision, it feels natural to grant the audience enough time to scan and appraise their appearance (primarily their face) without having to cut away quickly again in order to conceal a cut in the interview dialogue. While there may be moments where we wish to cut away like this for deliberate, frenetic effect, these kinds of cuts usually feel very distracting and unnecessarily 'busy.'

I try to find sections in my interview clips where the subject can stay in vision for whole phrase or sentence at least. I then tend to cut in and out of the interview in between sentences or at other natural junctions in the interviewee's train of thought.

There are instances where we may wish to avoid seeing our contributor in vision at all, using their voice alone to tell the story. This can sometimes help the audience to focus on what is being said without the distraction of (perhaps less than satisfactory) pictures. I have found this approach works well when something of particular significance or perhaps very personal import is being said.

Tip! At times it can be difficult to appraise a join in an interview without becoming distracted by the awkward picture jumps. In these moments, I find it useful to look away from the screen while playing the clip, listening only for the sense of the spoken words. Once it sounds good, I can then set about fixing the pictures.

Key Points

- We want to make our interview contributors look as good as possible.
- Keep voices sounding natural. Match the energy of adjoining clips.
- Cut as little as possible. A few "ums" or "ahs" are okay.
- Establish where, if at all, to keep interviews in vision.

WORKING WITH ACTUALITY

Actuality material is perhaps the single most important and persuasive component in our storytelling armoury. This is because it speaks directly to our audience as authentic testimony ('evidence') whilst, at the same time, offering appropriate context to the narrative argument. Actuality *shows* our audience what is happening (the camera appears to simply follow the action), rather than *telling* them, as interview or voiceover might. This lack of *obvious* editorial filtering (or absence of overt bias) encourages our audience to engage with the story first-hand and to form their own views without the appearance of intervention on our part, even though we have, of course, selected our actuality from rushes in a way which best supports the argument we want to make. As always, truth is a matter of perspective.

However, while actuality is a powerful and effective storytelling device, it can be difficult to make it work alone. First, it takes time to understand actuality and requires investment on the part of the viewer in the scene that the actuality is illustrating. Given the viewing habits of modern audiences—which more often than not require more immediate gratification—such investment cannot be simply taken for granted. Further, because actuality usually requires a degree of interpretation and 'effort' on the part of the audience, the actual import of the message is not guaranteed to be unambiguous or crystal-clear. This can, of course, be a strength—particularly if conveying complexity is the purpose of the scene—but it can also lead to unintended consequences: generating an element of confusion which may impact on the clarity of the narrative overall.

For these reasons, actuality is frequently used in combination with interview, each complementing the other's storytelling strengths. Indeed, interview is greatly enhanced by actuality and actuality by interview in what can be a highly effective symbiosis. For if we *show* our audience the interplay between characters and events (through carefully selected actuality), we can then help guide their thoughts and reactions with carefully selected interview materials.

24 Hours in A&E,[10] for example, is a series predominantly built on this interplay between actuality and interview. The actuality shows the action, urgency and emotional interplay between events and characters, while the interview gives the actuality context and meaning, by allowing the characters to express their feelings (their fears, worries and frustrations) as well as supplying important expositional material required to aid the audience's understanding of what is happening. Taken together, these two contrasting but highly complementary forms give the audience a more complete and engaging picture of the event.

In this sense, actuality and interview live happily alongside each other in our film, each informing and supporting the other.

Key Points

- Actuality provides evidence and context to our narrative argument, which earns our audience's trust. It enables them to see things for themselves.
- Interview and voiceover tells the audience; actuality shows them.

WORKING WITH VOICEOVER

> "What differentiates a documentary film editor from a feature film editor is that a documentary editor is also the film's scriptwriter."
>
> —David Tedeschi[11]

Regardless of how skilfully we are able to select and order the interview clips for our scene, we will usually be left with a number of gaps between them. These 'gaps' are jumps in the story logic, which are not explained through the interview sync, actuality or pieces to camera.

These gaps could be where two interview clips do not follow on logically from each other, where a leap in the story's development has occurred between two clips or where an interviewee introduces a new idea or concept that is crucial to the audience's understanding of the story.

More fundamentally, we might find that we discover large story gaps during the editing process, if we need to embed a completely new story idea into our film—for example, one that had not been thought of prior to the edit. In this instance, we may not have the necessary interview material to explain and develop the storyline that we now wish to elaborate.

I experienced exactly this scenario while editing *The Treasure Hunters*.[12] The series explored the great treasures to be found across the world, such as gold and diamonds. The director and I were struggling to connect our scenes together as a meaningful whole, trying to make the film more than just a loose assemblage of isolated stories. The 'solution' that materialised was to construct a plausible overarching thesis in voiceover. In this way we badged each story as a 'raw treasure' that you only have to scratch the surface of the planet to find. The end result wasn't entirely brilliant but it helped!

Even on a basic level, without more significant structural problems to address, interview clips alone will rarely cover every aspect of the story in a neat, comprehensive and engaging way.

An effective way to bridge these gaps, thus both clarifying our story and linking the various parts together, is by using *voiceover* (also known as *guide commentary*). Voiceover is any spoken words that are written and recorded in the edit (via a microphone) and then positioned between the unconnected interview clips in the edit timeline. Voiceover provides a tailored means of bridging gaps in our story, as we can write any words we require to connect the thoughts together.

It is worth remembering that not all documentaries use voiceover (particularly actuality led, observational films) and in these instances, story gaps must either be lived with, solved by the rearrangement or deletion of material, or in some cases, title captions (which perform a similar job to voiceover).

Voiceover is particularly useful for:

- **Linking two ideas or thoughts together.**
  Voiceover can be used to link two separate ideas (or story threads) together by finding an expression that they both have in common. The line of voiceover will effectively make up for the missing step between the two ideas.
- **Linking whole scenes or acts together.**
  Voiceover is particularly useful in recapping larger story points, unifying disparate ideas and summarising thoughts between scenes and acts. These sorts of connections might otherwise be hard to establish with interview or actuality alone.

  Voiceover, when used at key turning points in our story, is an effective means of re-engaging our audience with our films central argument.
- **Simplifying tricky concepts.**
  Documentaries will often tackle subjects that involve complicated concepts, theories and terminology. Interview contributors are rarely good at explaining such things, as they tend to use overly technical and/or elaborate language (jargon), and often mumble or speak too quickly/slowly, missing out on important steps in the exposition they are struggling to convey. This usually results in a tedious and sometimes confusing experience for the audience.

  However, a few precisely focused words, in the form of voiceover, can provide a simple means of explaining these tricky story ideas.

  Similarly, we can also use voiceover to deliver simple facts that would not otherwise have a means of expression within our story.
- **Giving another texture to our film.**
  Some films work incredibly well as a succession of interview clips, with pictures and music in between (i.e., without voiceover). However, many others, particularly more complicated stories, do not. Interviews alone can sometimes make for a slow and laboured exposition.

  Voiceover can add energy, variety and pace to our story and its sequences. Through voiceover, we can drip feed and regulate the flow of information. We can create patterns and rhythms in our words. We can choose interesting punctuations and edges. This all adds up to exciting changes in pace and mood, and creates an element of variety and unpredictability in our narrative.

Furthermore, this variety of pacing can help the audience digest the story more easily. We can create space between our lines of voiceover, allowing time for thought where needed, or equally we can use shorthand expressions to move things on quickly in other instances.

Because voiceovers are scripted (and often supplied by well-known voiceover artists), they possess a tone quite different from that of ordinary interviewees (who tend to be more idiomatic and generally less considered in their expression).

There are two styles commonly used to express voiceover in documentary films. The first is referred to as the *Voice of God*, due to its third-person status, prominence and natural authority in the film. Such voices (even if not famous or identifiable) are lent a natural authority by virtue of their status and prominence in the film. *Planet Earth*[13] uses the Voice of God (albeit with David Attenborough's highly recognisable voice). His is a disembodied omnipresent voice, exuding absolute mastery and knowledge and clearly outside the spatial and temporal boundaries of the world the film depicts. This approach is also frequently used in documentaries such as Discovery's *Deadliest Catch*.[14] Whilst this Voice of God can be used to advantage—a point made during a voiceover is likely to come across as an objective truth and might be a useful summary of the story thus far—it also has its dangers in that, wrongly used, voiceovers can appear to diminish the contributions made by interviewees or, at the very least, 'trump' their contribution. Careful thought should be given then to the nature, duration and tone of any voiceover if a proper balance is to be maintained.

A simple rule for remembering how to use voiceover is: we say (with voiceover) what *happened*, and they (the contributor) tell us how it *felt*.

The second style commonly used to express voiceover appears in presenter-led films, where the voice heard during the voiceover is clearly the presenter's own. Here the voiceover is a continuation of the presenter's point of view and remains a personal opinion, where freer, more personal and idiomatic expression is required. It is quite different from the more traditional, and often rather more rigid, Voice of God. This personal approach works well where the personality of the author is part of the construction of the film as it is in the films of

Obscure, quirky man walking through the grass looking for poo in Richmond Park. Format intro shot – same frame as people in street, but surrounded by green – Graham looking straight down the lens. **GFX 1A Labels for Prof Graham Man** Graham chatting with the deer behind him.	*Graham Man upsync:* *... poo ...* **COMM:** **This is Graham Man. Professor of Immunology at University City College.** *Graham upsync:* *... where was it? There's got to be some deer poo here somewhere?* *There's some poo of some sort there.* **COMM:** **His theory explains how organisms so small that they're invisible are changing our physiology.** *Deer poo . . .* **And they're making us allergic.** *Graham Man:* *It is calculated that the animal kingdom deposits on this planet something like fourteen billion tonnes of faeces per year. Now faeces contain an enormous number of bacteria and also an enormous number of bacterial spores.* **COMM:** **But these bacteria aren't just found in faeces.**
Graham is standing in the middle of Richmond Park. **GFX 1B labels** multitude of bacteria in the air around Graham Use the macro – ground, flowers, dirt etc where needed.	*Graham Man:* *Well of course the micro-organisms, bacteria in particular are absolutely everywhere – even the air is full of bacteria.* *I mean there are at least, on a day like this in this park, I don't know... a hundred thousand or maybe even a million per cubic meter of air.* *And if you're in the vicinity of animals, if one were in amongst the herd of deer over there would probably be ten million.* **COMM:** **But these micro-organisms don't just live in the air, they live on us too.**

Figure 2.2 Script Extract

A script extract from one of my documentaries. The left column is a suggested visual treatment from the director and the right column contains the spoken material.

Michael Moore (for example *Capitalism: A Love Story*[15]), and in those written and narrated by Jonathan Meades (such as *Ben Building: Mussolini, Monuments and Modernism*[16]). In a similar vein though slightly unusual, Alex Gibney in *The Armstrong Lie*[17] adopts a second-person singular approach to his voiceover.

The writing and recording of voiceover, regardless of its form, is usually taken care of in the most part by the director. The director will devise and write the voiceover into the script during the edit. They will transcribe any spoken material (be it interview, actuality or piece to camera) that has been selected and placed in the timeline to work with it. Once written, this voiceover is recorded into the edit (as a guide) so that the script and edit sequence remain mirrored (see figure 2.2).

Whilst editors do not have to be master voiceover writers, it is still important that we are capable of assisting the director by spotting story gaps which need fixing and helping to work out the essence of what the voiceover needs to say. Being a competent scriptwriter is simply a bonus.

Key Point

- We say what happened, and they tell us how it felt. Voiceover should be used for factual exposition, while contributors (as well as presenters) are good for conveying emotional content.

DECIDING WHERE VOICEOVER IS NEEDED

Voiceover, like most other filmmaking devices, should be used as sparingly as possible. Our aim should always be to allow the audience as much freedom as we can to interpret the story through their own encounter with the characters, pictures and sounds.

While a few carefully chosen and positioned words can have immense impact, in general, the more we say, the less people will listen.

So, we now have a neat sync pull for our new scene. This contains all of the important interview clips. We have trimmed these clips to make their words clearer and more succinct, and have placed them in a dramatic yet broadly logical order.

We can now decide if and where we are likely to need voiceover to progress the scene.

I begin doing the following:

- **First, I ask, where are the gaps between my interview clips?** It is worth listening through your sync pull to ensure that your interview clips follow on from each other seamlessly and logically. If they do, then we can begin to plan voiceover to better link sections together.

  You will recall that when I first assembled my sync pull, I deliberately chose to exclude much of the expositional parts of my interviews. These were the parts of their interview that dealt with the mundane processes, mechanisms, and technical workings in the story (but probably badly, dully or confusingly stated). While that was a good move, it is likely that information important to our story was lost in the process.

  We are now going to restore some of this information in a shorthand form, using voiceover.

  Second, it is also worth asking if there is anything that was not covered in the original interview, which may be important to the story now. This information could be the location in place or time of the scene at hand. Adding context, or clarifying that part of a contributor's *backstory* which contextualises their contribution is often vital to the overall storyline itself.

  Any information that is likely to reinforce the significance and veracity of our story as well as reinforce the credentials of those involved in it may be worth including as voiceover. Is your contributor a world expert in their field? Or a unique witness to the event? Did the incident take place at a significant moment in history? In the middle of a civil war? In this way, our voiceover is going to enhance the expositional elements of the scene and any relevant and supporting details, at the same time, explaining the process succinctly and clarifying the structure of events.

  If we are unable to find a satisfactory way to link two interview clips together, we should try to find another place for the clip to live in our sequence, find another point in the clip(s) to make the cut between them, or cut the clip out altogether. I often find that removing a clip from my sequence creates a much more effective link to the next part of the story (and saves valuable screen time).

- **Second, I ask, could some of the information in an interview clip or actuality sequence be better explained with voiceover?**
  I am always keen to keep the story moving and for each 'beat' of the story to add to the last. If the delivery of a particular interviewee is slow or laboured, perhaps the point could be better made with a line of voiceover.
  I will always aim to preserve clips where an interviewee expresses a strong personal opinion or exhibits a distinct emotional response. Voiceover is no substitute for this kind of expression. However, if the contributor is saying something which is purely expositional in a less than clear and entertaining manner, I would be tempted to cut them out and replace what they say with a short, simple voiceover.
- **Finally, I ask, if we cut this part of the scene out, would the story still make sense?**
  We do not have time to explain every single aspect of our story. The story would become too long, too complicated and too dull. Therefore, we must be selective of the information that we choose to explore and work around the information which is less essential.
  I ask, if I cut this part of the scene, would the story still make sense? Would the thoughts expressed on either side of the cut points link up just as well?
  Sometimes we have to be tough with our clips for the greater good of the film: cutting out parts of our story which are nice enough in themselves or which we happen to like, but which do not strengthen the finished film.

At the end of this process, we will have a good idea of what information is missing from our sync assembly and may be developing a much firmer grasp on what we really want to say.

Key Point

- Voiceover should be used as sparingly as possible. The more we say, the less our audience will listen.

VOICEOVER WRITING BASICS

There are very few rules in documentary editing, and this is also true for how we use voiceover. However, there are a few principles I have adopted which help me use voiceover effectively, thus keeping my storytelling clear, concise and engaging.

- **Voiceover works best when used for exposition.**
  Voiceover is a very efficient way of conveying information. It is highly effective when used to convey the information-rich and information-centric, factual elements of our story.
  Voiceover is not appropriate to emotional storytelling. It is not a device that works well for communicating feelings. Perhaps this is because we cannot see the voiceover artist who is speaking (though we may recognise their voice) and are unable to read their facial expressions so that their dispassionate voice can seem too authoritative and even authoritarian.
  For this reason, confine the use of voiceover to explaining the functional parts of the story, and use real people, through interviews and actuality, to communicate the emotional content.
  For example, we may wish to use voiceover to begin a scene: what is the purpose of this scene in supporting the overarching theme of our film? Who is this interviewee and what qualifies them as the best person to tell us what they are about to tell us?
- **Keep it simple.**
  Voiceover works best when it is delivered in straightforward, short, conversational language. We are creating a piece of entertainment, not a written textbook, so keep it snappy! The more characterful and chatty we are able to make our voiceover, the more personable and companionable it will seem and the more effective it will be.
  I find it helps to imagine I'm in the pub (or some such relaxed social environment), explaining the story to a friend. What sort of language would I use? I would probably avoid complicated words and jargon. How would I reveal the information, breaking it down to help my friends understand and be entertained by what I am saying? Where would I pause for dramatic effect? What would I leave out? Remember, too, the intended

audience: if I were speaking to a child, rather than an adult, I would simplify my language still further.

Remember: no one is likely to complain because you've made something too easy for them to understand.

- **Drip-feed information. One step at a time.**

It is likely that our audience will know little about the subject of our film, and a great deal of what we say will come as new to them. Therefore, we must regulate the flow of information throughout our scene and avoid overwhelming them with too much in one go.

Break down your sentences into short digestible chunks, each taking one small step at a time.

An added bonus of this approach is that by holding information back, we can hook our audience in to watching the scene to its end, allowing them to figure out some of the subtle missing pieces for themselves and granting them space to guess what will come next.

Screenwriter Andrew Stanton calls this concept The Theory of 2+2. He says,

> Good storytelling never gives you four, it gives you two plus two. . . . Don't give the audience the answer; give the audience the pieces and compel them to conclude the answer. Audiences have an unconscious desire to work for their entertainment. They are rewarded with a sense of thrill and delight when they find the answer themselves.[18]

Contrary to this wisdom, many filmmakers (particularly in the higher executive echelons) fear this approach because it leaves room for and may even require interpretation—but that's the whole point. Interpretation is the mechanism whereby the audience becomes actively involved in the narrative. It doesn't alienate the audience—it does the opposite: it engages them!

This is particularly true at the beginnings and ends of scenes. I like to begin and end my scenes in an information-light manner, giving the audience a chance to ease in and out, much like the warm up and down in a running race. Once I sense the audience has been warmed up and is comfortably alongside, I feel confident I can add weight and detail to the story.

- **Don't give everything away at the beginning of the scene.**
  When we have great stories to tell, it can be tempting to start our scene with the most startling revelation: going straight to the denouement without the 'appetiser.' While this form of instant gratification could be seen as an easy way of capturing the audience's attention, it leaves very few places to take the story thereafter, effectively killing it before it has begun.

  We should, therefore, ensure that we structure the story in a way that allows it to be revealed gradually, with a clear beginning, middle and end. We want to build a sense of anticipation in the audience, keeping them 'short-changed' initially, then excited and finally engaged enough to want to discover what will come next.
- **Avoid unessential detail.**
  Almost any subject has the potential to become too wide-ranging for its own good and our treatment of it sprawling. We need to keep our story focused to fit the time and space we have. So we cannot include and explain everything. Avoid information that does not directly serve the story (or central argument) at hand, and when you do introduce new information, do so once you have created the need or desire in the audience to know.

  For example, I have recently been editing a documentary series about slavery, and in one particular scene we look at Britain's involvement in American slavery. The opening voiceover first read: "The North American state of Virginia. It's hard to believe, but for almost 150 years Virginia and twelve other states were part of the British Empire." On closer inspection, the director and I realised that some of this information was unnecessary. We subsequently changed it to read: "The North American state of Virginia. For almost 150 years it was part of the British Empire." Since it was working, the first line stayed the same. In the second, we subtracted two things. First, we thought it was better not to assume that the audience would find it "hard to believe." We want the audience to decide for themselves, rather than project our own feelings onto them, which may not be the same. Second, we did not need to know that "twelve other states" were once part of the British Empire. The scene was primarily about Virginia. By saying that there were twelve other states, this only begs the question, "Well, what were the twelve other states?" There is no strict need to know this information—it just gets in the way—so we cut it out.

This need-to-know basis for voiceover delivery could be triggered by something which is said by an interviewee if, for example, they introduce terminology or a concept which is new, yet essential, to the storytelling. We must always be aware when new terms are introduced and ask ourselves if the audience is likely to understand them immediately or require assistance before they can process the information they have been given.

- **Deal with everything once only.**
  You should only have to introduce a concept once in a film. If you find that you need to remind the audience of what something is, or reintroduce it all together, then something has gone wrong. Is your story in the right order?
- **Back up voiceover statements with evidence.**
  It is easy to write anything in voiceover. Our audience is smart, and if we are to convince them that our point of view is valid, then we must support our case as convincingly as possible.

  This evidence could be a piece of interview, where the contributor confirms a statement we have made in voiceover, a piece of archive (historical footage connected to the story) or even a picture or sound bite which illustrates our point.
- **Avoid superlatives.**
  Superlatives, such as *amazing* or *incredible*, are a facile—and ultimately ineffective—way of strong-arming our audience into buying our story and our particular take on it. The problem is that hyperbole and any other language that exaggerates the significance of any claim we make usually comes across as fake. Further, it betrays a fundamental lack of confidence in the narrative's (and rushes material's) power to tell its own story in its own way. By overtly (or even covertly) editorialising in this way we are intruding: denying our audience the right to form their own opinions based on their own contact with the original source materials.

  In general, I believe we should avoid adjectives altogether and, wherever possible, let the audience form their own conclusions without our intervention. If we present the story well, the audience will likely come to the same conclusions we ourselves have, but from a place of authenticity and trust.

- **Write voiceover with your picture sequences in mind.**
  If a picture is worth a thousand words, then what about a sequence of pictures? Placing two shots together creates new and often unanticipated meanings, which neither picture alone could describe. For example, a picture of a chicken says very little. It's just a chicken. Cut this together with a picture of a knife being sharpened and now we have the beginning of a story. We have created drama. A sequence of pictures connected like this offers more opportunities still.

  Most picture sequences that we craft as editors will have an optimal order and structure, based on the flow and development of the pictures and the meanings they impart when placed together. We must be aware of the importance of this natural picture flow and respect it when writing our voiceover. There are several reasons for this.

  First, we can write anything, but we may not have the pictures to illustrate what we write in a properly satisfactory way. Furthermore, arranging our pictures only to fit a certain sequence of words usually results in a meaningless, fragmented and ugly jumble of images. These generally translate into a graceless and enervating experience for the audience.

  Moreover, experience suggests that people do not generally listen to words very carefully, as they become increasingly absorbed in the general flow and energy of the film. I believe they are more likely to be put off a film by a confused, poorly flowing sequence of shots, than drawn to it by a determining, fixed choice of words.

  Voiceover should be written to support what is contained within your picture sequences and not *vice versa*. We should be *writing to our pictures*.

  This means that in most instances we will construct a sentence so that the reference to what is on screen comes near the start of the sequence (or is led into from the end of the previous sequence), setting up our audience for what is to come.

- **Know your audience.**
  Your use of language must be appropriate to your audience. The way we explain something to a child is obviously very different to an adult. What a fourteen-year-old adolescent finds funny may not appeal quite so much to his grandmother.

It is important that when we choose our words, we use a tone and vocabulary that is appropriate to our audience.

- **Tell your story for the big screen.**

  Most of us will have grown up watching cinema films in one form or another. On the whole, most of us will regard feature films as the pinnacle of quality, dramatic storytelling and audience experience.

  Documentaries are real-life dramas, real-life feature films. We should aim to tell our story in the most cinematic way possible, emulating appropriately the storytelling and craft of the bigger screen.

  As documentary makers, there is nothing to stop us dramatizing our words to create the richest, most suspenseful or heart-warming narrative of which we are capable.

  For example, I once cut a documentary about the British weather, which in truth was (like the British weather) inherently rather dull. However, we were able to breathe some life into it by crafting the voiceover in the manner of a murder mystery. The weather event became the crime or murderer, and the various factors which contribute to bad weather became the suspects. We looked at the bits of evidence in turn, made our deductions and identified the 'culprit' rather as Hercule Poirot might have done. It worked!

  Again, on a similar note, I try not to address the audience as though they were gathered together collectively as if in a stadium and in the first person plural. When people watch your film, they are likely to be alone, or in a small group. Imagine you are speaking directly to them, one human being to another in the second person singular. This principle works particularly well for the Voice of God style of voiceover—giving it an encouraging softness and warmth.

- **Never write a line of voiceover where you can create a visual expression.**

  Some films can, and do, work wonderfully well without voiceover at all. It is a kind of ideal, and, conceptually at least, we should always be striving to make a film which works without voiceover. To achieve this, we must be sparing in our use of words avoiding them wherever possible. Let the pictures tell the story.

  Ask, if I took this line of voiceover out, will the story still make sense?

- **Above all, be truthful.**
  As filmmakers, we are in a highly influential position over our audience. We choose the line of our story, select the information which supports that line, and we present it all in an order which most clearly and dramatically serves our intention. Further, we are at liberty to write almost anything we choose to further justify and 'sell' our chosen line.

  We have a duty to our audience to represent accurately and fairly both our story and the people who are part of it. Integrity must be our byword.

  Any information we include in the programme must always be thoroughly researched and sourced from trustworthy sources and not just looked up on Wikipedia! This information must be carefully fact-checked again at the end of the edit to ensure accuracy and identify any sins of omission or commission. The director and their assistant producer will usually take care of this process, though as editors it is still important that we remain vigilant in all that we do. After all, it is we who, as editors, have lived with and scrutinised this material a thousand times more carefully than anyone else. If something does not sit right with you, then speak up!

  Finally, it is worth noting that whilst truthfulness is of paramount importance, the truth is often simply an opinion convincingly stated. For this reason, editing is inherently manipulative. As Wolf Koenig said, "Every cut is a lie. It's never that way. Those two shots were never next to each other in time that way. But you're telling a lie in order to tell the truth."[19]

  Interview contributors freely express their opinions on camera, and those opinions are the lodestone of our film. In this way, each contributor has his or her personal 'take,' and the only way in which we can remain objective and mitigate any bias in our story is to present these multiple points of view as honestly as we can. We make films for audiences. Tell them the best story you can and have the confidence to let them make up their own minds.

Key Points

- Voiceover works best for exposition. It is not an appropriate way to convey emotion.

- Keep it simple. No one will ever complain that you've made something too easy to understand.
- Use conversational language and avoid jargon.
- Drip-feed information and do not give everything away at the beginning.
- Voiceover should be written to support your picture sequences, not the other way around.
- Write in a style and with a voice appropriate to your audience.
- Ask, if I took this line out, would the story still make sense?
- Tell the truth.

MANAGING A VOICEOVER RECORDING

Voiceover is recorded into the edit via a desktop microphone. This voiceover is then placed where required in the edit timeline.

The words of the voiceover will likely change many times during the editing process as the story itself evolves, so at this stage—while we are still playing with our story ideas—the voiceover we will record serves purely as a guide. It is usually voiced by the director, or sometimes, the editor. In broadcast television, once the film is finished (known as *picture lock*) the final voiceover is then re-recorded with a professional voiceover artist in a controlled studio environment. This new voiceover then takes the place of the guide voiceover in the finished film.

Regardless of whether our guide voiceover record will make the final cut of the film, it is still worth making the quality of the recording, and most importantly the quality of the read, as good as possible. By doing so, we can best imagine and see the film as a finished product from an early stage and make any screenings with outside contributors—such as directors or executives—as representative of the edit's quality and as enjoyable and convincing as possible.

Some simple principles to consider when recording guide voiceover are:

- **Speak slowly.**
  Most of us tend to speak too quickly when we are being recorded or if we feel someone is listening to our voice. I suspect this has something to do with nerves. Unfortunately, this doesn't work well for voiceover recording, as our words become unclear and sound unnatural.

So, make sure that you speak slowly and articulate clearly, keeping the delivery of each word evenly paced. When you reach a full stop, count to two before continuing. When you reach a comma or other punctuation, count to one. Focus on keeping your energy levels up and your voice bright from the beginnings to the ends of your sentences.

Note! It is likely that your director will read the voiceover—as they will have written most of it. While most experienced filmmakers will be aware of their pacing, if necessary, do not be afraid to (politely!) ask if they could say that again more slowly.

- **Speak with presence.**
  You must project your voice with power and energy. By doing so, you can help instill a sense of authority to your words. Your voice must be in a tone appropriate to the mood of the scene.
- **Voiceover does not have to be perfect first time.**
  You can rewrite and re-record your voiceover as many times as you like during the edit. There is no need to become concerned or fixated on making your words and sentences absolutely perfect the first time.

  As a principle, I find it works best to write and record something quite quickly at first. I simply ensure that the sentence has the right overall meaning and it is about the right length—the more concise the better. I then go ahead and record it there and then.

  This way, I am always moving forward in painting the broad brushstrokes of the film, and crucially, I am able to get into a steady rhythm early on. This rhythm or, better, sense of flow, which—if we are lucky—we experience when we become totally immersed in our work, allows us to achieve much higher levels of productivity and to decant many of the ideas we have into the film quickly and with ease. I am able to fashion the rough shape of the scene in a single 'stroke' without becoming bogged down in the detail.

  Further, on a pragmatic note, I am also well aware that these words are unlikely to survive into the final edit, so I do not wish to waste time tinkering at this stage.

Once I have recorded my voiceover line, I move on to the next one, without delay. I will come back and review it later on, in the context of the whole scene, and decide where, if at all, it needs refining.

- **Get your final words placed into the edit before picture lock.** Once the film is effectively picture locked and everyone is happy with the rest of the content, take some time to review the script and ensure the words work in the way you intended. If any changes are to be made, re-record them and place them into the edit timeline.

  Odd as it may sound, I have worked on many films where the voiceover has been substantially rewritten *after* the film has been picture locked and not laid into the edit against the pictures *at all*. Unfortunately, some people (mainly executives in truth) do not really understand the significant effect that changing words, and ultimately their duration and connection with the pictures actually has.

  In these circumstances, it is difficult to ensure that the new words will fit into the spaces occupied by the old ones. As a result, the pauses and breaks which once existed between sentences are squeezed or removed to fit everything in. This seriously damages the pacing and delivery of the sequence, and the film can lose much of its feeling in the process. Worse, it may look to outsiders as though the editor hasn't done their job properly at all!

We must ensure that we pace our words carefully and respect the spaces between them. The spaces contribute as much and, I would argue sometimes more, to the narrative as the words themselves. They create opportunities for the audience to absorb, think, feel and care about what they are seeing and hearing. Making space for the emotional needs of our audience in this way greatly enhances the power and effect of our story. Silence can indeed be golden!

It is also worth remembering that are many films that work well without any voiceover at all. In these films, the interview sync sound and actuality alone tells the story, occasionally assisted by title captions to provide any other information essential to the narrative. We should be aiming to make films which are as sparing with voiceover as possible.

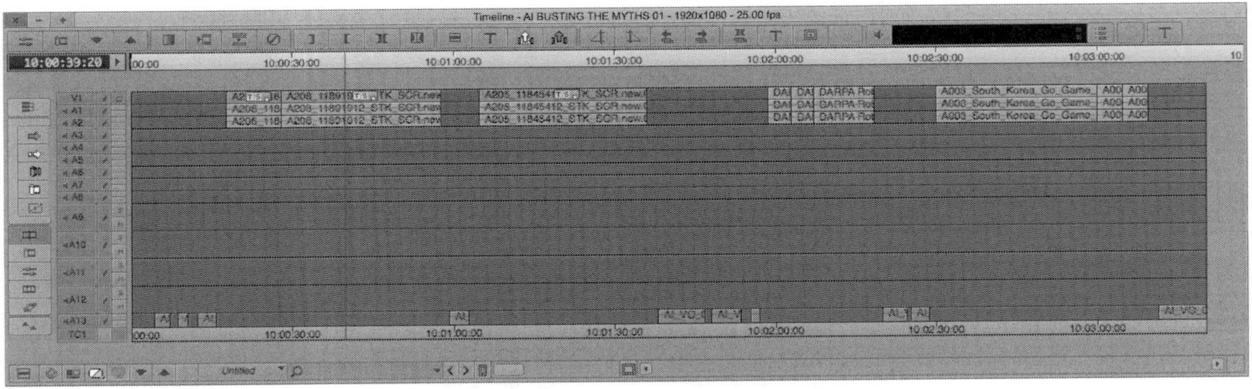

Figure 2.3 Sync & Black Assembly

The scene is blocked out and we're ready to start cutting! Interview sync is on A1&2 and the guide voiceover is on A13.

Key Points

- Speak slowly. When you reach a full stop, count to two. When you reach a comma or other punctuation, count to one.
- Voiceover does not have to be perfect the first time.
- Get your final words placed into the edit before picture lock.
- Pace your words out deliberately.

So, we now have a spine for our new scene and a framework from which we can build our film. We have an understanding of the principles that help us structure our film and the elements that comprise it (see figure 2.3).

This spine, consisting of interview sync, actuality and voiceover in between is known as a *sync and black assembly*. At this stage, it is a structure made up of spoken elements (much like a basic radio programme), and the only visual element comprises the interview clips and actuality with empty black spaces in between. However, since I have previously viewed the other supporting rushes for the scene, I will already be thinking of how the visuals may work to support this assembly and where each sequence of shots may work best.

We are now ready to focus our efforts on these more obviously alluring elements of the editing process, that of cutting picture sequences, as well as working with music and sound design.

This is where the fun really begins.

NOTES

1 Gabriella Oldham, *First Cut: Conversations with Film Editors* (University of California Press, Berkeley: 1995), 117.
2 Simon Smith, *Welcome to Romford* (Halcyons Heart Films/Channel 4, 2011).
3 Werner Herzog, *Grizzly Man* (Discovery Docs/Real Big Productions/Lions Gate Films, 2005).
4 Douglas Gordon/Philippe Parreno, *Zidane: A 21st Century Portrait* (Universal International, 2006).
5 www.izquotes.com. Accessed 23 October, 2016. http://izquotes.com/quote/284652
6 Martin Johnson, *Countdown to Life: The Extraordinary Making of You* (BBC, 2015).

7 www.televisual.com. Accessed 23 October, 2016. www.televisual.com/blog-detail/The-art-of-the-edit_bid-465.html
8 Nat Sherman, *Inside the Human Body* (BBC, 2011).
9 Martin Johnson, *Countdown to Life: The Extraordinary Making of You* (BBC, 2015).
10 *24 Hours in A&E* (The Garden Productions/Channel 4, 2011).
11 Aniruddha Guha, "A Documentary Film Editor is Like a Scriptwriter: David Tedeschi." Accessed 23 October, 2016. www.dnaindia.com/entertainment/report-a-documentary-film-editor-is-like-a-scriptwriter-david-tedeschi-1608154
12 Dick Taylor, *The Treasure Hunters* (BBC, 2014).
13 Alastair Fothergill, *Planet Earth* (BBC, 2006).
14 Thom Beers, *Deadliest Catch* (Original Productions/Freemantle Media/Image Entertainment/Discovery Communications/Debmar-Mercury, 2005).
15 Michael Moore, *Capitalism: A Love Story* (Dog Eat Dog Films/The Weinstein Company/Overture Films, 2009).
16 Francis Hanly, *Ben Building: Mussolini, Monuments and Modernism*, presented by Jonathan Meades (BBC, 2016).
17 Alex Gibney, *The Armstrong Lie* (Kennedy Marshall Productions/Jigsaw Productions/Matt Tolmach Productions/Sony Picture Classics, 2013).
18 John Yorke, *Into the Woods: How Stories Work and Why We Tell Them* (Penguin, London: 2015), Kindle edition, 113.
19 www.documentaryisneverneutral.com. "Quotes on Documentary." Accessed 23 October, 2016. http://documentaryisneverneutral.com/words/docquotes.html

3

PICTURE EDITING

VISUAL STORYTELLING

> "Obviously great directors give you great material to work with. But the ultimate film that you see is the edited version and the editor is greatly responsible for that."
>
> —Tom Rolf[1]

It has been my experience that as soon as I begin to cut shots together in sequence, which is to say to place them in a running order in my timeline, the film immediately comes to life. For the first time, I am seeing something that feels like the real film; something that the audience will one day see on their television screens. Further, there is a surprising, almost magic effect: I am struck by an overwhelming sense of the architecture and flow of the film that could not have been imagined prior to the edit. This surprising concatenation of shots—so pregnant with meaning—is a unique product of the edit, and the editor is very much responsible for it.

A single shot in isolation will usually have one simple, discrete and unambiguous meaning. For example, a close shot of a grown man crying will communicate sadness. This shot, or unit of film language as we might think of it, will take on an entirely different and potentially more complex meaning when placed next to another shot. If, for example, our shot of the crying man is followed by a shot of an ice cream cone lying on the pavement and melting into the gutter, then we suddenly get the picture: the man has dropped the ice cream and is acting like a child. Now, rather than feeling sad, we might laugh and even wonder whether he is entirely sane. In just the same way, the cone alone would mean very little but juxtaposed with other shots it becomes ripe with narrative possibilities.

David Mamet said, "You always want to tell the story in cuts. Which is to say through a juxtaposition of images that are basically uninflected."[2] In other words, our film is a simple succession of clearly delineated single shots put together, each building on the meaning of its predecessor and all cumulatively propelling the narrative line through towards its end.

It is hard to appreciate the sheer power which two well chosen shots, cut together at just the right time, can have until you do it. I am frequently so struck by their power that I sit in my cutting room, my legs shaking and even laughing out loud! There isn't an experience quite like it!

This is just the beginning of the wonderful process of cutting picture sequences. Combining these shots with the right sound and, where required, the right music creates something utterly surprising and enthralling.

Note! In order to explain the process of cutting picture sequences as clearly and as comprehensively as I can, I will discuss picture cutting first, then sound and then music.

However, I cannot stress sufficiently that in practice I would advocate assembling your sequences in the *reverse* order this suggests—i.e., music, then sound and then pictures (with some wiggle room back and forth if required). The reason for this will be explained as we go along.

THE KULESHOV EFFECT

The remarkable meaning inferred by the simple cutting together of two shots was tested at the turn of the twentieth century soon after the invention of cinema by Soviet filmmaker Lev Kuleshov. He edited together a short film in which a shot of an expressionless face—that of Russian silent film actor

Ivan Mosjoukine—was cut in alternation with three other shots: a plate of soup, a child in a coffin and a scantily clad woman. The film was shown to an audience who believed the expression on Mosjoukine's face was different each time he appeared, depending on whether he was 'looking at' the plate of soup, the woman or the child in the coffin. His 'changing' expression displayed, they believed, was hunger, grief and desire respectively.

In truth, the footage of Mosjoukine was precisely the *same shot each time*. See my recreation of the Kuleshov Effect in figure 3.1.

The experiment revealed a human need to identify meaning in the materials we encounter. If an audience is presented with disparate images, they will, as far as possible, assemble them into a meaningful statement. By simply editing each of the shot pairs together, Kuleshov had encouraged his subjects to do this, 'tricking' them into projecting their own interpretations onto the

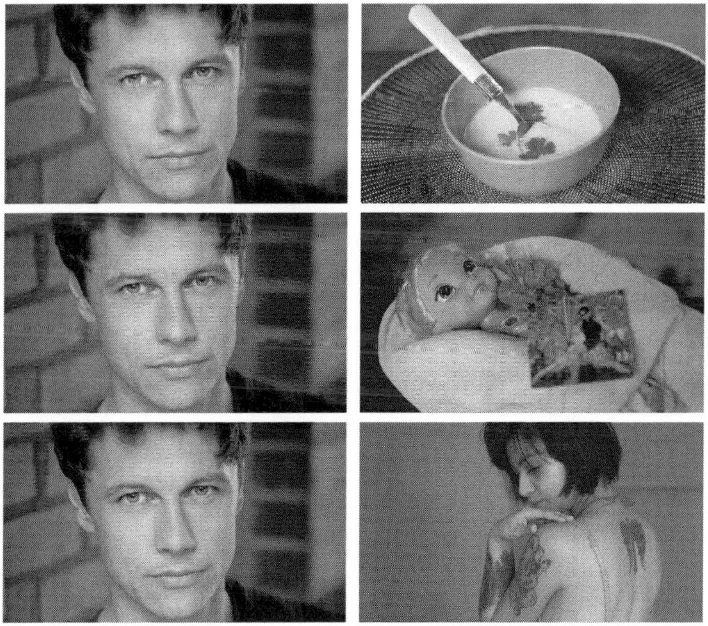

Figure 3.1 The Kuleshov Effect

A recreation of the Kuleshov Effect.

neutral materials; which is to say, exploiting a natural instinct to transfer their own emotional understanding onto the face of the impassive Mosjoukine.

Key Point

- Two shots placed together infer an entirely new and greater meaning than each single shot on its own.

TYPES OF PICTURE SEQUENCE

There are limitless ways in which we can cut together our picture sequences. Whatever we can imagine (from the available rushes) can be created. However, there are a few common types of sequences that are used in documentary and indeed all forms of film editing:

- **A chronological, straight picture sequence**
  Rushes from a single location are cut together into one sequence. The purpose of this sequence is to explore an event as it unfolds. The rushes for this sort of sequence will usually have a clear and inherent beginning, middle and end. For example, a sequence of a sword being forged may begin with a cold block of iron, progress though the heating and forming of the metal, and eventually conclude with the finished article. This kind of sequence is held together through a unity of *location*.
- **An intercut sequence**
  Two separate sequences and sets of rushes are interwoven. Two separate events are unfolding in parallel action. This kind of sequence can be used to create tension; the assumption being that the two events are likely to come together. For example, the craftsman may be steadily forging the sword, while intercut in parallel, the presenter is journeying to the forge by car, getting ever closer. The sequence concludes as the presenter enters the forge on foot and the craftsman places the finished article on a worktop. This kind of sequence is held together through a unity of *time*.
- **Montage**
  Rushes from a number of different sources, places and times are cut together into a single sequence. This builds an overall sense of time passing and an accumulated sense of story journey. For example, we

may cut together a sequence of our 'best bits' in the pre-title of our film to illustrate the scope of the subject we will explore and the breadth of places we will visit. This kind of sequence is held together through a unity of *meaning* or *story theme*.

All documentary sequences will fall in to one of these three categories. Even seemingly more unusual sequences, such as dream sequences, flashbacks or flash forwards are merely versions of the above.

Experience suggests that the best directors usually shoot their rushes with sequences in mind. The reason for this is the inherent structure necessarily present in specially shot sequences. The audience has a subliminal sense of the sequence and the journey that will unfold and they know that ultimately it must resolve both in place and time. Knowing that there is a resolution to be found at the end of the sequence and knowing at what point along that path they are, situates, reassures and compels an audience.

TYPES OF SHOT

In order to craft an effective sequence, we first need to understand the types of shot we have to work with. The best and most desirable documentary rushes consist of many different types of shot and use many different shooting techniques.

Below are a few key examples:

- **Extreme Wide Shot (EWS)**

  The *extreme wide shot* captures the environment or context in which the scene and characters are set from a distanced perspective. The purpose of this shot is to show the audience where the action is taking place. This kind of shot is also useful for creating a sense of scale.

  This shot is often referred to in documentary as a *long shot* or an *establisher*, as it is used to establish the geography of a location (see figure 3.2).
- **Wide Shot (WS)**

  In the *wide shot* the subject takes up the full frame; their head almost at the top of the frame and their feet at the bottom. There is a small amount of 'safety' room above and below the subject—ensuring that no part of them are accidentally cut off or missed (see figure 3.3).

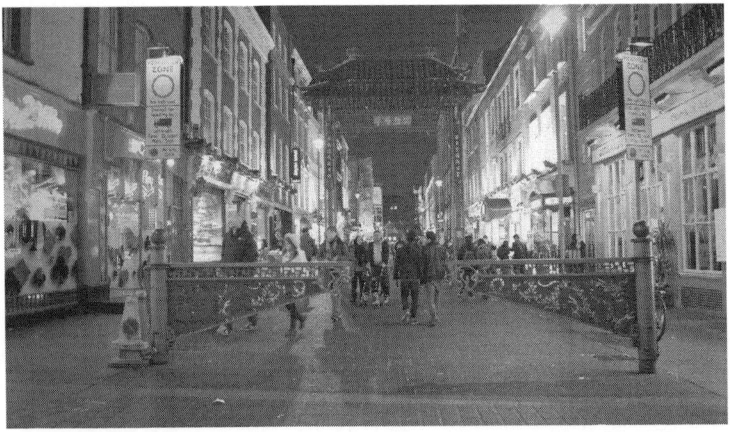

Figure 3.2 Extreme Wide Shot

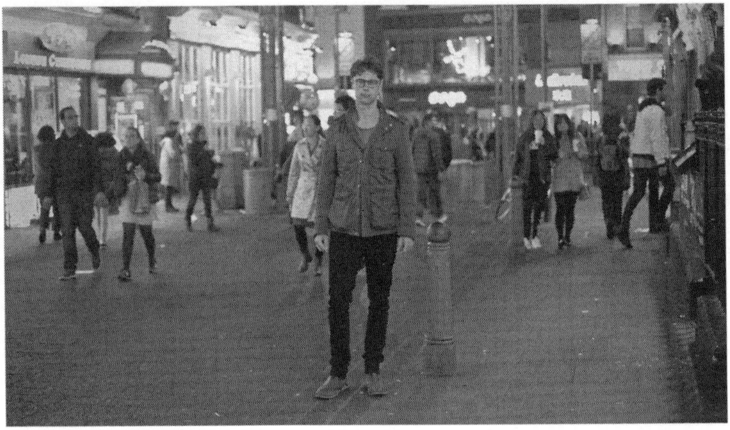

Figure 3.3 Wide Shot

- **Mid Shot (MS)**

  The *mid shot* captures the subject in more detail, whilst still showing enough for the audience to feel they are seeing the whole subject. This shot is an approximation of how you would see a person 'in the flesh' if you were having a conversation with them. You would not be paying much attention to their lower body, so that part of the subject is excluded.

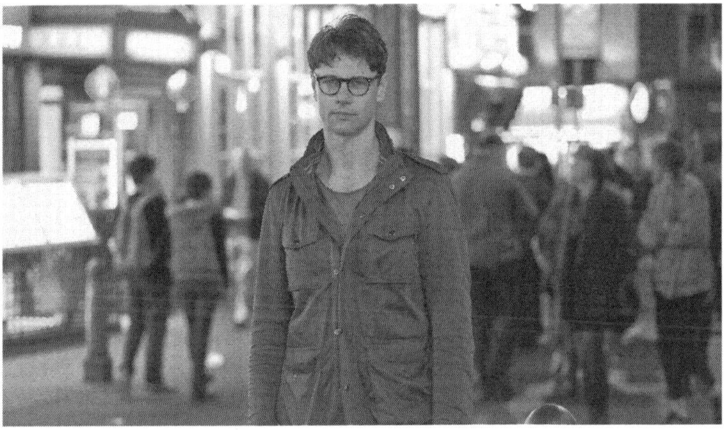

Figure 3.4 Mid Shot (MS)

The mid shot is useful when the subject is speaking in a relaxed and straightforward manner and without too much emotion. For this reason, it is frequently used when filming presenters.

As well as being a comfortable, emotionally neutral shot, the mid shot allows room for hand gestures and occasional movement (see figure 3.4).

- **Close-up (CU) Shot**

  In the *close-up shot*, a required feature or part of the subject takes up most of the frame. A close-up of a person usually means a close up of their face.

  Close-ups are useful for showing detail and especially effective in conveying emotion, since facial expressions are made more obvious. The audience is drawn towards the subject and made more aware of their personal feelings.

  Close shots work well for action-led sequences, as movements within the frame feel bigger, faster, more energetic and powerful. They also work well for intimate moments in a story, where emotional expression is key (see figure 3.5).

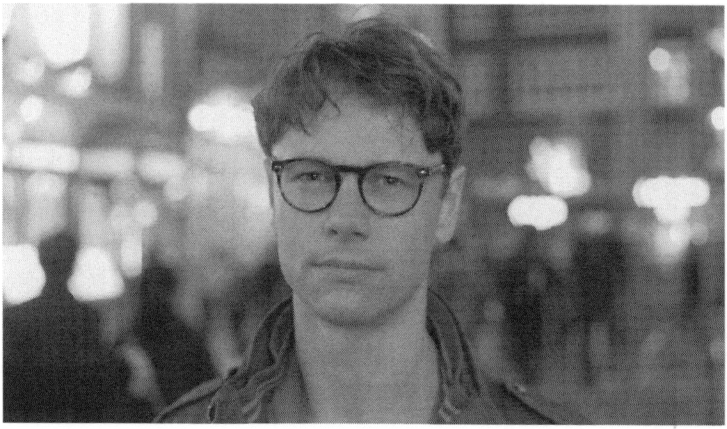

Figure 3.5 Close-Up (CU)

- **Extreme Close-Up (ECU) Shot**
  The *extreme close-up* is a very tight shot that shows extreme detail. It is often used to show intense facial expressions, as it is too close to show general reactions or emotion (see figure 3.6).

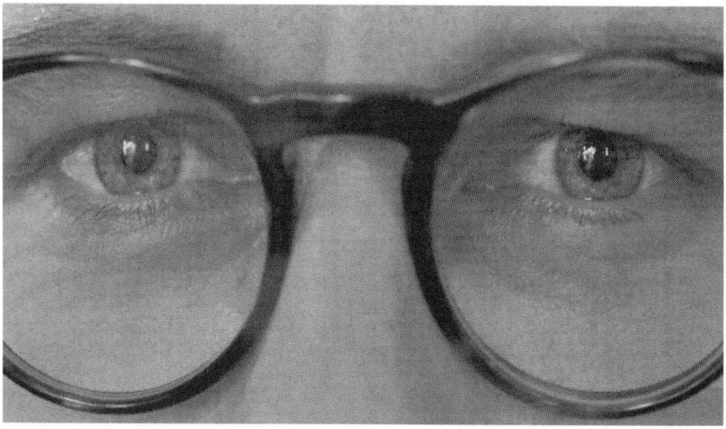

Figure 3.6 Extreme Close-Up (ECU)

- **Two Shot**

  The principle of the *two shot* is to fit two people comfortably into the frame, usually side-by-side. This kind of shot is often used in interviews and is a natural way to introduce two people.

  Two shots are good for establishing a relationship between subjects. If you see two presenters standing side-by-side facing the camera, you know immediately that these people are going to be the programme's co-hosts.

  Two shots are also useful for allowing two people to interact without the potentially distracting and noisy effect of having to cut between them in separate shots in order to make the same point (see figure 3.7).

- **Over-the-Shoulder Shot (OTS)**

  The *over-the-shoulder shot* is taken from the perspective of the close back of one person facing towards another. The back of head and shoulder is used to frame whatever (or whomever) the camera is pointing toward.

  This shot helps to establish the position of each person, as if looking at one person from the other's point of view. This shot is often used when two people are having a discussion (such as in interview or actuality): it helps to establish the position of each person. It is common to cut between these shots, alternating the view between the different speakers (see figure 3.8).

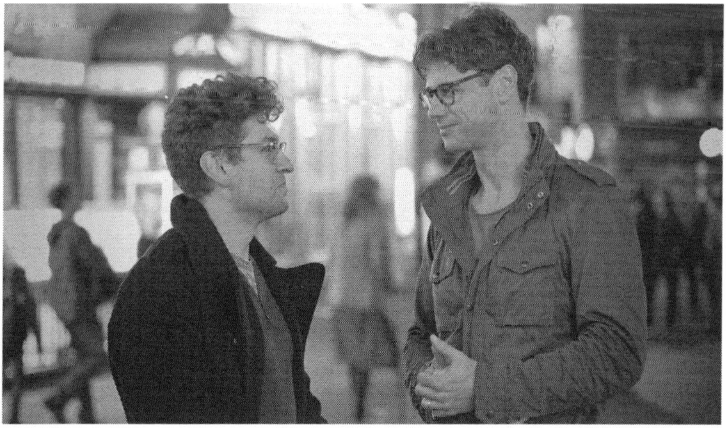

Figure 3.7 Two Shot

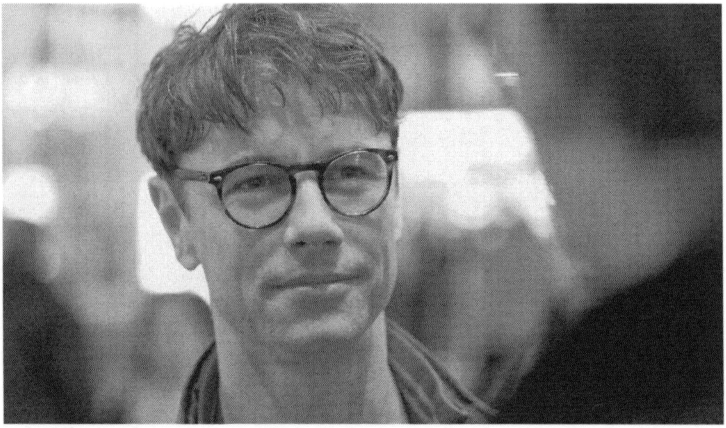

Figure 3.8 Over-the-Shoulder Shot (OTS)

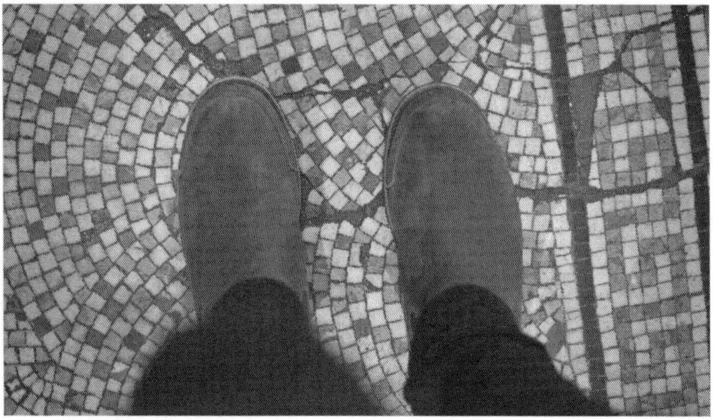

Figure 3.9 Point-of-View Shot (POV)

- **Point-of-View Shot (POV)**

  The *point-of-view shot* shows what the subject is looking at from a first-person perspective. It gives the audience a sense of standing in their shoes, even being in their head. In some senses it is similar in feel to the *over-the-shoulder shot*, though more intimate. POVs can feel disorientating and dizzying; though, when used appropriately, they can add variety and energy to a sequence (see figure 3.9).

These shot types can also be combined with a variety of camera angles, for added effect:

- **Low Angle Shot**
  A *low angle shot* (figure 3.10) is a shot that is positioned anywhere below the eye line. The psychological effect of the shot is to make the character or object look big and powerful.
- **High Angle Shot/Top Shot**
  A *high angle shot* (figure 3.11) is where the camera looks down on the subject from up high. High angle shots can make the subject appear small and vulnerable.

  A more extreme version of this shot is the *aerial shot*, where the camera tracks the subject from much higher up, as a bird might see the action, either by using a helicopter or drone device.

There are many variations on these basic shots, some even wider, some closer, some panning, tilting, tracking, zooming or *on the Dutch* (a tilted angle shot, which is somewhat out of fashion at the moment). Each shot type meets a particular requirement and conveys a specific feeling to our audience.

It is this great variety of shots that, if present in the rushes, allows us as editors to create rich, colourful and dramatic sequences and by so doing, create compelling and engaging narratives.

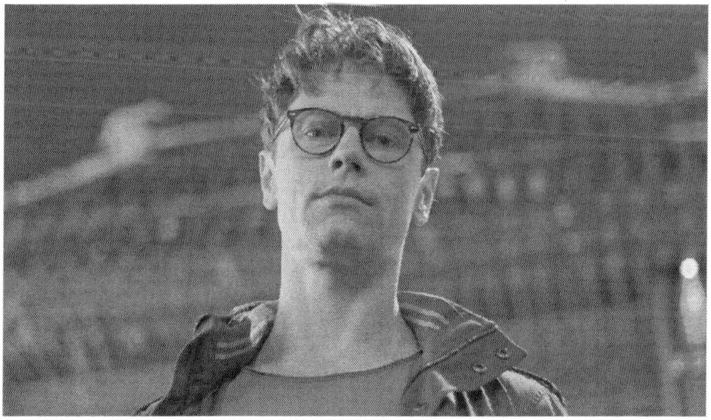

Figure 3.10 Low Angle Shot

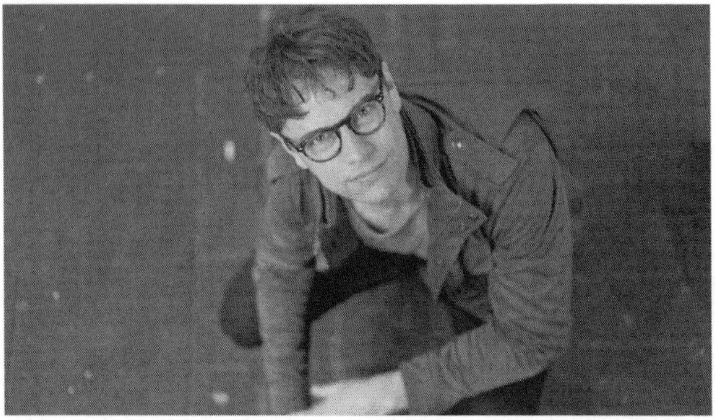

Figure 3.11 High Angle Shot/Top Shot

STRUCTURING A PICTURE SEQUENCE

We can order our sequence of shots in a number of different ways. In fact, the possibilities are near endless. As we begin to put our sequence together, the range of options we have can feel overwhelming. When we have a great wealth of beautiful rushes, where should we begin? The choices we make are subjective and there is no right or wrong answer. It is easy to overcomplicate this and, in so doing, lose perspective and with it our instinctive sense of the rhythm and flow of our work.

Over time, I have developed a number of simple principles that help me at this potentially daunting stage. They have allowed me to make consistently good choices, which have, in turn, yielded clear, dramatic, surprising and beautiful sequences. By applying them, you will be able to craft sequences faster and with more confidence.

- **First, picture sequences must tell their own story.**
  Pictures are the most powerful storytelling device that we have as filmmakers. When considering the order for your shots, think how they can tell their *own* story. Each shot should build on the previous one, presenting the audience with new meaning and propelling the story forward.

  There should be an inherent logic to the order of your shots. I like to think, if I turned the sound off, and so did not have a guide as to what is happening, the sequence would still make sense (i.e., the pictures would tell their own story). I do sometimes do precisely this towards the end of the edit process so that I am forced to focus on the pictures alone, without the distraction and overload that comes with sound and pictures combined. It is amazing what suddenly stands out.

Remember! Do not allow picture sequences to become overly dictated by voiceover or other spoken information. This usually makes for dull sequences, which lack energy and drama, since their natural rhythms are confounded.

- **Keep it simple.**
  We should aim to use as few shots as we can get away with. This does not mean we must cut everything slow! It means that every shot must serve a narrative purpose and be present for a good reason. This may still mean a fast, pacey sequence with many shots, in the case of something heavily action orientated. Equally this could just mean a single shot.

  Carefully consider which shots most contribute to the meaning you are trying to convey at this point in the story and look to remove any shots that are unnecessary or needlessly repetitive. Sometimes it helps to place similar shots together in sequence deliberately to emphasize the significance of a particular action, though generally I look to move the story on directly with each cut.

Remember the Kuleshov Effect! Our ultimate aim is to do just enough to allow the audience to exercise their own imaginations.

- **Start your sequence with the most visually arresting shot.**
  I like to start each sequence in the most intriguing and arresting way I can. This does not necessarily mean starting with the shot that is most

descriptive of the sequence and scene that follows. While there should be an inherent logic to the order of your shots, the story we are telling does not have to be revealed immediately. Rather we should allow it to become clear over time and certainly by the end of the sequence. For example, if mystery is an important component of the sequence, we might deliberately choose more obscure and merely suggestive shots to begin with, so that the audience does not know what is going on until we are some way into the story.

In documentary, our aim is to intrigue our audience through the composition of our sequences so that we keep them keen to watch and anxious to discover what will come next.

- **Cut at the speed of human thought.**

  Our audience is intelligent. This is true regardless of their age and interests. They are often a step or two ahead of us in understanding what is happening and where the story is likely to go. As a result, we must disregard the notion of time as we experience it in ordinary life and omit, wherever possible, steps in the sequence that are unnecessary to the meaning of the scene or simply make it hang fire. As Alfred Hitchcock said, "Drama is life with the dull bits cut out."[3] In effect, we must cut to the chase.

  Take this for example: a girl walks towards a door, opens it, walks through the doorway, closes the door on the other side, and then proceeds to walk across a room and sit down in a chair. Do we need to see all of these steps to understand what the girl is doing and where she is going? Perhaps simply seeing her turn the door handle, walk three paces and sit down is enough.

  Discontinuity of time is key in editing and vital in keeping the sequence alive and snappy.

- **Avoid editing material destined for the cutting room floor.**

  Beautiful editing takes time. As a result, we really want to try and focus our energy on the sequences and rushes material that will count in the end (i.e., those which are likely to make our final finished film).

  It is hard at the beginning of a project to determine which parts of the film will likely make the cut. However, we know that overall time constraints mean that each scene will have to be only a few minutes in length.

I begin by adding up all of the scenes I have, and then dividing the film's final duration by that number. For example, a sixty-minute film with ten scenes would produce an average scene length of six minutes each. Now I know this will vary depending on the requirements of each scene and any number of 'extra' scenes which we may require (such as a pre-title or an end sequence); however, in the beginning at least, it is a good rough guide.

On a basic level, once I have blocked out a new scene with sync and voiceover, and before I invest serious time cutting it with pictures and music, I will measure its duration against the target (average) length allowed for it in the final film (e.g., six minutes), always remembering that I do not want the first cut of the scene to be more than about 25 percent longer than its ultimate duration is likely to be. So, in the case of the six-minute scene, I do not want the first cut to exceed eight minutes. I am also aware that first sync and black assemblies of scenes will almost certainly grow in length once filled out with pictures and music.

If it is obvious at this stage that your scene is going to be significantly longer, then look for effective cuts to bring it down to length. There is no point cutting a sequence of twenty minutes for a scene that will end up as three!

Ask yourself, is this information necessary to tell the story? Is this sequence or scene doing the same job as another in the film? The more disciplined you are at this stage, the quicker you will have a first working edit of your film.

Remember! Not all scenes have to be uniform in length. Base your decisions about duration on the merits of each scene. However, it is worth cutting obvious fat from your sync and black scene assemblies *before* you start cutting sequences.

- **Cut neatly on your first pass.**

  When I cut a sequence, I aim to make it as perfect as possible on the first pass. This way, when I watch it back, I am better able to judge if it is working and then improve it further. Also when I show the sequence to my director or anyone else who cares to watch, they can be confident the film is working, and they can experience it as an audience would, without the distraction of untidy artefacts.

  It is not uncommon to find editors who prefer to work by putting down a few shots in a quick and rough succession in order to get an initial feel for the sequence before moving on, with a view to coming back to the scene later to polish it up. While I can understand their logic, I find this approach perilous. Quite simply, the more I view my cut, the less sensitive to it I become, and more blasé about its merits. It follows that the more I watch an imperfect sequence, the more likely I am to overlook its flaws and accept them, rather than fix them. Further, once the edit progresses, things can get pretty busy, and it will become difficult to find the time to come back and fix every little thing—always assuming that you can remember what needed fixing in the first place.

  Avoid this pitfall and just get it right the first time!

  That said, I like to put down the *broad* brushstrokes of each sequence first, without too much attention to detail and without *unnecessary* finesse, just to ensure the right blocks are hitting the right marks in the right order. At this stage I am free to move things around as ideas evolve. It also helps get into a working rhythm to avoid wasting time on the details of each frame. I then go back over it with a greater eye for detail once the elements are in place to make sure that the cut points and timing are perfect.

> Remember! You can only focus your energy on cutting one sequence at a time. Focus on getting each sequence right before moving on to the next.

- **Once it is working, move on.**

  Once you've cut your sequence and had a good pass over it, resist fiddling around with it further.

  I like to watch the sequence back once or twice, usually with my director if they are present, and make a few obvious tweaks there and then. I then 'park' it and move on to something new. Later I'll come back with fresh eyes and refine it again.

  I try to resist viewing my sequence too frequently early on, as I want to keep the material fresh for as long as I can. Tinkering endlessly leads to diminishing returns and simply wastes time, particularly in the early stages of editing when we are still finding the overall 'shape' for the film.

  Bearing this in mind, if you're cutting a sequence and get stuck or unsure where to go next, or you are missing some of the shots you need to make it work, resist spending too much time thinking about how to solve the problem there and then. Move on to something new instead. Often enough, the answer will spring to mind later on, perhaps while cutting something else, relaxing, or even in the shower! You can always go back to it with fresh ideas.

Key Points

- Sequences should tell their own story. Do not allow voiceover or other dialogue to dictate the flow of the sequence.
- Keep it simple. Our ultimate aim is to do just enough to engage our audience's imagination.
- Start with the most visually arresting shot. The story we are telling does not have to be immediately obvious to our audience, as long as they get the message in due course.
- Cut at the speed of thought. Discontinuity of time is key in editing.
- Beautiful editing takes time. Do not spend time on material which is only likely to hit the cutting room floor.
- Cut neatly on your first pass. Focus on getting each sequence right the first time.
- Once your scene is 'working,' move on. Tinkering wastes time. You can come back later with fresh eyes.

SEQUENCING SHOTS

While it is worth re-emphasising that you can order your sequence of shots in any way you feel works best for your story, experience has taught me that there are certain 'templates' which work well as a general starting point.

For example, I often like to start a scene with a close shot: something which does not give away everything about the location or meaning of the scene straight way. This shot effectively acts as a tease for the sequence and story which follows. I usually select a close shot which has an intriguing feel to it even if, on the face of it, this might feel almost random or out of context. I will then think how I can visually unpack the story from this place. Perhaps with another series of close shots each adding a further impression of where we are and what is happening. Once I have 'teased' the scene in this way, I may decide to cut back to something wide, which shows the geography of the location—as if to say—hey presto! Now you get the picture!

This sequence would look something like figure 3.12.

There are instances where we might choose to reverse this order by starting with the wide shot. Particularly if the content of the wide shot and what is going on in it does not give everything away, or if the dramatic scale of the shot is of great importance to the meaning of the scene. For example, I may choose to start with a wide shot if there was something in the distant horizon coming towards us: say, a lone horse rider or if there was such a mass of people within the frame that at first it simply looked like a swarm of ants. We do not have the full picture of what is happening immediately, but we soon will. In this case, one shot is doing the work of two or three close shots in conveying emotion and meaning to the audience. From this wide shot, I might go to a series of close shots which now begin to fill in the gaps in the audience's understanding of the place and time.

This sequence will look a bit like figure 3.13:

In a character-led sequence, we may wish to present the scene from their point of view, as if we are somehow 'in their shoes.' In this instance, I may start the scene with a POV shot, to place the audience immediately inside the head of our character. Then I might reveal exactly who's eyes we are looking through, with a clear close shot, which matches the size

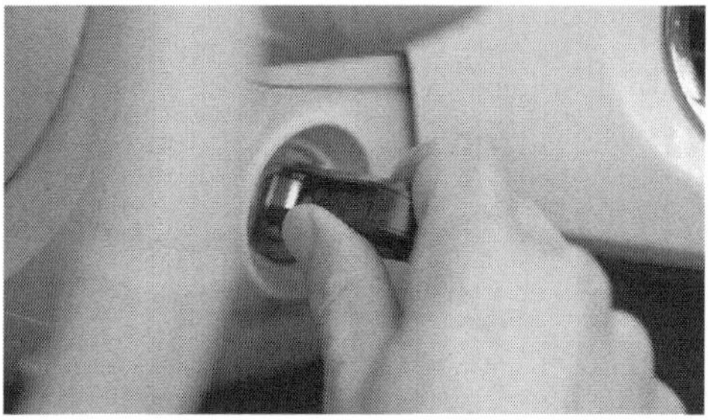

Shot 1

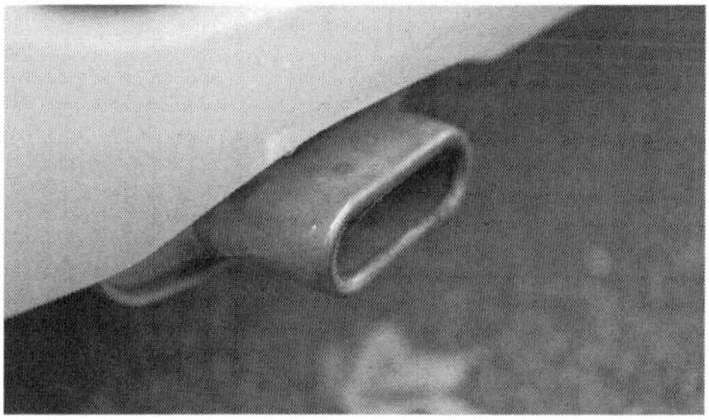

Shot 2

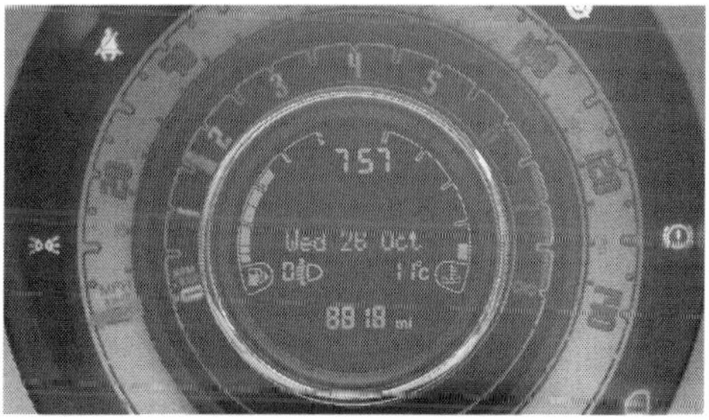

Shot 3

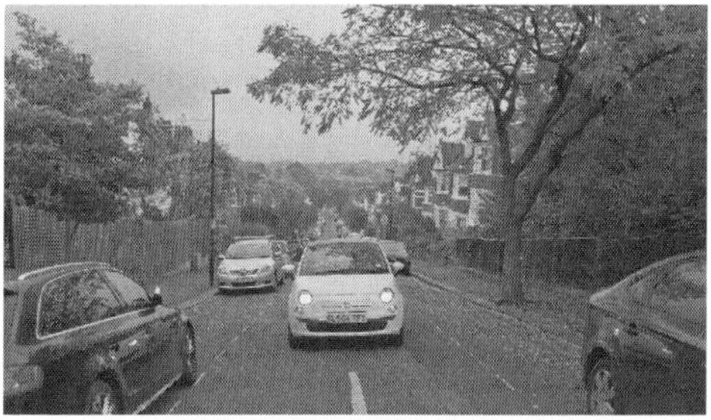

Shot 4

Figure 3.12 Picture Sequence Building Out to Reveal

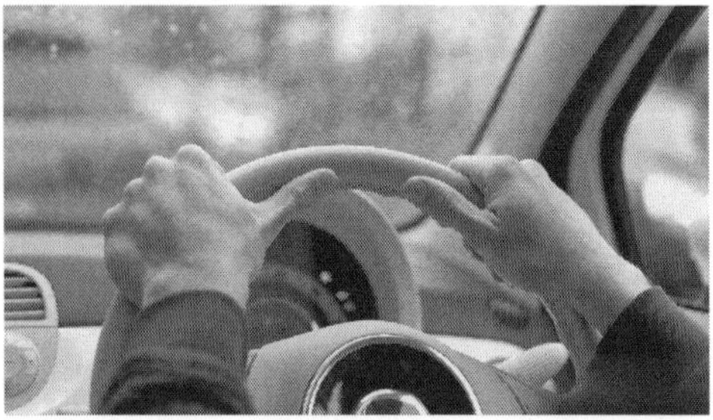

Shot 1

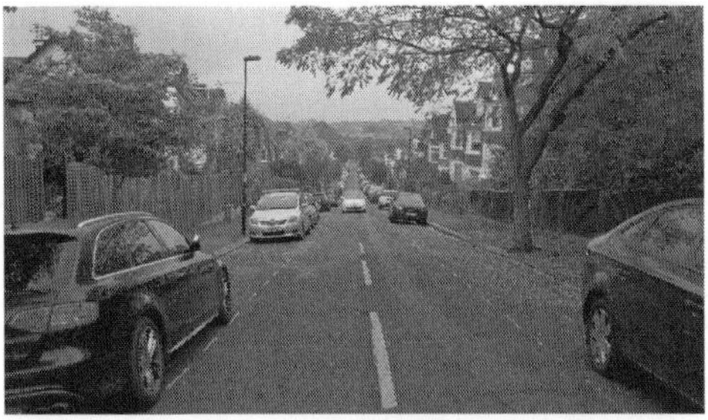

Shot 2

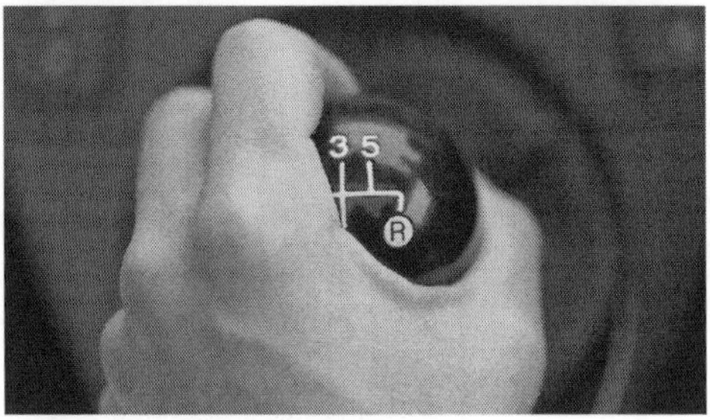

Shot 3

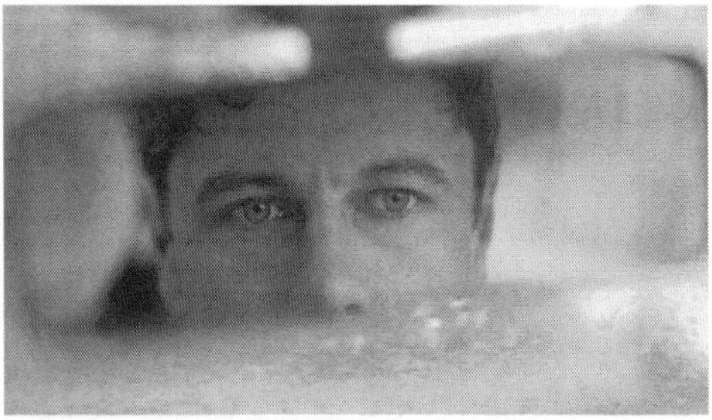

Shot 4

Figure 3.13 Picture Sequence Starting Wide to Close

and dynamics of the first. Perhaps from there, I will choose to establish the context of the scene—to tell the audience where they are and at what time. The question of why they are there at all might then logically follow on from here.

This sequence will look something like figure 3.14:

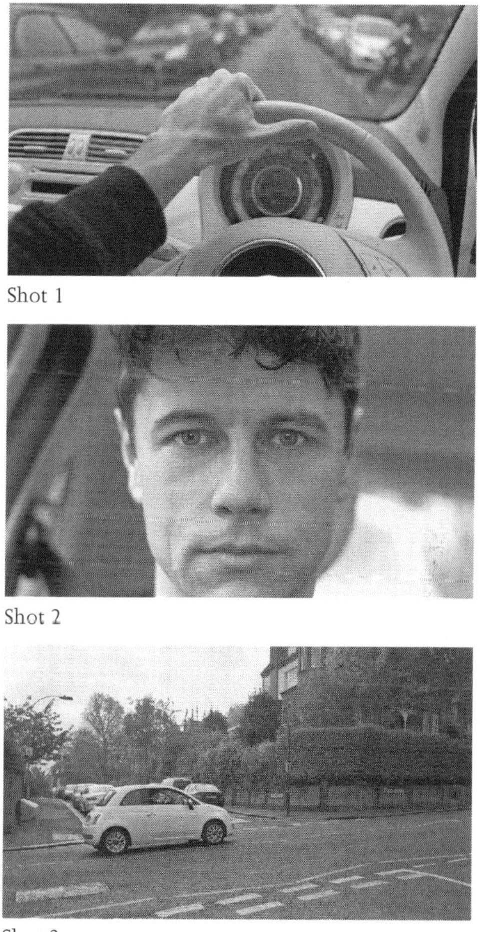

Shot 1

Shot 2

Shot 3

Figure 3.14 Point of View Picture Sequence

Every sequence will be different, and each will depend on the rushes you have and the story you are telling. It is also worth remembering that the order of your shots, particularly what you decide to start and end your sequence with, will depend on the shot with which the previous sequence ends as well as that with which the following sequence begins. For example, if we are ending one sequence with a wide shot, we may want to start the next sequence with a close shot (they'll probably cut together better, as we'll soon discuss).

These are just a couple of basic ideas you can think about. Using the principles outlined in the previous chapter, start placing shots in your timeline and think how they connect.

Tip! When building up your sequence, you can place the shots in your timeline out of sequence. If you know a certain shot will work well in a particular place in the timeline, put it there, and then work backwards to decide which shots will allow you to arrive at this point.

Part of a sequence will often become clear once you know where it needs to end and what critical points you must hit on the way.

A PRACTICAL METHOD FOR BUILDING A SEQUENCE

1. Open the sequence that contains the sync and black assembly for your new scene. This is the basic skeleton for the new scene, consisting of interview sync, and if required, voiceover, which we built earlier on. We are about to flesh out this skeleton.
2. In parallel, open the rushes assembly sequence that we created at the beginning of the edit, which contains the supporting shots for the scene.
3. Skim through the rushes assembly sequence to find the shot you think will work best as the opening for your scene. Something arresting!
4. Duplicate this shot into your sync and black assembly and place into position.
5. Repeat this process until you have built up a sequence of shots.

Remember! Do not remove or edit shots from the original rushes assembly sequence. This original sequence must remain strictly a read only resource! You will rely on this sequence again should you need to recut your scene and you may require additional or different shots from it, so ensure everything stays together.

I suggest working from a new sequence timeline when cutting a scene for the first time. Once I have a satisfactory cut of the scene, I migrate it back into a master sequence which houses all of my completed scenes in order and which will effectively become my completed film.

By creating a separate sequence at first, I have the freedom to play with the shots and move elements around easily, without the fear of accidentally knocking something else out of place.

The master edit remains a locked sequence that contains complete scenes. If I need to get back to the nitty-gritty cutting of a sequence again, I will again copy it out of the master sequence and rework it before slotting it back in.

THE ART OF THE CUT

> "I'm on a barge for two days trying to get the shark to look real, and the sad fact was that the shark would only look real in 36 frames and not 38 frames. And that 2 frame difference was the difference between something really scary, and something that looked like a great white floating turd."
>
> —Steven Spielberg, on *Jaws*[4]

So far we have only discussed the general principle of structuring a sequence of shots for their narrative exposition—for the meaning generated by each shot in sequence. We have not considered the equally important matter of aesthetics—the artistic principles associated with sequence editing. Aesthetic considerations include: the kinds of shots which work well together, the best place for each shot to begin and end, how cuts between different kinds of shots work and how different kinds of cut impact our audience.

While we all accept cuts (instantaneous changes of one shot for another) as a convention of filmmaking, and are very used to seeing them, they are in fact a quite remarkable and 'unnatural' artefact.

Until the invention of cinema editing at the start of the twentieth century, no one had ever seen a cut before. We experienced life as one continuous real-time stream of consciousness—interrupted only by our own blinking and sleeping.

Remarkably—and despite their novelty and fundamentally alien quality—cuts are accepted by our eyes and brains without issue. Many theories exist for why this is so. Some point to the way we blink—producing momentary cuts of a sort—and others to the way in which we dream—our brains randomly darting around between images as we sleep. Regardless of how this acceptance has come about, one thing is certainly true: we can all instinctively tell, if only on a subconscious level, when a cut is a good one and when it is not.

WHAT MAKES A GOOD CUT?

The general aim when deciding where and when to cut is to make the cut feel emotionally correct in the context of the sequence and its logic or feeling. For example, when the action is conveying a sense of unease or violence, we may want the cuts to be sharp, surprising and jarring, which is to say uncomfortable and ugly like the action itself.

Often, however, we will want shots to join together as naturally and invisibly as possible. In managing this, we are allowing the audience to focus on the story experience rather than distracting them with the technical means we have used to get there. As a result, the audience will have a more immersive and natural viewing experience.

The factors which determine the feeling and quality of our cuts are:

- Where in the frame the action is taking place on either side of the cut.
- The camera position, shot size, style and movement on either side of the cut.
- The rhythm and pace of the action on either side of the cut.
- Where each shot begins and ends.

So what makes a great cut? Most editors consider the ability to make good cuts an instinctive talent that can be refined over time, through practice. This is certainly true to an extent. As with anything in life, practise makes perfect, and it is through practise that we begin to feel, somewhere in our bones, when and where the cut 'works.' However, I also believe there is a science to making beautiful cuts: a science that can be analysed and learned.

> Note! I consider picture and sound editing as two separate, yet connected processes in cutting a sequence together. I will always strive to get the sound working first, as this usually determines the timing of our cut. Only when this is satisfactorily accomplished do I deal with the picture cut point.

In terms of picture edits, here are a few practical ideas:

- **Wherever possible, cut in movement.**
  Our eyes naturally follow action in the video frame. Wherever there are clear shapes or patterns moving, our eyes will follow. For example, if a car is speeding around a racing track, our focus will be primarily on the car rather than the background or anything else peripheral within the frame.

  This action acts as a sort of magnet, drawing our attention away from everything else in the frame. Once our eyes have computed and understood the action, we may then begin to shift our gaze towards the rest of the content in the frame, especially if the shot is long enough to allow this to happen.

  Understanding this principle is important. If we select shots with movement in the frame, we can control where the audience will be looking at any time. We can then choose our cut points between shots with greater precision and certainty, to create cuts that are either invisible or deliberately obvious depending upon which is preferred.

  Generally speaking, I like to cut in and out of a shot at a point where there is a clear, defined movement taking place within the frame. This can be something as simple as a person picking up a coffee cup. I will choose to cut at the point where the cup is being lifted, so that at the cut point, the audience is hardly aware of any other action within the frame. In short, they hardly notice the cut itself since their eyes are already following the movement of the coffee cup.

In this respect, when cutting in to a shot like this I usually like to cut at the very beginning of the movement itself without any frames of inactivity beforehand. Some editors I know like to cut mid-movement: for example, when the hand is half way up the mouth already (i.e., at the point of maximum energy in the movement). However, I much prefer the cleaner and crisper feeling of capturing the movement as one whole.

Equally, when cutting out of a shot, it can be very effective to cut at a point where there is motion, particularly a quick moving one which fills the frame. This could be a natural wipe across frame as an object passes through and fills the frame or any sudden and surprising action.

Whatever you decide, position your cuts at a point where there is movement or action within the frame. The bigger, closer and swifter the action, the better. This will help to conceal and smooth your cuts.

- **Observe eye trace.**

Imagine there is a little red dot on the screen. Wherever your eyes are naturally taken around the frame, the dot follows. This is known as *eye trace*.

As figure 3.15 shows that as we watch shot A, the red dot moves around the frame along with the action. When we cut from shot A to shot B, the red dot remains where it was from the last frame of shot A, to the first frame of shot B.

If the position of the action in shot B references the position from shot A, our eyes will be more accepting of this change as we do not have to hunt for a new focal point in the frame. This results in a cut that

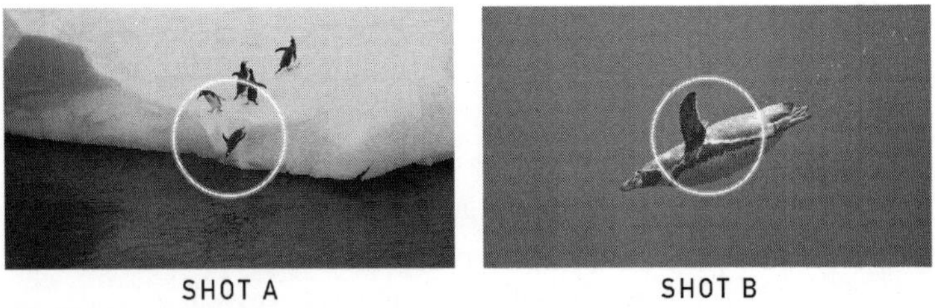

Figure 3.15 Matching Eye Trace

is more continuous, smoother and more natural on the eye. We can then carry this dot on to wherever the action in the frame next takes it.

Understanding this principle allows us to position the action between shots in harmony, determining the audience's focus through our picture sequence. Alternatively, we can deliberately choose to put the dot somewhere different between shots for deliberate intended effect.

For example, if we wish to create a sense of chaos or disorder, we may wish to throw the dot to the opposite side of the frame: up above or low down. At the cut point, the audience is forced to readjust their gaze, creating a momentary sense of disorientation and discomfort. This chaotic way of cutting may be effective if, for example, we were cutting a boxing match. The action is flying in all directions, punches here and there. It is tense, uncomfortable and dangerous, and we don't know what is going to happen next. The cuts heighten the sense of aggression, disorder and menace in the scene (see figure 3.16).

Through our choice of cuts we are now determining how the audience *feels* about the sequence. We are cutting *emotionally*.

Note! I also find when cutting a two-way conversation or using two interview clips side by side, it works best to have each person on the appropriate sides of the frame in each cut. If the first person is on the left, then in the next shot I will ensure that the second person is on the right. We are simulating the position that each person would adopt during a conversation whilst facing towards each other.

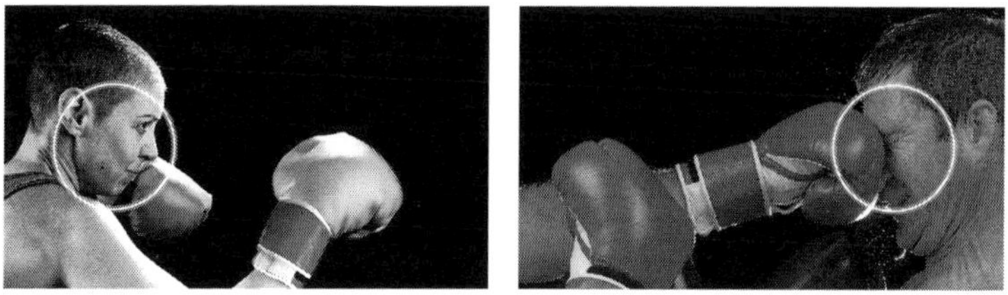

SHOT A SHOT B

Figure 3.16 Opposing Eye Trace

- **Cut for emotion first.**

  We must prioritise the likely emotional impact of our cuts upon our audience when choosing how we cut between shots.

  We do not always need to follow the traditional rules of visual or temporal continuity, putting together our scene in the exact manner of the original event—as in, say, a courtroom account or a live game show. While certain films might require this punctilious adherence to elapsing time, most of the time we are at risk of producing a flat and boring sequence. Instead, we must strive to convey the feeling and spirit of the event, through whatever cuts are necessary. Our cuts should be interpretive and intuitive, working more for feeling than for pure exposition.

  If I was cutting a scene in a prison cell, for example, I might choose to cut between extreme close-up shots of the cell's contents, the dripping tap, the rattling window through the bars etc. and, initially at least, exclude wide shots of the room itself. While this style of cutting does not establish the whole geography of the location and so tell the audience precisely where they are, it gives an emotional force to the scene, emphasising its unpleasant claustrophobia: a much more telling effect.

- **Next, cut for story development.**

  Every cut we make must move the story on. We are cutting so that every shot progresses the story towards its ultimate end. This cut can be one that develops the emotional tone of the scene, emphasising unspoken qualities, or it could be a cut in a piece of dialogue that furthers the expositional content of the film.

  We will often find ourselves with an array of beautiful, peripheral shots from which we could build the sequence. However, unless they are serving the purpose of the story, we must not use them. Directors will often say to me, "Wow that shot is so beautiful; we must use it!" Whilst I wholly agree that wherever possible we should make use of our best shots, I often find the 'prettiest' shots do not make the cut for precisely this reason; they do not connect adequately with the narrative and simply end up getting in the way.

  Prettiness is rarely sufficient reason to use a shot.

- **Continuity is not that important.**

Continuity editing refers to a style of editing that maintains a sense of continuous space and time between shots, when in fact each were shot out of sequence. This style of editing is very smooth and closely simulates the way in which we usually encounter the physical world.

Lack of continuity (which we refer to in editing as *continuity issues*) are such things as differences in the position of people or objects between shots—or even the position of the camera itself. Continuity relating to the position of the camera traditionally has its own conventional guiding principles; epitomised in the the *180° Rule* shown in figure 3.17.

The 180° Rule is a cinematography guideline that states that two characters in a scene should maintain the same left/right relationship to one another.

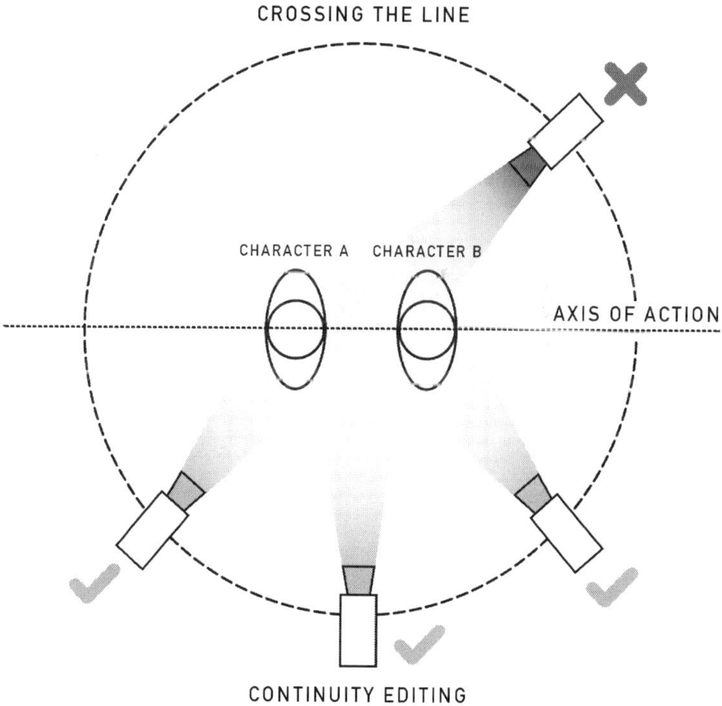

Figure 3.17 180° Rule

When the camera passes over the invisible axis of action connecting the two subjects, it is called crossing the line and the shot becomes what is called a *reverse angle*. Cutting from a shot of character A on one side of the line, to character B on the other, could undoubtedly be confusing. Since the audience's viewpoint is shifted so radically, the geography of the scene can become confusing, disorientating and ultimately uncomfortable (unless discomfort is the specific emotional aim of the scene).

For this reason, many filmmakers maintain that continuity is highly important: after all, how can an edited sequence come across to an audience as believable, if it does not look and feel like real life (which does not contain jumps in time or sudden repositioning of space)? There are moments of course when continuity of this nature is important; for example, during the conversation outlined above between characters A and B. Here, jumping around in space would create an unnecessary level of distraction when the real intention of the scene is to allow the audience to listen and understand.

However, while it is logical to think that we must always maintain perfect continuity in order to make the cuts we have made as real and viable, the truth is that most of us focus more on the overall flow and feeling of the sequence than on the extraneous details which generally define its continuity.

Unless blatant, as in the case of crossing the line during an interview, people do not usually notice gaps in continuity.

Indeed, jumps in time and space are often exciting and energising for the audience. They allow the audience to transcend the real, occasionally mundane, physical world and enter a magical space where anything becomes possible. We can play with time and space liberally in the edit, cutting for emotion, rather than strict sense, as we have previously discussed.

However, there is one form of continuity that I am usually very keen to maintain when cutting a sequence of shots. When cutting a picture sequence, I almost always ensure that there is continuity in the rhythm between the shots. For example, if I were cutting a sequence where an individual is walking along, I will ensure that the cuts between shots keep the rhythm of their footsteps and the flow of their motion.

Similarly, if two individuals are playing tennis, I would observe and maintain the time between hits as a natural rhythm, unless, of course, I was choosing deliberately to unsettle the sequence for deliberate effect, with an offbeat rubato tempo.

In this respect, it may help to keep in mind that editing is, in an important sense, 'musical.' The pace of our cuts should establish a rhythm that is sympathetic to the action and movement exhibited in the shots.

- **Wherever possible, keep the action in the frame.**
  By keeping the action within the frame, we are maintaining the energy of our sequence.

  It often surprises me how, in some documentaries, a presenter will walk out of frame after delivering a piece to camera, leaving us with an empty, unfocused background at which to look. This may last for a number of frames and sometimes even seconds before the cut. In these instances, I wonder, like the audience at home (whether they consciously realise it or not): "What am I supposed to be looking at here or reading in to this?"

  Usually the answer is nothing! This is just a waste of time and a leeching of energy!
- **Every frame counts.**
  Our aim is for every cut to be perfect. The cuts should be appropriate to the feeling of the sequence of which they are part. Every frame makes a difference. There is a perfect cut point to be found for every shot in every sequence.

  Any slack at the beginning or end of a shot is dead time. We must strive for every frame in our sequence to be essential.

  Equally, we must ensure that every shot has as much time to register and to 'speak' as it needs. Every cut that comes too early disturbs the natural rhythm of the sequence. It prematurely removes images that our eyes have not yet fully digested, creating a feeling of vague dissatisfaction. Of course, there are times where we may wish deliberately to cut shots short in order to create this discomfort, but in general, the shot lengths should be appropriate to the tone and feeling of the sequence, which is itself truly reciprocal to the rhythms and pacing evidenced in each shot it contains.

The effect of mistimed or badly timed cuts is cumulative, and this can become seriously damaging over the course of an entire film. When cuts are repeatedly too loose, the film will falter, feel slow and lethargic. When the cuts are repeatedly too tight, the film will feel choppy and frenetic.

- **Cuts are all you need.**

  We have an abundance of tools at our disposal that we can use to blend and connect shots together. These are known as *transitions*. Examples of transitions are *cross dissolves*, where the two shots fade between each other, or a *push*, where one image is nudged out of the way by another.

  Transitions do have a place in filmmaking. For example, *Star Wars* made great use of *wipe* transitions, where one shot replaced another by travelling along a line across the frame. They were used to good effect to suggest passages of time and to divide scenes.

  However, while transitions can occasionally be effective, they are best deployed sparingly, if at all.

  There are many reasons for this. First of all, transitions tend to cheapen the look of a film, especially if overused, and placed without proper thought. Second, transitions tend to look digitally generated and so unnatural. They do not replicate how we experience real life, which in my opinion is the ultimate goal of good documentary editing. Finally, I find that transitions can be distracting. They draw attention to themselves, rather than to the shots and the story, and blur the connections between the juxtaposing images.

  If we decide we do wish to use a transition, then we must think of what precisely it is adding to the sequence. A *cross dissolve* can be a way of suggesting time passing. A *dip-to-black* can suggest the end of scene or act.

  On the whole, I believe that a simple cut, deftly placed, is all we need.

- **Do not cut unless you have to.**

  We should only be cutting to make a point that is essential to the progression of the story: the logical, surprising yet vital next step.

  This does not mean that we must always cut slowly. When I cut *Jetstream*,[5] a film about trainee fighter jet pilots in the Royal Canadian Air Force, we had nearly 1,200 cuts in a single forty-six-minute film. An average cut rate of one every 2.3 seconds! The justification for this is that the film was largely action based, and each cut gave the audience something new to consider whilst maintaining a feeling of frenetic action essential to conveying the overall tone of the film.

Conversely, when I cut *Dawn Chorus*[6] (for The BBC's *BBC Four Goes Slow*), a film about birdsong at sunrise, we had around 180 cuts in a single fifty-nine-minute programme. An average cut rate of every 19.6 seconds—nearly ten times fewer cuts! Indeed, one shot of a sunrise lasted a whole two minutes, which utterly confused the executives present, used as they were to faster, more heavily produced films. After we had viewed the edited film for the first time, they just looked at each other and shrugged. They had little idea whether this ultra slow form of filmmaking could really sustain the audience's interest over the whole span—and to be fair neither did we, since there were few if any precedents to which it could be compared. However, whatever one may think of this extreme example, the purpose of the film was clear: to focus attention on the birdsong and to allow the viewers to do so without distraction. This could not have been achieved with frequent 'noisy' cuts.

Some may argue that the huge cut-rate now favoured by many films is simply a way of distracting the audience and disguising fundamental flaws in the story and its telling. One sometimes suspects that, in extreme cases, there is simply no real story at all, or that what there is has been lost somewhere along the way. In Britain, we rather irreverently refer to rescuing a film through these shallow and self-serving means as *turd-polishing*. In essence, as previously discussed, we can help a bad story though clever cutting, but if there isn't a worthwhile story to tell, nothing can ever truly save it.

So, to repeat: we should only ever cut for *meaning*. On this basis, the very definition of *bad* editing is *cutting for the sake of it*.

Finally, it is worth saying again that all of these choices being matters of feel, taste and aesthetics are, necessarily, personal. You must create your own rationale for making cuts and for deciding if they work or not. The suggestions above should serve only as a basis for finding your own style and developing your own filmmaking philosophy.

Tip! Use keyboard shortcuts wherever possible when editing. Particularly when adding edits, as well as marking in and out points around clips. Being able to press a key, rather than using a combination of awkward mouse clicks, frees you up to make much more instinctive and natural moves. You will begin to feel your cut points and where to move between shots much better this way. The keyboard is also a lot faster and probably easier on your arms, hands and fingers, too.

Key Points

- Wherever possible, cut in movement.
- Observe eye trace.
- Cut for emotional impact first. We must prioritise the emotional impact of our cuts when choosing how we connect shots.
- Every cut we make must move the story on. Prettiness is not usually reason alone to keep and use a shot.
- Continuity is not usually that important.
- The pace of our cuts should establish a rhythm that is sympathetic to the action and movement exhibited in the shots.
- Wherever possible, keep the action in the frame and the energy level high.
- Every frame counts.
- Cuts are all you need.
- The definition of bad editing: cutting for the sake of it.

WHAT SHOTS CUT WELL TOGETHER?

Whilst there is no rule for deciding what shots to put together, it is fair to say that certain types of shots cut together more successfully than others. Here are a few ideas for the kinds of shots that tend to work well together:

- **Close-up to close-up shots, rather than wide to wide shots**
  Close shots tend to cut well together in sequence. My theory is that our brains have less to process in close shots—in effect, there is less

information to assimilate, and our eye trace is limited to any object or movement that fills the frame.

On the other hand, cutting from wide to wide shots is challenging for the audience since wide shots present us with a lot of information to process and our eyes are likely to move around the frame, making details harder to hone in on.

However, cutting from close to wide and then close again usually works very well. The contrast between the shot sizes is visually appealing.

- **Shots with movement in the same direction**

  The physical movement of the camera itself, whether tracking, tilting or panning, also has a major effect on how well the cut works. For example, when shot A is panning from left to right, we are wise to continue the direction of this panning motion in shot B if smoothness of the cut is our objective. The momentum of the shot is already taking us this way. If, however chaos and discomfort is our objective, we may wish to cut the opposite way in the next shot, for a more jarring effect.

  Once we include a panning shot, this does not mean that every subsequent shot in the sequence must therefore pan in order to keep the motion smoothly flowing. We can simply cut to a static or fast-moving close shot which takes our eyes elsewhere.

- **Shots of the same pace and rhythm**

  Fast action shots cut well with other fast action shots. The opposite is also true. If we choose to cut a fast shot next to a slow shot, this will give an abrupt feeling of 'braking' and, later, stasis. This could of course be a powerful effect if used deliberately: perhaps to draw attention to something within the slow frame. It could also help with the dynamism and variety of the sequence, keeping the audience excited and guessing where we will go next.

- **Shots of similar colour and luminescence**

  If we wish to keep continuity and unobtrusiveness in our sequence, then we should look to match the colour and lightness of the shots. If I was cutting a sequence of dawn over London, I would look to keep the orange hues joined up between cuts, perhaps slowly lighting up as dawn breaks.

JUDGING PACING AND THE RHYTHM OF SEQUENCES

> "What you cut on is everything for creating tension. It's amazing how expanding a shot by five seconds can just ruin the tension."
>
> —Sean Durkin[7]

The pace and rhythm of our sequences has an enormous effect on how an audience experiences our film. Our choice of pacing can stimulate our audience into feeling almost any range of emotions, from tension to wonder, excitement to sadness. The emotional response that we engender in our audience is communicated through our choice of shots, the order we place them in and where we decide to cut between them.

Our ability to coordinate these elements into sequences that feel coherent and genuine has led many to compare the editor to an orchestra conductor. Indeed, as I have said, editing is highly musical. The editor must be tuned in to the rhythms, flows and movements within the rushes, make connections and cut them into meaningful sequences. Further, these sequences must have variety, surprise, pace and dynamism. In order to achieve this, the editor must have a keen sense of timing, pacing, rhythm and tone.

The pacing and rhythm of our sequences is determined by the following:

- The level of action taking place within the shots
- The speed and number of cuts we make between these shots
- The choice and tempo of the supporting music, if music is used at all (we will discuss music in a later chapter)

Pacing is the fuel that energises our film. Pacing generates the emotional current of our scene and helps the audience to connect more profoundly with the unfolding story.

But how do we determine the right pace for our sequence? I offer a few principles that I believe will help you find a satisfactory answer:

- **Cut at a pace appropriate to the natural rhythm of your rushes.**
  A good starting point when deciding how to pace a new sequence is first to re-watch the rushes you have selected to cut with. The level of

action and the energy within them will give you an indication as to how fast they should be cut.

For example, a bull fight with rapid, sharp, unpredictable movement will lend itself naturally to faster, crazier cutting. On the other hand, a serious conversation between mother and daughter with little action and movement in the frame will lend itself to fewer cuts and slower pacing.

By cutting in a manner that is sympathetic to the internal movements of the rushes, we allow our audience to focus on and experience the story without technical distraction.

This link between speed of action and speed of cutting has been explained by the level of brain activity we would need in real life to process the same actions as those we are witnessing in the film. A group of Japanese scientists conducted an experiment in which they showed an audience a video story.[8] They discovered that the audience's blinks were generally suppressed during a passage that required visual attention and tended to occur immediately before or after the passage when the timing of its onset and offset were explicitly signaled. In other words, the audience would blink in synchronisation at the beginning or end of a significant movement on screen and every time each audience member had a new and discrete thought or emotion to process.

In this sense, faster moving action has more frequent and broader movements and there is, of course, much more to process, as well as many more emotional cues within the action. As a result, we are compelled as an audience to blink more often. In calmer or less busy situations, where the movements and emotional cues are fewer, the opposite is true and we blink less.

The team attributed the audience's blinks to our brain's ability and need to create emotional punctuation by breaking down each chunk of data it receives into manageable packages, so that we can understand and process them with greater ease. In short, where there is more to understand, we blink more, and *visa versa*. (Interestingly, this rather reinforces the 'blinking' theory as to why we are able to accept cuts in films as a 'natural' way of seeing.)

Understanding how our brains process 'environmental' information in this way is key to understanding where and when to place the cuts in our sequence. Our cuts should be placed at those moments where the on-screen action naturally causes us to blink (i.e., at the beginning or end of key movements, separating out shots to form a sequence in the same way our brain separates out thoughts with blinks).

- **Change the pace in every sequence.**
  As documentary editors, our aim is to both educate and entertain our audience. An important way of keeping our audience engaged (and willingly paying attention) is to keep them continually surprised and guessing what will be coming next.

  So once you have established a pace and emotional current within your sequence—be it slow, fast or anywhere in between—be prepared to change it again in the next sequence. We want our film to have as much contrast as possible, and variety in pace helps enormously. If one sequence is cut slow, pick up the cut rate in the next. At the end of a fast cut sequence, slow it down again, or certainly change it in a way which the audience will notice, or better 'feel.'

  If we choose to ignore this need for variety and allow adjoining sequences to continue at the same pace, then the engagement and impact that we are always aiming to generate will be diminished. The audience will already be used to the feeling of scene A, and so once scene B 'arrives' there will be little to engage them further. If continuously slow, the film will begin to feel monotonous and sleepy; if continuously fast, the audience will become first blasé and then fatigued by the action.

  An additional benefit of changing the pace between sequences is that it creates a clear visual marker to separate your scenes and give your story definition, as well as ever-important breathing space. This editing grammar helps to divide and organise the key components of the story.
- **We should vary the pace within each sequence itself.**
  While it is important for each sequence to have its own distinct pace, we must also look for appropriate opportunities to create variety of pace within each individual sequence.

  Once we have decided upon a tempo for our new sequence, it is tempting and easy enough to simply keep it going. While this will work well for a while, our audience is always ahead of us and in some way guessing what is going to happen next—and our job is to surprise them as best we can. In order to help this along, I look to create micro changes of pace, much like visual punctuation marks, to keep the sequence alive. These rhythmic changes, sometimes known as *stings*, work on a micro scale *within* sequences in the same way that changes of pace *between* sequences work on a macro scale.

Imagine a piece of orchestral music. The melody ebbs and flows, twisting and turning but building to smaller and larger climaxes, making a sort of journey for the listener and creating a story of its own. This principle applies to the way we cut our picture sequences, too—varying them makes them thrilling, emotional and suggestive for our audience.

Here are a few suggestions about how we can approach this.

- ***Punctuate your sequences with quick, short groups of shots.*** Break up your dialogue and other action with surprising bursts of pace, before settling back into the overall pace you have established—or even change the pace again. These quick-fire shots will help to create space in your sequence and give them an extra visual dynamic.
- ***The rule of three.*** Quick shots in groups of three feel good. They have a neat natural rhythm and a nice balance to them. Shots in groups of two can give a feeling of abruptness, whilst single, sustained shots generally feel poignant and add a sense of *gravitas* as our attention is first focused and then held in a single moment.

- **Change the emotion in every scene.**

In the same way that we aim to change the pace between our sequences and scenes, our films should also strive to convey emotional variety and contrast wherever possible. If one scene has finished on a negative note, then we are usually wise to turn this around and contrast it with something more positive in the next scene.

This contrast of emotional tone, similar to changing pace, urges our audience to engage with each movement of our story with freshness and renewed insight. The negativity of scene A is dissipated by the positive arrival of scene B, which will likely come as welcome relief. If we ignore this principle, joining one scene positive in tone with another of a similar tone, for example, then the intended emotional impact of scene B will be greatly diminished.

This said, we cannot always anticipate exactly how our audience will feel when they watch a scene. We are all different and precisely how we react to a film will depend on our personal life experiences as well as our prevailing mood and circumstances when we sat down to watch the film. However, we can make a pretty good guess at the impact any scene will have (based on our own feelings, experience and common sense), and as long as we stay true to the implications of that guess as we work through our sequence, things will likely turn out much as we hope.

- **Leave space.**
  Documentaries are usually packed full of information, and so it's vital that we regulate the speed at which we reveal that information, always acknowledging the audience's need for time to digest what they have seen. Pauses, absent of dialogue or other spoken information, allow both music and pictures time to 'breathe' and can have a very powerful positive impact. They are one of the most important devices for regulating and releasing emotional tension within a film: allowing an audience to absorb and/or question the narrative and making the experience a deeper and more impactful one.

  Particularly useful places for pauses are:

  - **At the beginning of a new scene**—giving the audience a chance to adjust to the new setting before any information is delivered.
  - **At the end of a scene**—giving the audience breathing space time to digest information and reflect before the next scene.
  - **At the major act breaks or junctions in the film**—pauses here should be extra large, to signify to our audience that we have reached a notable point in the narrative.
  - **At the beginning and end of the film**—again, these pauses should be elongated in order to show the audience we are at a place of significance and to allow them extra time either to settle in to the story or to reflect finally upon it.
  - **After a big statement has been made at any point during the film**—for example, when an interview contributor says something

of particular emotional weight and significance, where a major story revelation has occurred or a large question has been posed.

These pauses can be anything from ten seconds to up to a minute in length—there are no rules—so judge what you feel is right for the situation.

As a device, pauses are a huge, but too often underestimated, part of the storytelling. Do not be tempted to fill them up with words!

- **End sequences with a big, visual full stop.**
  It is important to create clear beginnings and ends to our sequences in order to keep them structured and defined. A good signal to help the audience understand we have reached the end of a story or sequence is to mark it with a big visual statement, or full stop.

  This is a single shot that is either dramatic in itself or synoptic of the preceding scene which has now reached its climax.

  We should always avoid letting any sequence drift into the next without punctuation and always strive to create clear markers through our film, thereby reminding our audience exactly where they are in the narrative.

Key Points

- Cut at a pace appropriate to the internal rhythm of your rushes.
- Change the pace in every sequence and scene.
- Vary the pace within each sequence and create moments of punctuation.
- Change the emotional tone in every adjoining scene.
- Sequences must have emotional breathing room. When needed, place pauses.
- Ensure your scenes have a clear beginnings and ends.
- End sequences with a big visual full stop.

ENHANCING THE VISUAL STYLE OF A SEQUENCE

Now we are getting a feel for how we can put our sequences together. We understand how our choice of shots, their order, and where they each begin and end will determine the overall shape of our film and its effect on our audience. We are developing some powerful and sophisticated tools for telling our story and learning how to convey complex feelings and diverse messages.

There are two final considerations when constructing our sequences, which can further enhance their overall impact and effectiveness.

- **Find an extra visual layer.**
  Most films benefit from having an extra visual layer. Typically, this visual layer comprises a set of stylised images (of contrasting colour and texture) which are distinct from the rest of the rushes in the sequence but which enhance the sequence's meaning and reinforce its direction. This visual layer could be made up from rushes from another sequence that corresponds to or otherwise 'references' the current sequence in some way.

  The purpose of this extra layer is to help brand the film and give it an identity and overall stylistic cohesion. While each sequence can have its own style and character (determined by the rushes assembled within it), the visual layer helps to create a common thread through the story as a whole. It ties everything together with a common set of pictures. Further, when used carefully, it can help signify key turns in the film, bringing the audience's attention back to the broader story and helping them to understand that each scene is a necessary and integral part of the broader narrative.

  While cutting *The Code*,[9] a series about mathematical patterns in the natural world, I discovered this extra visual signature for the series by first taking some general shots of our presenter, Marcus du Sautoy, simply walking around a rural landscape (artfully photographed with a shallow, shifting depth of field) and then intercut them with quick close shots from the previous scenes. I placed these short montage sequences at key story turns in the film (primarily at act junctions), as if to suggest Marcus was reflecting and puzzling over the mystery of the film—searching in that very moment for the answers. In order to help emphasize the other-worldly feel of these moments (as they were essentially asides from the main body of the programme), I shifted the colour of the images (known as *colour grading*) to a dark, deep blue. This gave them an added dreamlike quality. I further reinforced their effect by overlapping the sound and adding plenty of reverb—as if they were in some sort of strange cavern. In the context of the film, it worked perfectly, and we used it across all three programmes to 'glue' them together, thereby branding the whole series.

Sometimes—though all too rarely—the director will specially shoot extra material for this very purpose. Where possible and if required, I will ask the director to shoot something new, especially if nothing within the rushes suits this purpose. An alternative strategy, though usually less convincing and harder to execute, is to search for stock footage to do the job instead (library footage, brought in 'off the shelf'). Ideally—and whatever their source—this set of images should have qualities rather imperfectly described as 'poetic' or 'symbolic,' by which I mean they should have a capacity to reinforce the meaning of the sequence in more abstract and allegorical ways (as a mild form of escape from the information-heavy body of the film). We must, however, ensure that these pictures are consonant with our existing rushes, or if meaningful and appropriate, make a virtue of their distinctive qualities.

Rather as great drama causes an audience to abstract wider generalities from the specifics of the action they have seen and the words they have heard, great documentaries encourage us to think beyond the confines of what we have just seen and been told and, as a consequence, take up more general positions based on the implication of the film as a whole. The extra visual layer described here can strongly support this aspiration, encouraging a more general reflection on the implications of the film as a whole.

For example, I once cut a film called *What Happened Before the Big Bang?*[10] As the title suggests, the film was about the contrasting, complex and crazy theories that scientists have constructed to explain what might have happened before the big bang. The very idea of *before* the big bang was novel in itself to many. In order to create an extra visual layer to tie the many disparate elements of the film together, the director, rather cleverly, shot each theorist in close up attempting to solve a Rubik's Cube style puzzle. Their attempts to solve the puzzle and their apparent frustration in failing to do so created an interesting parallel to their attempts to answer the question of what happened before the big bang. While the puzzle was in no way the subject of the film, it had a good—because appropriate and visually arresting—connection to the story. It also provided welcome relief at key moments and signaled to the audience a common thread through the narrative.

In *The Trouble with Space Junk*, a documentary that explores the threat of human-created debris in the Earth's orbit, we created an extra visual layer throughout the film by taking old space archives and inserting quick flashes of the material at near random intervals through the sequences. The intention of this was to tease the audience into thinking that their television signal at home, transmitted from a satellite in orbit, was itself being interrupted by rogue space debris.

These layers often work best when they are held back for key moments in the film, such as the beginning and end, as well as the key junctions and turning points between scenes. They can stand alone as sequences in their own right or be cut together with other shots from within the scenes, depending what feels right for your story.

- **Cut in a style appropriate to the emotion of your scene.**
  Obvious as it may seem, it is worth emphasising that we must consider the emotional thrust of our sequence and cut in a style that is supportive of it. For example, if a scene is about something uncomfortable and violent, I will cut in a way that is equally brash and sharp. I might choose to draw attention to the cuts and make shots collide more obviously, rather than making everything smooth and invisible.

  Jump cuts are sometimes useful in this way. This is where we cut two shots from the same setup and framing next to each other, creating a noticeable jump in the action. They give a feeling of quick-fire, disjointed activity.

  Alternatively, if I was cutting a scene where tension was the driving emotion, I would wish to create an ominous feeling of mounting threat. This could be achieved by intercutting one character's set of actions with that of another; suggesting that the two will shortly 'collide' and the action reach its climax. Additionally, I might create the sensation of a countdown to this moment, either by using shots containing a reference to time counting or a sound design and music which gradually increase in speed and intensity.

  Equally, if I was cutting a scene of lovers walking through a meadow. I would probably cut this a lot slower, lingering on shots that show the couple's affection for each other, for example, a close up of their hands entwined and their eyes staring deeply into each other's. In this way, we can create a sense of time slowing down and the couple entering a dreamlike state.

Key Points

- Find an extra visual layer to support your sequences.
- Cut in a style appropriate to the emotion of your scene.

WORKING WITH CUTAWAYS

Early in our project we made selections of our best interview clips. These sync pulls were then structured into the framework of a scene: the *sync and black assembly*. When we made selections from the master interview, we made cuts in the interviews, which to the naked eye almost certainly looked ugly and awkward.

Now that we have begun to craft our sequences that will build together to form our entire scene, we can look to conceal the cuts in the interview clips and also help the interviews where needed with visual illustration.

In short, we will use the supporting B-roll and actuality for the scene to cover the edits in our interview. This work is primarily a picture editing task, though some finer audio adjustments may be needed.

The mechanism of covering cuts in interview with cutaway shots is simple, but it isn't necessarily easy (see figure 3.18). There is an art to doing it well, an art which I feel many editors either undervalue or in some cases neglect entirely.

I have come to realise:

- **We must ensure that interview cutaways progress the story.**
  It can be easy to use a cutaway for the sake of it. Many editors will use almost anything to cover an interview cut—often something repetitive or altogether meaningless. This simply says, to me at least, "Well I had a cut to cover here, what else did you expect me to do?" This kind of cutaway merely interrupts the flow of our film and is, in the end, generally detrimental to it.

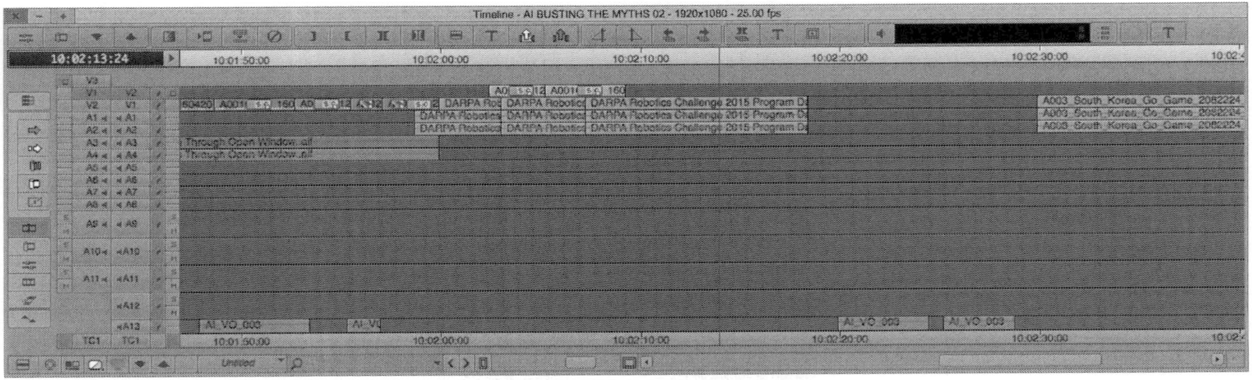

Figure 3.18 Interview Cutaways

There are two cuts in the underlying interview clips (which are placed on V1). These cuts have been concealed with two shots on the video layer above (on V2).

Cutaways must feel *necessary*: included because they serve the purposes of the film, not because they cover an awkward picture edit. Remember: we want to progress the narrative with every cut.

I find the best way to achieve this effect is to consider the last shot in the previous sequence, before we came to the interview, and then find a shot which connects to that as the next logical story 'beat.' This way, the interview feels integral to and propelled by the action, not a driver of poorly orchestrated and misdirected action.

Any cutaways we need to cover further cuts in the interview must then be a continuation of this action, and a forward link to the sequence that follows on from the end of the interview.

- **We must re-pace interview sync to allow breathing room for cutaway shots.**

Now that we have the makings of a fleshed-out and viable scene, we can further improve the effectiveness of our interview sync clips by matching them to the flows and rhythms in the supporting sequences. The use of cutaways should not be constrained by the nature and timing of the words that they cover. We should be prepared to cut up and pace out our interview sync to fit around and support the pictures and sounds that we have.

In more considered scenes, let the interview clips breathe and create space to allow their easy assimilation. In fast-paced action sequences, cut out the pauses and deliver the interview sync in a more quick-fire fashion.

- **Cut interviews in and out of vision at sentence breaks.**

I find it easiest to cut in and out of interviews between discrete sentences or thoughts. This makes the interview clips feel more natural, neater, and more deliberate—and consequently easier for the audience to accept. Cutting in or out of vision mid-sentence can be jarring and ugly.

In addition, I will try to ensure that any sections of interview in which the contributor exhibits a strong physical gesture remain in vision. Our contributor's body language is vital to our understanding of what he or she is trying to convey and hugely influences our audience's understanding of their feelings.

If there are no natural breaks to cut in and out of vision, then consider playing all of a particular piece of sync *out of vision*. This technique is also useful when a contributor is so poor that in order to salvage their contribution (if it is really worth salvaging) we have to make multiple detailed cuts in their sync. As a result of this extensive editing, we may not have any clear and sustained points where we can show them in vision. We might choose to make a stylistic virtue of this impediment, keeping them 'deliberately' out of vision throughout the scene.

Key Points

- The choice of cutaways must be motivated by the needs of the story (pushing it always towards its end) and not by the technical need to cover an awkward picture edit.
- The use of cutaways need not be determined or constrained by the original structure and pacing of the words that they cover.
- Cut interviews in and out of vision at sentence breaks.
- Keep strong emotional expressions and body language in vision.

WORKING WITH STOCK FOOTAGE

Stock footage, also known as *archive footage*, is film footage brought into the edit from an outside source. It is often taken from other films or library sources that license its use to multiple films. The term *archive footage* tends to refer to old film footage, often of historical events, while *stock footage* is intended to match and supplement present-day rushes. Documentaries make frequent and varying use of both, though some do not use it at all, using specially shot rushes only, whilst others are built entirely out of archive materials.

Stock footage is useful to filmmakers in many ways. It can save the expense of shooting new material, where perfectly good footage already exists. It can be a useful way of obtaining one-off, high-quality shots that would otherwise be difficult to recreate, such as aerial helicopter footage of a landscape. Archive footage is also essential for sourcing shots of historical events. For example, the first moon landing or the Queen's Coronation are—obviously—only available as archive.

Archive and stock footage are useful tools for editors to have at their disposal and, in order to get the most out of it, its use must be carefully thought through. In films that are not primarily stock-footage-based and where stock shots are being used to supplement and support your rushes, remember the following:

- **Only use stock shots that match your rushes.**
  When using stock shots to supplement our rushes, we are attempting to pass off the shots *as* rushes. We want our stock shots to look as though they are part of the sequence.

  In order to achieve this, we must identify stock footage sources that were shot at a similar time, on a similar camera and under similar lighting and weather conditions. An archive film researcher is extremely useful in achieving this, as they will have a good knowledge of the film material that is available worldwide.

  Recently I watched a documentary (I dare not name the programme) where the presenter is seen skimming along the Amazon river on a speed boat in crisp high-definition, shot with prime lenses with a shallow depth of field: all visually arresting and beautifully crisp material. The film editor then cut back to a wide of the Amazon rain forest shot on 16mm cine film. The shot looked as though it had been filmed about thirty years earlier! It was yellow and grainy. So, rather than enhancing the storytelling (giving us the geography of the location and a sense of it's scale), its technical disparity *vis-à-vis* the more recently filmed sequences constituted a major distraction, posing far more unwanted questions than answers.

  The aim should be for our stock shots to blend into our sequence seamlessly so that they do not draw unnecessary attention to themselves or distract the audience from the main matter in hand.
- **Keep the use of stock footage to a minimum.**
  Whenever we use stock footage, we introduce continuity issues. These continuity issues can be anything from issues of technical quality (as in the example above) to matters of lighting or the time and place from which they came. As a result, we must be careful how we select and place these stock clips, since whenever we use them, we run the risk of unsettling our audience and even causing them to question the authenticity of our account.

As a result, we should aim to limit the use of stock shots and wherever possible make a virtue of our rushes. After all, our rushes were shot with our particular story in mind and should give us most if not all of what we need to craft a sequence.

There are instances, of course, where films require some stock or archive materials to 'rescue' them. The director may have encountered problems on the shoot and had been unable to get what he or she needed. Occasionally, the story can change so radically from the shoot to the edit that major picture gaps emerge and stock footage provides a solution, when reshooting is not an option.

- **Explain your archive sources.**
  As well as using stock footage to supplement our rushes, there are many occasions in documentary when we wish to draw attention to our historical archive as a deliberate statement and for specific reasons. For example, in the case of very old film archive, where we get a window into another time and way of living.

  In these instances, since the archive footage will almost certainly appear novel and even arresting to the audience, it is often helpful to explain the source. This could be a simple title card (perhaps in the lower third, bottom edges of the screen), if voiceover is too distracting.

Another reason to be wary of historical archive is that we usually have to license it. We have a legal duty to pay the copyright holders royalties for the use of their footage. This is usually paid according to the number of seconds used or, in some cases, per shot. These licenses are often valid for a certain number of years only (at which point the license must be renewed, at further expense, failing which they expire, rendering it impossible for the filmmaker to exhibit the film in later years). Furthermore, these licenses may have territory restrictions, meaning broadcast is limited to certain countries and on certain platforms. Stock footage, on the other hand, is usually paid as a one-off fee with perpetual single-use granted thereafter.

It is essential then, if we are to use archive footage, that we have a clear system in place to catalogue and account for every archive clip used in our film. The information of most importance in order to license and manage the footage will be their source (the origin of the footage), their timecode start and end (if present in the source, or often 'burnt in' vision on screen, in the case of screener copies from the master libraries) and overall duration. This information can usually be exported directly from the edit software into a text format—which can be read with relative ease.

We should ensure that all sources have been verified and cleared for licensing before the film is complete so that we can be sure that all footage is legally usable, within our budget and ultimately available for screening.

Key Points

- When using stock shots to support rushes, only use shots that match.
- Keep the use of archive and stock shots to a minimum.
- Explain your sources, when relevant.

WORKING WITH STILL IMAGES

There are almost endless ways in which to use still images in documentary filmmaking. Most commonly, documentary uses stills to help tell the story when rushes and other archive materials are not available. Still images can in themselves have great style and beauty and can add significantly to the aesthetics of a film. They can create a strong emotional response in our audience, especially when combined with other still images in montage. Equally, if used poorly, stills can slow a film down to a near fatal halt.

Dropping a still image into your timeline is easily done, but making it flow and blend into your film takes skill. There are many techniques available to editors for working with still images. Here are a few ideas:

- **Rostrum movements**

  A rostrum movement could be a zoom in, tilt, pan, rotation or any perspective shift applied to the still image. Giving our still images some movement, rather than leaving them static, is an easy way to add energy and dynamism and maintain a sense of ongoing motion. Movements such as a zoom can also be used to draw the audience's attention to a specific detail within the image. Zooming in on a point of interest or zooming out to give the wider context takes the audience where you want to take them, directing the viewer's gaze towards a certain part of the frame and making a significant point in doing so.

Filmmaker Ken Burns has made such extensive use of rostrum movements in his films (such as *The Civil War*[11]) that the very technique has become known as *The Ken Burns effect*!

- **Making cuts to form a picture sequence**
  We do not have to take a single image as one single shot. We could make several cuts within a single still image, each cropped to a different part of the frame to create the impression of a picture sequence as well as an impression of the wider frame. In this way, we can use a still image much like we use rushes footage.

  Note, this technique will only work with very high-resolution images, which hold up to extreme magnification.
- **2.5D**
  A sophisticated and effective way of using stills can be to cut out each element of the still as a separate layer. We then independently move each layer, creating movement and perspective, to simulate the appearance of 3D.

  I first saw this approach adopted in the film adaptation of Robert Evans's *The Kid Stays in the Picture*,[12] though it has been taken a lot further since, particularly in television commercials.
- **Shoot the stills in situ**
  A final idea for using stills, which I have found highly effective (when the option is available), is if the director is able to shoot still images on location in the environment in which the rest of the scene is set. For example, the director could ask an interview contributor to hold their photographs up to the camera or even go through them in an album. This way, when we are editing the footage, we do not have to 'interrupt' the flow of the sequence by cutting away to a stark, digital version of the still.

  In Niall Ferguson's *Civilization: Is the West History?*[13] the director projected stills onto walls and buildings to similar effect.

NOTES

1 Andrew C. Evans, GBFTE. "Should Editors Have Any Rights to Joint Authorship of Their Work?" *First Frame: The Guild of British Film and Television Editors Magazine* (Spring, 2015).

2 Ira Nadel, *David Mamet: A Life in the Theatre* (Palgrave Macmillan, New York: 2012), 157.

3 www.quotationspage.com. Accessed 6 September 2016. www.quotationspage.com/quote/268.html

4 Wendy Apple, *The Cutting Edge: The Magic of Movie Editing* (A.C.E/BBC/NHK Enterprises/TCEP Inc., 2004), Part 1.

5 Dale Drewery, Laine Drewery, Leslie Lucas, David Massar, Kelly McClughan, Lori Smart, Tyler J. Smart, & Bruce Thorston, *Jetstream* (Paperny Films/Discovery Channel Canada, 2008).

6 Nigel Patterson, *Dawn Chorus: The Sounds of Spring* (BBC, 2015).

7 www.brainyquote.com. Accessed 23 October, 2016. www.brainyquote.com/quotes/quotes/s/seandurkin510530.html

8 The Royal Society Publishing. "Synchronization of Spontaneous Eyeblinks While Viewing Video Stories." (29 July 2009) Tamami Nakano, Yoshiharu Yamamoto, Keiichi Kitajo, Toshimitsu Takahashi & Shigeru Kitazawa. Accessed 23 October, 2016. http://rspb.royalsocietypublishing.org/content/early/2009/07/24/rspb.2009.0828

9 Stephen Cooter, *The Code* (BBC, 2011).

10 Peter Leonard, *What Happened before the Big Bang?* (BBC, 2010).

11 Ken Burns, *The Civil War* (Kenneth Lauren Burns Productions/Florentine Films/WETA-TV/PBS, 1990).

12 Nanette Burstein/Brett Morgen, *The Kid Stays in the Picture* (USA Films, 2002).

13 Adrian Pennink, *Civilisation: Is the West History?* (Chimerica Media/Channel 4, 2011).

4

SOUND EDITING

WORKING WITH SOUND DESIGN AND MUSIC

> "Films are 50 percent visual and 50 percent sound. Sometimes sound even overplays the visual."
>
> —David Lynch[1]

So far we have discussed picture editing. There is of course a whole other side to editing, which is as important—perhaps even more important—and that is sound.

We rely on sound for so much of our storytelling. We need sound to deliver dialogue and voiceover (the fundamental narrative components of our film), for the musical score, and just as importantly, we depend on sound for creating the atmosphere of our scenes.

This atmosphere is created through a process of sourcing, selecting and manipulating or generating audio elements, to create a desired effect or mood, and is commonly referred to as *sound design*. Sound design can be used in documentary to a varying extent, depending on the genre of film. For example, an observational documentary with an ultra-realistic foundation in the natural world may require very little, if any additional sound. Ambient natural sound (which is captured in the field), dialogue and perhaps the occasional sound effect (commonly referred to as a *spot effect*—which could be something as simple as a door bell) will probably be enough to tell the story. On the other hand, a film about particle physics, where there is likely to be little or no obvious sound available to support the intricacies of the narrative, will be likely to require a lot more imagination if sound is to be deployed in support of the narrative structure.

Good sound design and music give our scenes much of their feeling. If you are in the slightest doubt about this, try watching a movie with its soundtrack muted, taking for example almost any of the memorable scenes in Hitchcock's *Psycho*. Without Bernard Herrmann's music and the other carefully placed audio signals, the shower scene or drive in the rain lose almost all of their power and go for virtually nothing. Of course, since the time of *Psycho* the sophistication of sound design and music has increased enormously, but the basic *raison d'etre* for the presence of sound remains much the same.

While the environmental aspects of sound (the ambient or background 'noise') may at first seem unimportant in comparison to the more narrative components of sound (dialogue for example), they are in fact a huge contributor to the success of our storytelling. Environmental sound tells us far more about where we are and what is happening in our story than the pictures alone can. Sound can also tell us what is happening *outside* of the frame as well as what is happening immediately in front of us. Because of its far-reaching and subliminal capabilities, sound design is one of the most powerful tools we have for connecting our audience with our narrative. In life, silence is rare and unnatural. Silence in film, unless used for deliberate effect, distances us from what we are seeing, whereas good sound design draws us in and opens us up emotionally to the message of the sequence or film as a whole.

Film sound falls primarily in to two groups:

- **Diegetic sound**

  Any sound that is represented as an original source from within the film's world. This can be on or off screen and can consist of the following:

  - Dialogue; such as interviews, discussions, interactions or arguments
  - Natural sound captured in the field, such as the environmental sound of a forest or a bowling alley

  - Incidental music; represented as coming from instruments within the story space
- **Non-diegetic sound**

  Any sound recognised as coming from outside the space of the story events. This can consist of:
  - Voiceover narration
  - Sound effects added for dramatic impact
  - Pre-recorded music (sourced from a commercial, composed or library-catalogue publishers)

These two sound groups are usually mixed together in filmmaking for optimum dramatic effect. For example, a play with diegetic and non-diegetic elements can be used to create ambiguity in genres such as horror or to delight the audience in comedy.

These different sound components work on two levels. Interview dialogue and voiceover narration work primarily on a conscious level, stating and clarifying the story, while sound design and music work mostly on a subconscious level, underscoring and enhancing the emotional tone of the story.

> Note! Whilst within this book I have explained picture editing first, it is important that we consider sound *in parallel with* and even *before* picture editing when approaching a new sequence.

UNDERSTANDING SOUND

Sound is a fundamental part of film, yet it is often neglected by documentary filmmakers. Perhaps this casual attitude prevails because we cannot see sound, and so it is easier to forget than pictures and, consequently, *seems* less important.

I maintain, however, that sound provides the defining aesthetic of any film in terms of the audience's viewing experience. I also believe that shaping the sound is one of the most important (and enjoyable) contributions that as editors we can make to our film.

However, from my experience, most editors struggle with sound and find it hard to master, often settling for clumsy and uninspiring sound mixes or shying away from it altogether. Yet despite the perceived difficulties of sound design, there are a number of simple and practical principles we can apply when building our mix which will make the process easier, more effective and much more fun.

- **First, start building each new sequence with the sound first.**
  Sound is such a foundation of our film that I generally believe we should consider its place in our sequence *before* we even begin to cut the pictures. This is because sound dictates certain temporal constraints (the length of a phrase), determines much of the flow of our sequence (its rhythm, pace and timing) and also influences significantly the *way* we cut our pictures.

  As explained earlier on, I begin by watching my rushes so that I understand the material I have to work with. I next block out my new sequence with dialogue, and where needed, voiceover to establish the scenes structure. Once I have this foundation and know something of the shape of my new scene, I next build in some of the basic sound design around it.

  Normally, I will choose a few sound effects that capture the feeling of the environment depicted in the sequence and how I would like the audience to apprehend or interpret it. I have a comprehensive library of sound effects which I have built up over many years. You will be able to access a similar sort of library online, or better still, purchase your own from an established provider.

  For example, if my scene is set on a wet night on a rough backstreet of London, I would first find some rain (on tarmac) and some distant traffic as a basic sound bed. I will then find a few extra effects to thicken it up and to 'animate' the sound, such as a distant dog barking, a car alarm, police siren or perhaps a single car passing close to us (splashing through puddles, too, if possible). As well as giving a strong sense of the obvious urban characteristics of the environment (the rain on tarmac and traffic sounds), the dog barks, car alarm and police siren add a sense of threat and unease: critical audio signals that establish a specific mood. Even though we can't see the car being 'stolen' or the barking dog, we will get the feeling. At a conscious or unconscious level, our brain supplies the missing images.

Where needed, I will open up the sequence and give space for these sounds to breathe and play out uninterrupted. Where there are spoken words in my scene assembly (by way of interview, actuality or voiceover) I will place the more distinct sounds in between sentence breaks or key phases whilst allowing the general sound bed (that of the rain and traffic) to run more or less continuously.

Once I have this framework in place, I will begin to cut my pictures in. I will build in more sound design as the mood and my imagination dictate.

Tip! Timing almost always comes from the sound (not the pictures). If you get the audio timing right first, then the pictures will follow.

While I believe this method of sound first and pictures later is an effective means of establishing a shape and tempo to a sequence, we must always be sympathetic to the inherent timing and rhythms of the pictures also—and not cut them strictly and only to the structure we have defined in sound. Once we have some notion of our sound bed, we must be flexible enough to adjust this once we start cutting pictures, to ensure each shot works in its own space. While much of our timing will come through sound, it must remain 'negotiable' and open, therefore, to the needs of the pictures.

- **Apply the law of two-and-a-half.**
  Prominent film editor and sound designer Walter Murch states that our brains are able to consciously track only about two and a half individuals sound 'layers' at any one time. As soon as we exceed these three elements, our brains can no longer readily distinguish between individual sounds and instead interpret them as more of a singular, collective group.

He says:

> My rule of thumb is generally to not present more than two-and-a-half thematic layers to the audience at any moment, because I'm interested in the balance between clarity on the one hand and density on the other. If you shove four simultaneous layers at an audience it just becomes a spectacle; they'll catch one or two things, but they won't enjoy the harmonic integration of all the elements, and the number of layers that seems optimal for this is two and a half. In other words: two full layers and another layer coming in or going out, all of this shifting every ten or 15 seconds. Ideally, it is like a good shell game where the audience is kept guessing about where the pea is.[2]

As a practical example, if we have a shot where a single person is walking, then we must ensure that the sound of their footsteps is in sync with the movement of their feet, otherwise the audience will be thrown by this discrepancy. Also, if there are two people walking in the shot, then each set of footsteps needs to match, too. However, if three or more people are walking, then *none* of the footsteps need to sync up.

On this basis and for general efficiency, we should limit the amount of sound design that we give to each component part of our scene to two or three individual sound elements.

I would suggest that while most audiences are not really aware of what they are listening to on a conscious level, they feel the emotional effect of the sound on a subconscious level: perhaps a more powerful contribution to the overall effectiveness of the scene than that made even by the pictures.

- **Sound does not have to describe the obvious.**

Looking at what is inside the frame and finding appropriate sound effects can be a very useful starting point when building up the soundscape for a scene or sequence.

However, I believe sound design is most interesting and exciting when it describes what is outside of the frame and portrays a world which the pictures alone cannot or do not show us. In this sense, the sound design is working independently to make our audience aware of the richness of the world they are in and to tap into their imaginations and, consequently, their deepest emotions.

When thinking about sound for a new sequence while looking at the rushes, I like to ask myself, "What is happening in the room next door?" If it is a suburban neighbourhood, there may be children playing and laughing in the street and the gentle hum of birds and lawn mowers. But, how big is the environment? In our suburban neighbourhood, the sound may be relatively tight and the elements individually distinct, but if the scene is set on a mountain, I might hear only a distant goat bleat over a thin, wide breeze, echoing through the otherwise empty landscape. All of this supplies an important sense of scale.

To create a specific emotional effect, I will often choose sounds that bear no resemblance to anything in the depicted environment itself: for example, a deep metallic rumble in a bright white room. Whilst the room looks mundane, the sound creates a real sense of unease.

- **Think primarily of the space that the sound is occupying.** Choosing the right sound effect can be a challenge. This is particularly true, for example, when hunting for a bird song. I must admit that all birds look and sound pretty similar to me, but to a *twitcher*, they are unique and getting them wrong would be a serious crime. If I did not take time to match the right call to the right bird, I could really spoil a bird lover's enjoyment of the film and cause them to distrust the rest of its content entirely. I know an ex-RAF pilot for whom the wrong aeroplane engine noise in a documentary about the Second World War led him to conclude that the filmmaker was an idiot and the film a complete fabrication. Clearly, the editor didn't know a Bristol Taurus engine from a Rolls-Royce Merlin! In general, however, I find that a car horn is a car horn. Once I have an effect that sounds good—to my ear at least—then that is good enough.

  On the whole, I find that it is the way the effect *sounds in the given space* that matters most, rather than the sound itself.

  For example, a car horn in a large empty garage will sound very different from a car horn in a dense forest, or a car that has crashed through the front window of my grandmother's living room. Once we have chosen the right effect, then we must next consider how we treat it. Here are a couple of examples of what we could do:

- **Apply reverb.** This gives the sound a sense of scale. You can make your audio sound bigger, as if it is in a hall or tunnel, making the environment in which it is sounding feel more open and expansive.
- **Use an EQ effect.** This effect will change the tonal balance of the sound. For example, we could use it to take out the bass. This makes the audio sound thin and tinny, as if it is coming out of the radio or an old television. Alternatively, we could use the same effect to take out all of the top end frequency. This makes the audio sound bass-heavy and dull, as if it is coming through the walls of the room next door or is underwater.
- **No sound at all.** This works particularly well in a busy action scene—at a moment of build or climax—adding drama and making the audience feel as though they are in the character's head. The audience can fill in the sound with their own imaginations: an extremely powerful device. This works particularly well if we have built to a climax in the sound mix, before effectively *cutting it off*. In this way, the audience can sense the dramatic change in environment.

- **Get sound design right as early as possible.**

I will always ensure that I have built up a comprehensive sound bed for each sequence at the very start of the cutting process; normally while I am assembling my first rough cut of the film. This is for two reasons.

First it helps in viewings with outside collaborators, such as executives. By ensuring, from the very first viewing, that they have a rich audio experience to match the visuals, executives can watch the film with far greater assurance, relating it more closely to the film as a finished product rather than an assembly of parts with any number of questionable and distracting loose ends.

Second, the ever-tighter budgets of most documentary film productions mean that the time that a film has for audio post-production (where a professional sound designer will enhance and progress the work of the editor after picture lock) is increasingly squeezed. It is critical then that we spend as much time as possible getting the sound design working in the edit, whilst we have time and the detailed knowledge of the project necessary to get it working effectively. We should not rely too heavily on outside professional help to save us later down the line.

Key Points

- Start cutting new sequences with the sound first.
- Get the timing right in the sound, and the pictures will follow.
- Two or three simultaneous streams of sound are probably all you will need.
- Sound does not have to describe the obvious. Ask, what is happening in the room next door?
- Think of the space that the sound is occupying, more than the effect itself.
- Get sound design right in the edit and do not rely on outside help to save it!
- Build your own comprehensive library of sound effects and take it everywhere you go!

WORKING WITH MUSIC

> "Music expresses that which cannot be put into words and that which cannot remain silent"
>
> —Victor Hugo[3]

Music is one of the trickiest yet most enjoyable parts of the editing process. Like so many aspects of editing, music selection and reactions to it are subjective and people's feelings about it vary enormously. What sounds great to one person can be a lot of noise to another. Furthermore, finding the right music for your film takes time and patience.

Music is also one of the only tools that the editor uses that the audience seems to recognise and readily engage with. Perhaps this is because we enjoy listening to music in our everyday lives and a particular soundtrack can come to represent and remind us of any number of our life experiences.

The film editor is usually responsible for sourcing, selecting and placing the music for the film. It is up to the editor to set the tone for how the music is going to be used throughout a film. As a result, it is important that we have a good understanding of music in general, as well as a keen sense of rhythm and timing.

WHY WE USE MUSIC IN FILMMAKING

> "Music is the shorthand of emotion"
>
> —Leo Tolstoy[4]

Music is an emotional storytelling device. It is used to underscore and enhance the emotional quality of a sequence. I say *enhance*, because for music to work best there should be a pre-existing emotional charge to the scene (which I will discuss shortly).

Music has a unique place in filmmaking since it gives us emotionally what the words and visuals cannot. As Jean Sibelius said, "Music begins where the possibilities of language end."[5] When used wisely, music can modulate and underscore the subtle currents in our story and bring new meaning and experience to our audience.

Music has a significant effect on any film. The same film would feel very different with a different music score. Furthermore, the power of music lies not only the track you use but also *how* you use it. The timing and positioning of our music most determines its effect on our audience.

Music can be used to:

- **Help with the pacing and rhythm of a sequence.**
  The rhythm of the music track can inspire the pace of the cut sequence. This does not mean we should always cut to the beat of the music (as this would be too predictable and robotic, unless, of course, you are determined to do so for deliberate effect.) There are many ways the pattern in the music can inspire the pattern of the cut, for example, cutting on the offbeat, cutting at double or half the speed of the music or just before and after the beat (in musical terms this is known as *playing in the pocket*).

Overall, however, our choice of music should be sympathetic to the rhythm of the pictures. For example, fast-moving action naturally lends itself to fast-moving music, whereas slow wide shots require slower and more graceful themes.

This said, fast music and pictures combined can quickly become fatiguing, and so there are times when using counterpoint (offsetting the tempo of the music and the pictures) can work extremely well. For example, slow graceful music can sometimes compliment fast moving action, creating a sense of suspended animation, poetic wonder and beauty.

- **Help with storytelling.**
  Music can be used to help support the story by supplying emotionally what the pictures do not. Music can tell the audience something is happening of which they may not otherwise be aware. This device is often used to create suspense: the sequence of pictures can be tracking something quite ordinary or neutral relatively speaking, whilst the music can suggest an accumulating sense of menace. This tells the audience that something is imminent and emphasizes a hidden threat.
- **Show we have reached a significant point in the story.**
  Music can be used to help segment and divide our film up into sections. This is a helpful way of indicating to the audience how far along the journey they are and can act as a sort of map, pointing out the key story points and junctions.

  A great way to do this is to choose a single track (and perhaps a number of variations of it) as a theme. This theme then becomes a symbol of the film's message, which we can refer back to at key story junctions. It gives our film a unity and identity it might otherwise lack.

  We may also consider having more than one theme for different story threads or characters. Sometimes called a *leitmotiv*, this technique derives from nineteenth-century German opera and was imported in to Hollywood soundtracks by the émigré composers who worked there in the 1930s. Characters have themes which identify them, and variations on their themes signal changes in their mood or circumstance. It is but one of many interesting ways in which film has inherited and still continues to work techniques derived from the stage.

Particularly good places to consider using themes are:

- At the beginning of the film.
- At the end of big scenes.
- At the ends of acts.
- At the end of the film.

SOME GOOD WAYS TO USE MUSIC

While our choices and uses of music are subjective and almost infinite, there are some ways to use music that I have found work better than others.

- **Music works best when used to channel an existing emotion.** First, music works best when used to channel an emotion that has already been established by the narrative. This rings truer in the audience's mind since it accords with their own experience of the scene, rather than being artificially imposed.

  Unfortunately, this is something that seems to confuse filmmakers, particularly in commercial television documentary editing. We often lead with the music in order quickly to establish a mood, and then try to back up that mood *afterwards* with pictures and story (by way of dialogue, voiceover and pictures). Perhaps this is because we do not have sufficient confidence in our narrative to do the job properly on its own. Alternatively, we may have insufficient faith in our audience to interpret the message properly, or perhaps we simply imitate the majority of mass television media that adopts this backward approach to music placement as a matter of routine.

  There are some instances where allowing the narrative to first establish the emotional temperature may not be easy or entirely possible. For example, most documentary opening sequences will require music of some sort, and obviously no emotion will have been established prior to this first sequence. Indeed, this sequence will be our first chance to establish that emotion. In instances like this we have a choice: delay starting the music until we have built a narrative hook for it or perhaps choose music which builds slowly, allowing the audience some opportunity to appraise and invest in the story before the music begins to do so for them.

Still, as far as is possible, we should avoid relying on music as the sole device for creating the mood and feel of our sequence. Resist introducing music for as long as is possible/necessary for the scene to play out uninterrupted and do not lead the scene with music, giving away its emotional payoff prematurely.

For example, in a scene where we are to learn that the subject has been diagnosed with cancer, it would be wise to avoid music that prefigures this. Telling the audience what is about to happen ("this music is sad and heavy, they must be about to get bad news") diminishes the effect of the revelation. The audience has already anticipated the outcome, and the film has been robbed of its emotional impact.

Personally, I would choose to bring the music in *after* the bad news has been given, at the moment when the penny drops and once the audience has assessed the situation for themselves. The music then underscores and reinforces this assessment, making the emotional response genuinely authentic and moving. This music can then carry the audience on to the next story beat.

- **When selecting music, ask, what is this sequence about?**

We have already asked this question in a different but related context, but it applies with particular force here. By now we should be reasonably adept at being able to identify the purpose of each scene and sequence within it. By understanding what our scene is about, we are able to judge its emotional tone, and this is crucial when selecting appropriate music tracks. The music track we select must support and reinforce that meaning.

The right music track does not always have to be the 'obvious' (such as sad piano music for a sad sequence). For example, when cutting *Guts*,[6] our presenter had various cameras inserted into his body to study how his body digested the food he ate. I contrasted the gruesome and occasionally painful processes involved in the study (such as the insertion of a wire camera up his nose) with playful, quirky music. So, while the pictures and other story elements suggested that the presenter was not enjoying the experience, the music added some much-needed humour which in turn made the scene more bearable to watch. It gave the audience permission to laugh and enjoy watching him squirm. *Schadenfreude* is after all a very basic human trait.

- **Music usually works best when it operates just below the consciousness of the audience.**
  Our choices of music must of course be appropriate to the style of film we are making and should reflect an awareness of its target audience. A film intended for a teen audience may lend itself to pop music more than a film aimed at a middle-aged audience. However, in general, I find that for most documentaries it is best to avoid making too many categorical choices based on stereotypes.

  It is safest to assume that our audience is knowledgeable and reasonably sophisticated, so most will have an interest in music. If we continually choose music that is easy to identify (and therefore probably already pregnant with association), we risk distracting our audience or evoking 'remembered' responses we do not intend. For this reason, I believe that music works best when it operates just below the audience's level of consciousness, supporting the action without overpowering it. In general, I will favour library music (often called *production music*) that is specially recorded and licensed for film and television use or composed music (of the highest quality) to support the narrative and reserve use of more distinctly identifiable music for choice moments in the story.

  For example, I may decide to use a trite, clichéd piece of music deliberately to draw attention to a particular moment in, or feature of, the story (usually for comic effect). I once used the opening theme to *Edward Scissorhands* to begin a science film about particle physics. Somehow it had a natural synergy, by way of its ethereal magic, and added to the feeling of the film without seeming too obvious. However, for most documentaries, use of commercial or otherwise recognisable music in this way should be kept to a minimum to preserve its impact.

> Tip! When auditioning music for a new sequence, before I lay anything into the timeline and cut with it, I find it useful to play potential tracks against my sync and black assembly. By doing so, I can quickly make a call as to how well the track is working. Does the track fit with the tone of the story? Does the pace of the music help the structure and suggest an interesting way of cutting the visuals?

- **Give music tracks a clear beginning and end.**
  It is important that our music is clearly delineated and has a defined place within our narrative structure. This means it should have a clear beginning, middle and end. Music works best when it frames a particular story beat.

  So while our music will likely start at a key emotional cue in our dialogue, our music track should end at the point at which the thought which it has framed comes to an end or when the next beat of the story begins.

  Personally, I like to give my music cues a clear and pronounced beginning and end by excising parts in the middle of the track so that I can use its own start and finish. I generally avoid fading music in and out, unless this is an intrinsic feature of the track I have chosen: it feels lazy, arbitrary and places in question the appropriateness of the original choice. I want the audience to notice or better 'feel' it when the music begins and ends and, even if not consciously, sense that it was there for good reason.

> Note! Be careful not let your music run on to the next scene, sequence or story beat. Letting music run on freely blurs the lines between the story segments and junctions. Keep your film's roadmap clearly defined!

- **Music works well to help change the pace and emotions between sequences and scenes.**
  Films work best when there is a continuous change of pace and emotion between sequences and scenes. This continual contrast keeps our audience guessing, engaged and entertained.

  Music can help motivate these turns when placed at the beginning of the new story beat or at the end of the previous one. It works as a sort of reset, regulating the energy level, cleansing the audience's palate and readying it for something new.
- **We should strive to use as little music as we can get away with.**
  This may sound rather idealistic, but when music is present it should feel motivated. It must be there for a clear, deliberate reason, providing

the audience with a strong signal that we have reached a significant moment in the story.

If we use a music track and then, at the end of it, immediately begin a new track, we begin to create a constant wall of sound: a whitewash. The effect of this is that the audience will tune into the specifics of the music less and less. The effect we are trying to achieve by having the music there (a rise and fall of both rhythm and emotion) will be greatly diminished.

Just as my definition of bad editing is cutting for the sake of it, my definition of bad music is music used purely for the sake of it. Ask, do I really need music here? If you are unsure, remove the music and see how the scene plays.

A principle that helps to guide this is to start the music as late as you can and finish it as early as you can. Furthermore, we should avoid letting music tracks clash by backing on to each other and always allow space between our music tracks.

- **Keep the music as varied as possible.**

We must strive to create contrast and change in each sequence and scene of our film. Our choice and placement of music is critical in helping to create and to delineate these changes. The way we can deal with this is simple: avoid placing music tracks of similar emotion, pace or tone near or next to one other.

For example, if we have a scene in which an investigation unfolds with mysterious music to accompany it, it would be unwise to use similarly mysterious music in the next sequence. The audience will feel as though they've just had this and the emotional effect for which you are aiming (engaging intrigue) will be diminished.

Instead, we may wish to hold off on further music until another specific need has arisen, or we might choose to pick up the pace with something different in tone and feel.

- **Build in plenty of breathing space.**

Most documentary films are packed with spoken information. We must ensure that when using music, we build in enough space to hear it without too much interruption. After all, music is a storytelling device in its own right and no other story element can substitute for it.

Here are some places to think about letting your music breathe:

- **At the beginning of a scene.** Ensure you allow a new music track a chance to establish itself before bringing in dialogue and voiceover. Personally I like to leave *at least* ten seconds at the start of a new scene for music to play out. As we get more into the body of the scene, I tend to keep these music breaks a little shorter, though I always ensure that they have their space.
- **At the end of the scene.** I find it is useful to reduce the amount of information delivered at the end of a scene. This allows the audience to reflect on what they have learned and reset before the next scene begins. Music can help achieve this. Again, I like to leave at least ten seconds for music to run on and create large pauses between dialogue and voiceover which allow the music to filter through.
- **At key story turns.** I like to ensure that music is present and allowed to breathe at crucial moments in the narrative. For example, when a character delivers something of particular import or significance, I like to introduce music and give it time to run freely. This gives the audience vital thinking time to digest and connect emotionally with what has been said.
- **At act junctions.** Music, when paced appropriately, can really help punctuate our film and communicate to our audience that we have reached a place of significance. In this way, I like to give music tracks extra time to breathe and run at key act junctions in the narrative. This breathing room tells our audience that we have reached an important part in our journey and again allows them time to reflect and reset before the next chapter. While I am never counting the time with any great precision, I like to make these pauses longer than usual, perhaps even as much as thirty or forty seconds.
- **At the very beginning and end of the film.** Much like act junctions or the start of any sequence, I will always give the audience a chance to settle in at the start of the film and enjoy the music (when I have decided to use music) at the very beginning and at the end of the film.

- **Keep the volume up!**

  If you have decided to use a piece of music, then make sure the audience can actually hear it. I appreciate that this might sound obvious, but I am surprised and frustrated by how often I watch a television documentary and struggle to hear the music. The sound engineer will often favour keeping the music low in order to keep the dialogue (the more obviously guiding components of the story) high in the mix, and whilst this makes sense (music which obscures important narrative information is either badly placed or its deployment entirely misconceived), if the music is important enough to be included, it must be audible in order to have its intended effect.
- **You do not have to accept a music track the way that it is.**

  If the music track you have chosen does not fit perfectly into your sequence, then do not be afraid to cut it up. By doing so, you can make your music punctuate your dialogue and story beats where it needs to and better support your narrative aims. There are no inviolable rules.

  However, when cutting up your music track, do be careful to ensure that you *beat match* your music. Ensure your music edits maintain the rhythm of the music track. This is less important, of course, for music where there is no rhythm (like a constant drone, where you can seamlessly fade between cuts) but essential for music with a solid, defined tempo.
- **Play with the space that the music occupies.**

  Your music does not have to sound as though it has come fresh out of the studio, perfectly balanced and level. As I have said, with the help of an audio equaliser effect, you can make the music sound as though it is coming from the car radio or make it sound as though it is coming through the walls of the room next door. You could even add reverb and make it sound as if it is coming from the top of a mountain if you like!

Music is very powerful and uniquely versatile. Whilst you can apply music almost anywhere in a film, I find it works particularly well for action-led sequences. Here it can help keep the cutting energy high and pace the sequence in order to allow much needed space for pictures and sound to work their individual and collective magic. I also find music works well for big emotional payoffs, where a significant turn or realisation has occurred in the story. The music allows the audience to appreciate the significance of this moment, giving them confidence in their own comprehension and carrying them on to the next story beat.

On the other hand, I find that music is often best avoided during dialogue-heavy scenes, such as interviews, where there is a great deal of intensive exposition taking place. Here music can *compete* with dialogue and detract rather than add to the storytelling.

Key Points

- Where possible, music should not tell the audience how to feel but rather channel their existing feelings.
- When selecting music, ask: what is this sequence about? We are looking for music that supports and develops the emotional current of our sequence.
- Music works best when it operates just below the consciousness of the audience. Limit your use of clichéd and overly associative music.
- Give tracks a clearly defined beginning and end (and avoid fades wherever possible).
- Films work best when there is a continuous change of pace and emotion. Vary your choices of music between story beats.
- Avoid letting music tracks back on to each other—and allow space between music tracks.
- Ask, do I need music here? Use as little music as you possibly can.
- Give your music plenty of breathing space.
- Keep the volume up.
- Do not be afraid to cut your music tracks up. Make them fit as you need them to. Ensure that you beat match all music edits.

A PRACTICAL METHOD FOR WORKING WITH MUSIC

1. First, I source a music track appropriate to the tone of the sequence. I will audition multiple tracks against my sync and black assembly first to find the right one. Once I have found a track that works, I stop and move on. I do not waste time looking for a 'more perfect' track.

2. I place the track into my timeline underneath the sync and black sequence assembly.
3. I cut up my sync and black assembly (as well as the music track where necessary) to ensure that the music hits the right story beats and that the sync sound is in rhythm with the tempo of the music.
4. I will begin to assemble my picture sequence to fit around this blueprint. I will continue to adjust music, sync and pictures where needed to refine the sequence.

AUDITIONING MUSIC

Selecting the right music track is perhaps the most challenging aspect of working with music. It can at times be hard to define what sort of music we are looking for and, even when we have decided what sort of music we need, it can be tough actually sourcing that track. After many years dealing with this challenge on a daily basis, I have developed a few ideas that will help you succeed when auditioning, selecting and refining your music choices.

- **First, always use expensive sounding music.**
  The music we select should highlight and raise the production values and enhance the quality of our finished film. For this reason, I like my music to sound as though it has come from the highest quality source. In short, I want it to sound expensive.
  First, I have a strong preference for music that has been recorded with real instruments, rather than synthesisers imitating real instruments. This is not to be confused with electronic music, which is a respected genre in its own right. There are of course cases where electronic music works really well and this should not be confused with a synthesiser, which is a cheap attempt to imitate an orchestra (without having to pay for an orchestra).
  Second, I am drawn to music that would not be out of place in a feature film, since I believe that cinema is the pinnacle of the visual arts and the music written for it is amongst the best being written for any platform.
- **Use music with a well-defined emotional charge.**
  Another reason for favouring music with real instruments is that, by utilising the full orchestral palate, they are capable of conveying—with

all the required subtlety or force—a broad range of very specific emotions. Orchestral scores usually contain a strong melodic line, which works particularly well for underscoring emotion.

I like music to reflect with precision the emotion I am looking for and to help in communicating this feeling to the audience. I avoid music that sounds generic.

- **Favour music that has its own variety.**
  I find that music that has an inherent shape: rises and falls, slow and fast sections, as well as quiet and loud passages work particularly well for cutting picture sequences. We can use these ebbs and flows creatively in pacing our film.

  Earlier we discussed the rhythm of cutting a picture sequence. We noted that by keeping the pace continually changing (both within and between sequences), we can keep our audience engaged and the emotional energy of our film running high. By selecting music which has this variety built into it, we can help ensure that our sequence(s) conform to these ideals.
- **Do not settle for anything less than perfect.**
  Never make do with a track if it is not working perfectly. I always come unstuck if I try. Music that is less than perfect will compromise the feeling of the cut sequence and will diminish or even ruin its impact on those who watch your film. More often than not, it will have to be replaced before picture lock.

  When sourcing music, take your time and be patient. Do not stop searching until you have the right track, and do not compromise. Once you have found a track that works well, stop searching immediately. Do not waste time searching for an even 'better' track, which may or may not exist. Get it in the timeline and start cutting.
- **Source music alone.**
  Music is very personal. We need to take time to think, listen and experiment with crazy ideas that may not work at all. This is best done alone, without any contributing voices from the back of the edit giving their (unwanted) opinions prematurely.

  However, I do find it prudent to ask my director at the beginning of the cutting process whether they have any strong feelings about the general style of the music. If they do, then I will take time to listen and understand in order to help me when sourcing music. Usually and thankfully, I find that most directors tend to shy away from the process of sourcing music, leaving me to get on with it alone.

Key Points

- Use expensive sounding music; the best quality you have available.
- Use music with a well-defined emotional charge.
- Favour music that has its own variety.
- Do not settle for anything less than perfect. When you have found it, stop and move on.
- Before you begin, ask your director if they have any strong feelings on the music.
- Source music alone.

COMPOSED, LIBRARY OR COMMERCIAL MUSIC?

There are three main sources of music available to editors.

- **A composer.** An individual or group who compose or produce music specially tailored to a film.
- **Library music.** An archive of music produced by a record label specifically for use in television and film. This music is produced and catalogued to fit a wide variety of different film production needs. It is not written specifically for the film in question.
- **Commercial music.** Any music produced by a mainstream artist and available through a commercial record label.

Each has its advantages and disadvantages. So how do they work?

Working with a Composer

Composers can provide a film with music specially (and in the best cases *perfectly*) tailored to fit the requirements of your story. Properly conceived and executed, such music can bring coherence and convey a sense of unity to all of the story elements of your film and create themes (*leitmotivs*) to underscore narrative points where needed. Because it is commissioned to a brief, the composer will aim above all to fulfill that brief and write music that fits in with your conception of your film and what you want the audience to take from it.

Good composers are also a valuable extra pair of ears when evaluating the many music-related decisions the editor must make. They can often interpret the brief in an original way, spotting something others may have missed and generally adding real value to the production.

Furthermore, composers can save the editor valuable time in not having to source their own tracks. Sourcing music from library or a commercial label is time consuming. Many fruitless hours can be spent looking for the perfect track before it is found.

Composers will often only begin working on the music for a film once the edit has begun and their work may continue even after picture lock. For this reason, I find it is usually best to begin cutting with good quality guide music (known as a *temp track*) until the composer has a chance to catch up. This temp track acts as a placeholder for the composer's score. It should be a good representation of the emotional tone and pace that the music needs to have at any given point in the film. By using a temp track, we are able to get on with cutting our film whilst the composer busies him- or herself with writing the proper score.

In order to get the composer up to speed and working alongside the edit as quickly as possible, once I have cut a few sequences, I will usually export these for them to view (as a low-resolution video clip). It helps to make this export *split-track*: with dialogue and effects on one audio channel, and music alone on the other. This way, the composer can turn the music on and off as they like and work with the export as guide when composing their own score, without the distraction of the temp track always coming through. Once I have exported a sequence for the composer, I usually try not to recut that sequence until I have a version of their music back in the edit. This way, I know their track will fit perfectly and that what they are working with is the same sequence that I can see, should remote discussions be necessary.

Once their music track is in the sequence in place of the temp track, I can recut the sequence as needed. Usually a composer will give tracks as a working guide and then re-master all of the tracks after picture lock to fit the sequence again and take account of any re-cutting. I will give the composer feedback on how well their music is working all through the edit and suggest improvements and new ideas where needed.

When discussing my musical needs with the composer, I always try not to be too prescriptive. I also avoid speaking in musical terms—since it is not my natural language—and I do not want to confuse or mislead the composer. I find it easier to talk in terms of general emotions and feelings that I hope the music will convey. Furthermore, I am always quick to emphasise that the guide track is really just that: a guide. If they wish to ignore all of my temp work and go their own way, then I encourage them to do so.

As editors, we do not have all of the answers; far from it. We must always ensure that whoever we collaborate with is given as much freedom in their own area of expertise as possible in order to get the very best out of them and ultimately the best outcome for the film.

Note! The more we listen to our temp track, the easier it is to fall in love with it. On the basis of this familiarity we may decide that we want to keep the temp track for the final film at the expense of our composer's work. While on occasion this bias may be justified (particularly in tricky instances where the composer is just not getting the brief), remember this *temp love* can blind us to the great benefits that a quality composer will bring to the film. We must always try to remain objective and judge the new score produced by our composer on its own merits, not in comparison to our existing score.

Working With Library Music

Library music companies provide editors with a large catalogue of music from which to choose. Library music covers many genres and styles. If you are keen to give your film a rich variety of music, as is often the case, library is a convenient and effective source.

Whilst the wide choice offered by library is a great asset when searching for the perfect musical score, it requires a great deal of time and patience to search through it thoroughly. Also, since library is an off-the-shelf solution, any selected music will probably require a degree of re-working by the editor to make it fit each sequence. Furthermore, it can be harder for library music to provide the cohesive soundtrack that a good composer can furnish at will.

There are a great number of library music providers, most of whom have their catalogues available to listen to and download online. Many also provide a supervisory service, helping you to source tracks that best fit your brief.

Working With Commercial Music

Commercial music is usually instantly recognizable to an audience. It can be a fun way of adding energy and colour to a sequence, helping to place the audience in a particular time and place.

For this reason, I find that commercial music is usually best reserved for making deliberate statements at choice moments in a film. Many viewers will associate a specific piece of commercial music with a particular time or event in their life (creating an emotional response in them which could be either positive or negative), and this can sometimes prove an unwelcome distraction. Some commercial music is used so routinely that it becomes a cliché in itself ("Eye of the Tiger" springs to mind), and unless cliché is precisely what is being aimed for, the over-familiar is generally best avoided.

While commercial music can provide the editor with a great deal of variety as well as instant 'canned emotion,' sourcing tracks that are film-friendly can be a challenge. A lot of commercial music is lyric-heavy, and these lyrics often compete with dialogue and voiceover (unless carefully cut around). Furthermore, I find that commercial music often lacks the variety needed for cutting dynamic sequences: the beat often tends to monotony with one climactic repetitive chorus. It can also be harder to create a film soundtrack that feels whole and cohesive from commercial music alone.

Tip! When cutting with lyric-heavy commercial music, look for an instrumental version of the same song to cut alongside the original mix. This way, you can cut between the two versions allowing lyric-free space for your dialogue and voiceover.

Commercial music provides an exciting and enjoyable solution to film music needs, providing you have the time and financial resources (in order to clear copyright) to make it work. Overall the decision you make where you source your music will be personal. I would suggest that if you can afford to engage a top quality composer, then do so: they can really bring something special to a film. That said, I would rather have good library music than employ and then have to live with the work of a mediocre composer.

NOTES

1 Phillip Halsall, "The Films of David Lynch." www.zenbullets.com. Accessed 23 October, 2016. www.zenbullets.com/britfilm/lynch/Sintro.html
2 Justin Chang, "Walter Murch's Simple Approach to the Rule of Six." www.masteringfilm.com. Accessed 23 October, 2016. www.masteringfilm.com/walter-murchs-simple-approach-to-the-rule-of-six/
3 www.goodreads.com. Accessed 23 October, 2016. www.goodreads.com/quotes/tag/music
4 www.brainyquote.com. Accessed 23 October, 2016. www.brainyquote.com/quotes/quotes/l/leotolstoy106870.html
5 www.wikiquote.org. Accessed 23 October, 2016. https://en.wikiquote.org/wiki/Jean_Sibelius
6 Alicky Sussman, *Guts: The Strange and Mysterious World of the Human Stomach* (BBC4, 2012)

5

STORY STRUCTURE

ORDERING AND CONNECTING SCENES

> "People have forgotten how to tell a story. Stories don't have a middle or an end any more. They usually have a beginning that never stops beginning."
>
> —Steven Spielberg[1]

We all have an inherent ability and need to tell stories. Further, we all understand that good stories have a beginning, a middle and an end. So once we have cut a scene—one part of our overall story—how do we decide where exactly it fits? What should come next? Or even what should come before? How can we decide on a clear pathway through our story and take our audience on that journey of discovery we always intended for them to experience?

The order in which we place our scenes—their *running order*—is a vital aspect of storytelling. The running order determines the point at which each part of the narrative will be revealed to the audience.

The same scene will feel very different (and have a very different impact) depending on where it appears in the film. Holding back a scene that reveals a key piece of information until late into the story could have a very powerful effect on our audience. Properly handled, it could keep them in a state of suspense or encourage them to keep an open mind about a subject until a pre-determined moment of (perhaps dramatic) illumination. Badly planned, however, holding back a key piece of information could leave the audience lost and struggling to follow the story at all. Just think of the difference between knowing and not knowing the end of a story and the way this colours our experience of any film: if we know there is a happy outcome, then we may enjoy the film for its heart-warming exposition of a comfortably familiar tale. If we are unsure, we may watch the whole on tenterhooks in a pleasant agony of uncertainty until all is revealed in a moment of climactic catharsis. Both are valid but utterly different experiences.

In documentary, we must first decide how we want to tell our story and then determine the order that best delivers this. As a rule, we are aiming for something that is dramatic but is also clear and easy to follow. We must balance backstory with present narrative and factual exposition with emotional human context.

Note! It is essential to establish a working structure for our film at the beginning of the edit and before we begin to cut our scenes. While the order of our scenes can be changed—to a degree—at any time, having a clear idea of the *likely* order means we can have a strong grasp on how each of our sequences and scenes connect. Understanding this means that we can ensure each sequence is different than the last in terms of emotion, pace and content.

COMMON DOCUMENTARY STORY STRUCTURES

Some documentaries are easier to structure than others, whilst some offer editors far less freedom for manoeuvre. Some films, for example, can only run in one chronological order and the placement of scenes is determined by the order of the events they portray. Other films are more a collection of individual scenes around a broader subject: a list of sorts that can go in almost any order.

In documentary, there are a number of common story structures. Three of the most common are as follows:

- A three-act structure
- An episodic (sometimes known as a *List Film*)
- A parallel narrative

The Three-Act Structure

The concept of a three-act structure will be familiar from an earlier section of this book where we discussed the basic construction of a film and the art of storytelling, but it is worth recapping here. The three-act structure is a dramatic and filmic way to structure a story, based around the principle of conflict and resolution.

The three-act structure, as the name suggests, is a film divided into three parts, or acts:

- Act 1—the initial setup of the story; specifically, the conflict at the heart of the story.
- Act 2—the attempts to resolve that conflict.
- Act 3—the resolution of the conflict.

In the following, I will set out in sequence the conceptual basis of the three-act structure, illustrating these concepts in each case with examples taken from *The Trouble with Space Junk*, a film I cut with the BBC some time ago.

Act One

The first act is typically used to establish the premise of the story and the conflict central to its argument. It is also used to introduce the main characters, their relationships and the world they live in.

During this first act, we explore facets of the central argument through individual scenes. Each scene builds on the action and tension of the last and ends on some kind of 'cliff-hanger.' This completely changes the course of the story.

In *The Trouble with Space Junk*, act one begins with a brief history of space flight. Space was once a pristine and empty environment. In a few short decades, we have filled the Earth's orbit with dangerous debris, old redundant rocket parts and other defunct man-made objects. This debris orbits at thousands of miles per hour. During the act we build up a picture of how this debris is a danger: strategically to national defence, physically to those who go into space, but also to each and every one of us in terms of its threat to the satellites on which we all depend for the delivery of GPS, mobile phone reception and so many other aspects of our daily lives. As the act progresses, we come to understand that the problem is getting worse as more debris gathers. At the climax of the act we learn from a key scientist that debris will likely kill an astronaut within the next ten years.

Act Two

The second act adds both tension and complexity, usually by depicting our characters' attempts to resolve the problem highlighted at the first act's turning point, but struggling to do so as they find themselves in ever worsening situations. They do not yet have the skills to deal with the forces that confront them. They must not only learn new skills but arrive at a deeper understanding of who they are, what capabilities they possess and what means they have (or will need to have) to deal with the predicament in which they find themselves. This journey of self-assessment and discovery changes, in turn, who they are and how we see them.

In *The Trouble with Space Junk*, in act two we meet astronaut Sandra Magnus, a resident of the International Space Station, and she tells us the story of her near miss with some orbital debris. The debris is so small and travelling so fast that the crew would never have known it was coming. Had it hit, it would have killed her and her crewmates. Fortunately, it missed. This time! We learn that the problem is set to get a lot worse as there is more debris being created all of the time. We need a solution and fast. We meet an ESA scientist who has designed a remote-controlled robot capable of doing what astronauts currently do—which may mean astronauts in the future will not have to risk their lives. But it's not ready yet, and it won't be enough to fix the existing problem. Another scientist has designed a harpoon that can catch debris. Though it sounds good, it could actually create more debris than in removes. Our narrative has reached a moment of crisis.

Act Three

The third act provides the (by now much-needed) resolution to the story. The conflict hitherto outlined is brought to its most intense point and then resolved, leaving the characters and audience with a new understanding of the subject and a sense of *enablement* based on what they now know and how they now view their own capabilities. Whether this resolution is optimistic and comforting or able only to point tentatively towards possible ways forward will depend of course on the nature of the subject and the filmmaker's decision to satisfy, disturb or provoke.

In *The Trouble with Space Junk*, act three explores a final possible solution to the debris problem. We come to understand that retrieving debris is too complicated and unrealistic, and our best method of handing the problem is to track and monitor the position of existing debris, to prevent future harm. We learn of a space surveillance system called Space Fence, capable of tracking most of the space debris in orbit. Although it won't make the problem go away, we stand a good chance of avoiding contact with the existing debris. There are limitations to the system, and the problem will likely get worse, but this approach is the best we currently have.

The three-act structure suits documentary narratives which focus on a single or multiple characters who share a common goal or are functionally connected in some way. This structure also provides an ideal method for exploring complex subject matter, providing the means to outline, dissect and interrogate the central conflict systematically in clear steps.

The Episodic

An episodic film juxtaposes story events that have no, or only casual, narrative relations. The meaning and connection between them is found through a central theme or thesis (e.g., the human body or planet Earth). Each of these somewhat disparate scenes explores a facet of that central subject.

Unlike a three-act structure, where narrative order is critical since each scene builds upon the last, an episodic can more easily be worked in any order, and thus, each story can be more freestanding. We can arrive at each scene with little prior knowledge and leave at the end having learnt something that has value in its own right. The message of an episodic film becomes clear in a broadly cumulative way rather than through structured linear exposition, the central theme 'emerging' as the audience assimilates and relates each of the stories to their predecessors. For this reason, as editors (working with our director where we can), we should always try to link them together by creating a central 'co-ordinating' argument, or thesis. This thesis is often manufactured in the edit suite not having been conceived prior to this point. Each scene is then designed to conform to this central thread, more often than not by judicious selection of dialogue. Since the narrative line through an episodic film is synthetically constructed, they are often heavily reliant on voiceover narration.

One result of this more synthetic approach to storytelling is that the scenes of an episodic film can usually be configured to appear in almost any order, that order being determined more by matters of dramatic pacing, contrast and aesthetics than any logical narrative drive. That said, the usual 'rules'—keeping the audience engaged, entertained and inquisitive—still apply.

An episodic structure works well for films that have many distinct and freestanding stories.

Forces of Nature[2] is a classically episodic series of documentaries. In one particular episode, *The Moth and the Flame*, presenter Professor Brian Cox explores such varying stories as: a sulphur mine, the Maasai Mara, cave diving, alpine ibex and thermal vents—all around a central theme of 'the building blocks of life.'

The Parallel Narrative

The basic premise behind a parallel narrative storyline is that multiple characters tell their own story with some common thread between them. Each thread is explored separately and individually though their own scenes, which are then intercut to provide variety, counterpoint and contrast. Typically, equal weight is given to each thread so that the balance between them is maintained.

Though a way of making a film in its own right, this type of structure will often work well *within* a three-act structure (or any number of other acts, depending on the number of key turning points within the story).

Parallel narratives work well for stories that draw comparisons between different people, groups and their points of view, for example, a film that explores a social problem which has a different impact on various cross-sections of society.

Life and Death Row[3] masterfully uses a parallel narrative structure. In one particular episode, titled 'Forgiveness', we meet Tyrone Trottie—sentenced to death for the murder of his wife and her brother. After twenty-one years on death row, he will be executed in three days—an imperative which drives the narrative tension throughout. Alongside Tyrone, we meet his only son, TT, who was eighteen months old when his mother was murdered. We follow Tyrone and TT's stories in parallel: how they first met and their differing views on the events that shaped their lives, as well as TT's forgiveness of his father. As an audience, as well as learning something of the meaning of forgiveness (under even the most extreme circumstances), we are challenged to consider the morality and collateral impact of the death penalty as TT, already a victim of his mother's death, becomes an orphan as the result of his father's execution.

While documentaries can be structured in any number of ways, I have found that the most successful stories usually employ a structure appropriate to and—critically—determined by the requirements of the story itself. Shoe-horning materials into an inappropriate narrative structure *rarely* works. Let the materials determine the form and, ideally, decide on the story structure before the edit begins (i.e., during the early stages of production).

WORKING WITH SHOOTING SCRIPTS AND PAPER EDITS

Fortunately, editors are not usually alone in making major structural and story related decisions. Editing is, after all, a collaborative art form primarily in partnership with the director.

Good directors are highly skilled at dealing with the narrative and editorial aspects of the storytelling, which is to say everything relating to the written and spoken word. Directors will usually arrive in the edit with some idea of the film's structure (often called it's *running order*). This usually comes planned out in the forms of a *shooting script* or a *paper edit*.

The shooting script is a written version of the film, as conceived *before* the edit and often even before the shoot. It is a blueprint for the film based on what the director and production team have been able to research, write and are likely to shoot. Usually at this stage the sync from interviews, as well as any other dialogue, has been fabricated on the basis of what is likely to be said and, where needed, guide voiceover written and organised into scenes.

Shooting scripts are just a working guide for the film (the film usually diverges significantly from the shooting script once the editing process takes over) but they are a great (and comforting!) resource at the start of the edit. If you have a shooting script, then it is a good idea to start cutting to it first and at least until you get a sense of how the film is working. Once you have built up your scenes side by side and you have something closely resembling a whole film, you can review and evaluate your story further.

On the other hand, a *paper edit* is a written version of the film (or any single scene or interview), put together after the shoot and prior to the edit. The director may use a paper edit to plan how they see the scene edited together (as best as anyone can prior to the actual edit) using transcriptions of the interviews, actuality and other materials—or occasionally from viewing rushes themselves. The paper edit details the order of events and where each piece of the story can be found in the rushes. This will usually appear as sections of sync with corresponding timecodes listed, so that the editor can simply pull the corresponding sections from the rushes.

It is worth emphasising that much like a shooting script, a paper edit is scarcely better than a starting point. While a paper edit can give us a more accurate means of establishing the initial structure of a scene (since we are working from real rushes, rather than theoretical rushes), it still remains hard to evaluate how any story will best work until we start editing. It is in the edit that we discover what works and what does not—and any number of serendipitous surprises that are likely to come along the way.

CHOOSING A RUNNING ORDER

> "What makes a film interesting and palatable to an audience, even though they may not know it, is the rhythm of the film, the way you structure the highs and lows."
>
> —Geof Bartz[4]

Whilst a shooting script or paper edit is an ideal starting point, as editors we must be sensitive and capable of reacting appropriately to the logic and connections in our narrative as they begin to emerge. Only in this way can we help the director (if we are not working alone) to improve the structure of the film. It is worth repeating that some of the most magical moments in any edit come when the materials begin to speak with their own voice, suggesting their own ways forward and, to a degree, shaping the story and even solving problems in utterly unforeseen ways. Whilst we must always be disciplined in our evaluation of where this takes us, being open to 'suggestion' in this way and working with rather than against the creative flow usually creates a better, more natural and effective film.

Here are a few ideas to help break down the many options open to you and to help you find the best possible running order for your film.

- **The order should be the clearest and most dramatic.**
  Generally speaking, we should start our film with the most arresting scene we have, both in terms of its emotional content and visual impact. This scene need not necessarily be the one that is most descriptive of the film which follows as long as it gives a sense of the story.

  If we can hook our audience with something compelling early on, then we can build on their intellectual and emotional investment from here on.

  If the most arresting scene you have has a critical role to play farther along in the story (i.e., later on in the running order on which you have decided), then consider splitting the scene in two: one section of the scene at the top of the film (as a tease) and the remainder (perhaps with a small reminder, by way of a reprise of the first part) later on where it is most needed and impactful.

- **Change the emotion and pace between every scene and sequence.**
  I have said it before but it is worth repeating: films work best when there is obvious contrast between sequences and scenes. This should come in the forms of contrasting emotions, visuals, sounds and pacing. For example, if you have a moment of quiet sadness in one scene, pick it up with something more positive and lively in the next. In this way, the audience is kept constantly on its toes, trying to guess what will follow. In film-making terms, this translates into excitement and engagement.
- **Scenes are usually linked either by a property they have in common or hold in opposition.**
  A key way of joining scenes together is to look for logical connections between their story threads. This may be something that they have in common, progressing the information and narrative of the previous scene, or alternatively something directly oppositional.

  The links themselves can work in several ways. First, as voiceover that summarises the first scene and bridges into the next. Second, as a piece of sync by way of an interview clip or piece to camera in the case of a presenter-led film. Finally, we could use a title card—also known in television as an *Aston*—which does the same job in written form as voiceover does in spoken form.

  The purpose of this link between the scenes is to bring the audience back to the central argument of the narrative. It summarises what has gone before and joins it to what is coming next.

  Sometimes, especially in the case of films without voiceover, we do not have the ability to craft tidy links. In these cases, it often works if we arrive at a new scene without any preparation and allow the audience time to fill in any gaps with materials contained in the new scene. In these instances, we should respect the audience's intelligence and allow them to join up the dots for themselves.
- **The story does not have to be chronological.**
  One of the most magical parts of documentary editing (indeed any editing) is our ability to play with time. We can go anywhere we like in a single instantaneous cut. This discontinuity of time is key to editing.

  Logic might tell us that we should start with the history of a subject and work our way through time to the present day. However, I often find that starting in the present and revealing the historical backstory subsequently is much more satisfying: once we have our audience hooked on our narrative in its contemporary context, it can be highly effective to go back in time and contextualise its early beginnings.

Remember that nothing is set in stone. Since the inherent meaning of each scene should stay broadly the same (though context can of course alter it), you can play with the order of your scenes until you reach a satisfactory outcome. Just pick up the block and move it. I like to think about the order of the scenes at the start of the edit and get a picture of the film in my mind. I do not labour over this plan though. Once I understand and accept the rough order of events, I get straight to work crafting the scenes. If necessary, we can change the game plan as we go.

Key Points

- Determine as much of the structure as you can before you begin cutting.
- The order you arrive at should be the clearest and most dramatic. Start with the most arresting scene you have.
- Change the emotion and pace between every sequence and scene.
- Link your scenes with something they have in common or hold in opposition. When considering your order, think: how are these scenes connected?
- The links between the scenes in a film should bring the audience back to the broader story at hand.
- Your story does not have to be chronological.
- Nothing is set in stone. You can move the scene blocks around as needed.

SCENE CARDS

Long-form documentaries consist of many scenes. Anything from six to sixteen scenes is common, depending on the broadcaster and intended audience. Deciding on an order in which to put these scenes can at first feel daunting.

One reason for this is because it can be tricky to hold a picture of the entire film in our heads. A useful way of getting to grips with the scenes we have and working out the best order in which to place them is by using *scene cards*.

Scene cards work like this:

1. Take a stack of sticky notes or postcard-size pieces of paper.
2. On the top of each, write a title for the scene (e.g., "Derek First Hospital Visit," "Derek and Wife Play Golf"). You may wish to write a brief description of what happens within each scene underneath, if that helps.
3. Lay all of the cards out in front of you.
4. Think of how cards link together and place them next to each other in a row. At the same time, consider how each of the scenes will feel in terms of pace and emotion. Ensure that scenes with a similar emotional conclusion (whether that be positive or negative) and beginning are separated by at least one card.
5. Once you have an order which you think flows, pin the cards up on a wall where you can see them easily.
6. Start cutting!

Note! You can use different colours or shapes of cards for different characters and story threads. This will help give you a quick visual representation of the energy and flow of your film. At a glance, you can see how the story threads are spaced out and balanced through the film.

I also like to mirror the setup of these scene cards on my edit timeline. Once I understand the working order for my scenes, and before I begin to cut, I will create a title card for each scene and lay them down in order in my master timeline. I can quickly spin through this timeline to see the order of the scenes. As I cut a scene, I put it in place of the title card, slowly building up the film. Where there is a scene that has not yet been shot, the card can also act as a placeholder showing where the proper footage will go (see figure 5.1).

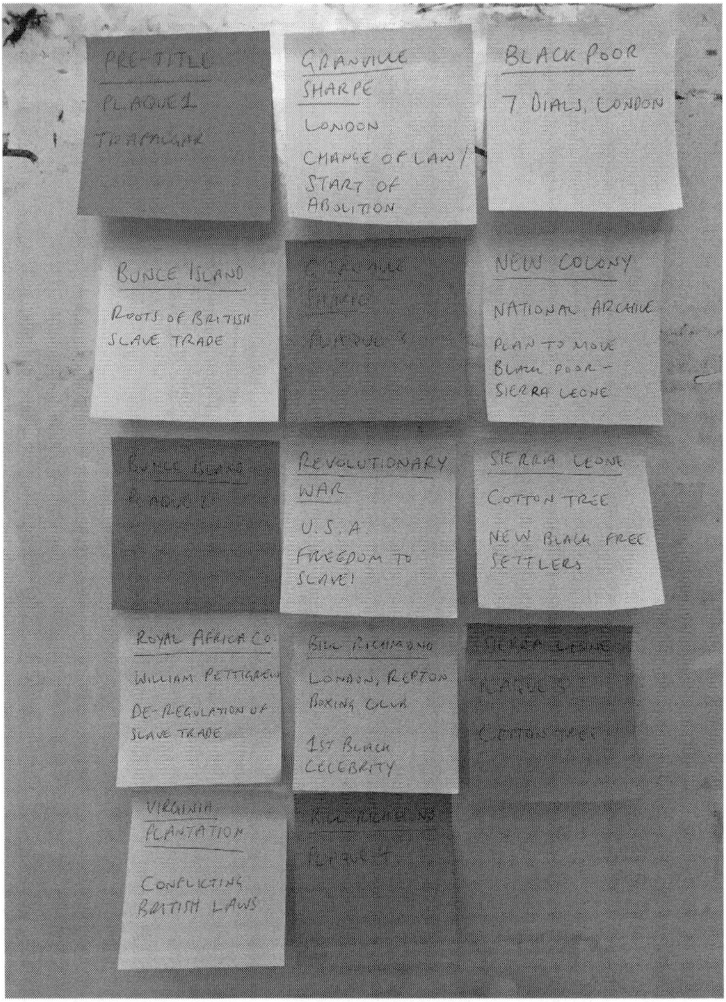

Figure 5.1 Scene Cards

Working out a structure for the film with some sticky notes on the edit suite whiteboard. The darker coloured notes are key scenes. The three columns of notes (from left to right) are the film's three acts.

WORKING TO A DEADLINE

The production of a commercial television documentary is almost always allotted, and is necessarily designed around a deadline by which it must be completed. This deadline is often referred to as a *schedule*. This schedule is determined by:

- **The programme's budget.** How many days of the director's time, the production crew and other supporting staff as well as editor time is affordable.
- **The transmission date.** The day and time when the finished programme is scheduled for broadcast. In an ever more digital, Internet-based world, this is simply a date by which the film must be finished and available to its audience.
- **The availability of on screen talent and other contributors to the film.** Professionals are usually busy people and are not always available exactly when the production team would like them. The schedule must work around this, which can mean delays and protracted timeframes for certain story elements.

The processes of editing a documentary does, of course, require time and patience. On average, I find that I am usually given around eight weeks to edit an hour-long commercial television documentary; though, if it is well resourced and high in its aspiration, I may be given as many as twelve to sixteen weeks. However, I have known projects to have much shorter allocations, even as few as one or two weeks! Wandering the streets of Soho, it is not uncommon to encounter bedraggled editors, exhausted and wholly disorientated having spent the night on the cutting room sofa whilst working around the clock trying to keep a film on schedule! It is not my preferred style of work and, I am grateful to say, not my normal *modus operandi*!

However, regardless of programme schedule, it is always worth looking ahead early on in the edit and planning carefully in order to meet immovable deadlines.

I usually find that a five-minute scene for a single well-budgeted documentary will take around two to three days to edit on a first, solid pass. This time will usually be broken down into:

- One day to view and organise the rushes for the scene, as well as pulling sync for interviews (on the broad assumption that I will have around six hours of raw rushes on average per scene, a couple of hours of this being interview material)
- Two days to structure and edit the rushes into a basic working story, incorporating voiceover narration, music and some practical sound design where needed

If the director is able to work from transcripts to pull interview sync for me, and record voiceover, then this process is helped along greatly—and likely two days will suffice to get a cut together.

On average, I have six to eight scenes for a commercial television hour (which is anywhere between forty-six and fifty-nine minutes in total duration) and on this basis, I can expect to have a first 'rough-cut' of the film in around five weeks.

Unhappily, we do not always get the luxury of five weeks uninterrupted editing time before other stakeholders in the film want to get involved. These stakeholders are usually eager executives and commissioners, keen to know that the film they have imagined, helped to develop and—crucially—financed is coming along 'to plan.'

I often find that the first viewings of these films take place around halfway into the schedule. On this basis, it is rare that I have the whole film cut in time for the first viewing.

We must therefore endeavour to look ahead at the schedule (and any likely points where others may wish to view the film) and break down the days into prioritised units of time to work on each story element and ensure we have the most important parts put together in time for this first mass appraisal.

How do we do this? While I like to start with something easy, I generally find from there on I work from the front of the film as much as possible—cutting those parts that are likely to appear early on first. In this way, when others view the film, they are more likely to get a proper sense—and form a favourable impression—of what the finished film will feel like. If later material is missing, at least they know what the film is about and whether it's broadly working. It is better to know that it is unfinished (but will be so along the indicated lines) than be unable to judge what it's about and where it all started!

I recall cutting a film many years ago to which eight weeks had been allocated for the edit. Our executive insisted that she come to view the film at the beginning of week three (around ten days into a forty-day edit). We had forty minutes of the show rough cut for her to watch, which the director and I were proud to have achieved—having cut four minutes a day, including viewing rushes and all. After watching the film, she said, "That's great! I'll come back tomorrow and view the rest of the show." I hesitated a moment and then said, "Well, which part of the rest of it would you like to see first?" (We still had about half an hour of programme to cut). She said, "Well I want to see it all." I told her, "I can't physically achieve that" and she said, "Well I need to see it." I said, "OK! You can have either, this, that or the other, but you can't have it all. If you want it all, come back in two weeks." She begrudgingly accepted, and the film was completed smoothly, on time and within budget, and everyone was happy. The point is this: executives are not always aware of the time it takes to edit a film, but because I had planned ahead and knew my timescales, I was able to give an accurate and convincing forecast which, though it may not have been what she wanted to hear, could not be gainsaid.

It is worth also noting that different kinds of films and scenes take different lengths of time to edit. Films with a lot of actuality can take longer, since the stories are often more intricate, whilst films with simple pieces to camera and long interviews with voiceover in between can be completed more quickly since there is less ground to cover with detailed editing and fewer overall cuts to make. I once cut an hour's film in three days. I was actually on another film, and we were ahead of schedule with all going well. The executive producer from one of the other cutting rooms came in and said, "We've got a bit of a problem. The editor next door has been cutting for eight-weeks and the programme is unwatchable. Do you think you could take a look?" True, the film was a mess. I did not have time to start again, familiarising myself with the rushes and 'working' the film as I would normally do. Instead, I just sat down and started cutting. I saw a nice shot, I put it next to one it sequenced well with. I needed music. I grabbed the first 'working' track to hand and just kept moving. Three days later they had a film. It wasn't a work of art, but it was respectable, and it worked. It went out and turned out—bizarrely—to be one of the most commercially successful documentaries I've had my name on! If this proves anything, it proves that the underlying story was fundamentally good and that the less than timely edit had managed to reveal that much at least. Equally, as I have said before, you cannot save a bad story with good cutting; you can certainly help it, but it will never be great.

Fundamentally, editing takes time and, ideally, as long as it needs to. Sure we can go slowly, or we can go quickly, but ultimately it is the quality that will suffer if we allow less time than the material demands.

Now we should have a good idea of how to build each of these blocks or scenes and appreciate how we must plan our time and look ahead to keep to schedule. We are ready to integrate and refine each of them into a more complete and polished film.

Key Point

- Look at the schedule early on and plan the days for editing each scene carefully in order to meet deadlines.

MAKING IMPROVEMENTS

> "It is easy to decide on what is wrong to wear to a party, such as deep-sea diving equipment or a pair of large pillows, but deciding what is right is much trickier."
>
> —Lemony Snicket[5]

We have now reached an exciting and, for some, a nerve-wracking part of the editing process. We have cut all of our scenes and they are linked together in a systematic running order on our timeline. In short, we have a first cut of our film.

In many ways, much of the hard editing work is done. Hopefully, we will have made the best of the rushes and accomplished most of the work in establishing the narrative, as well as setting the style and tone for the film.

However, it is unlikely that this first cut will be perfect or complete. This is always a disappointment, but don't worry! There will be more work to do in improving and refining its content, structure and style before we are ready to present it to an audience.

We must now enter the second phase of the editing process: the process of reviewing and improving our film.

We are viewing our film to:

- Clarify the story and, where needed, enhance the drama.
- Take out narrative redundancies and duplicate information.
- Ensure that the links between scenes are working well and meeting the narrative aims of the film.
- Get the film to its optimum length. Broadcast documentaries have a required duration, which usually means losing time but can occasionally mean adding time in.

I find on average that half of the edit time (the first four weeks or so of the average television documentary) will be spent cutting the scenes for the first time whilst the second half of the edit time (the remaining four weeks) will be spent improving and making changes to the edit.

VIEWING A FILM FOR THE FIRST TIME

> "The best books, just like the best movies, are a collaboration. They're only as good as the compromise made between the artists involved."
>
> —Viggo Mortensen[6]

It would be nice to think that all we need to do at this stage is sit back, watch our film almost as if watching any other piece of television or cinema and simply wait for the accolades; however, the viewing process, properly approached, is quite challenging and requires a skill that comes ideally with practice.

The first challenge we face when viewing our film is to watch it with absolute objectivity. Whilst our audience will probably watch our film just once, as the editor we will have already watched it many, many times and will watch it many times more. By the end of the editing process, familiarity may have bred if not contempt then at least a casual insensitivity (or worse a partisan commitment), which makes it very difficult to identify flaws and look for improvements in both the narrative and the craft and quality of the cut sequences.

The second challenge is also part of the solution to the first problem. This lies in the collaborative nature of viewing a film. The viewing and improving stage is actually the point in the editing process where the collaboration really begins as others outside the 'charmed circle' of the editor/director partnership begin to show an interest. Producers, series producers, executive producers, commissioners, channel controllers, the channel controller's seven year old nephew and any number of other people may wish to view the film and give feedback. Indeed, I have worked on productions with eight or more layers of management outside of the cutting room (and above us in the filmmaking hierarchy) who have wished to view the film, each insistent that their feedback be incorporated.

One person's idea may conflict with another, and so we must find ways to make each feel satisfied. Sometimes we will be asked to make changes that seem ridiculous. I once edited a scene that told the story of an unprecedented storm which swept across rural Canada, cutting off roads and electricity and starving entire communities to near death. Upon viewing, the executive producer said, "Oh I felt very nervous when I watched that scene. Can we make it 'happier'?" Baffling. In an instance like this, it becomes our job (as well as that of the directors) to convince the executive that what we have is in fact worth keeping and that making the scene 'happier' would go against everything it stands for. At the same time, we have to be diplomatic enough to make the executive feel that their misgivings have been understood and not simply dismissed out of hand. This is no easy task.

A great deal of patience is required as we try to balance a number of disparate opinions and comments and attempt to react as positively to each as we can. It is important to remind ourselves that the ultimate aim of this collaboration is to produce the best possible film. As editors, we must be prepared to swallow our pride and resist a natural inclination to defend each and every one of our decisions just because we like the film the way it is. Admittedly, as a junior editor I used to feel quite wounded when receiving any criticism of my work—something which only got easier with experience. Whilst it is right to defend decisions where there is good reason to do so, we must appreciate that 'our' film is not really ours at all: it belongs to everyone who has invested time, effort and money in bringing it to the screen.

It is also worth remembering that while we may collaborate with many others when viewing and refining the film, our allegiance is always to the director. They are our primary workmate, and we must support them in seeing the film to its completion in a form as near to their conception as we can manage (and convince others to accept).

Though screening our film to outside contributors can be challenging, it can also force us to see it afresh: to pay full attention once again and regain the objectivity we inevitably lose the more familiar we become with our sequences. Viewing the film with others may well make the hairs on the back of your neck stand up as you see the film in a whole new way.

However, as a result of the outside pressures which collaboration can bring, viewings can be quite scary at first. Fortunately, there are some systems and tricks we can use not only to get through viewings in one piece but also improve our films significantly.

- **The first time you view, view alone.**
  Without doubt, there will be a great many improvements you can make on a first appraisal of the *whole* film. It is better to correct these before you show your film to anyone else Not only will it make subsequent viewings easier to take (saving us, for example, from the irritation of having pointed out to us something so obvious we could and should have seen for ourselves), but it will also give some assurance that the film is working properly as a whole.

  After this you may welcome a fresh perspective.
- **Imagine there is an audience watching with you.**
  The hardest part of watching a film alone is that it is easy to become lazy and de-sensitized.

  Sometimes when I am watching my cut I will spot something which could be improved, and part of my brain says, "Oh I'll fix that later." The danger—and likelihood—is that I will never have the time and recollection to come back and deal with it properly. I could just let it slip. However, if I watch my cut with someone else present, it's amazing how much my senses are heightened. Every little imperfection stands out like a huge blemish, and I feel embarrassed that everything is not perfect.

Imagining someone is always behind me, over my shoulder, tricks me into paying attention to the many imperfections which my early rough cuts have and ensures that I fix them as soon as I see them and with full attention.

If your film still feels good after viewing it in this context, then you are probably doing okay!

Remember! We are always aiming for perfection. Do not let things just go by. Every aspect of the film—every shot, cut, sequence (pictures and audio)—must be as near perfect as we can make it. While the audience may not notice a single minor error here or there, they will notice the cumulative effect of lots of little errors. It will undermine their confidence in the quality and integrity of the film.

- **Physically sit back from the keyboard.**
  Viewings can be fidgety times and sitting close to the edit machine in this tense fashion can make us focus on the technical aspects of the viewing rather than the impact of the film as a whole. Watching the play-head on the timeline move slowly along and anticipating what is coming next takes us out of the normal viewing experience and distances us from the perspective of the ordinary viewing public.

  A good solution to this is to sit back physically from the edit machine, well out of reach of the keyboard and the software interface. This forces us to see the film for what it is. In so doing we are better able to make objective judgments and improvements. I like to watch the film in large sections, making *careful* note of any flaws I spot. I then come back to fix them as soon as I have finished viewing.

  However, once the viewing has ended and before we begin setting about changes, it is worth staying well clear of the edit workstation until our discussions with fellow collaborators have concluded. We should be listening to their ideas and understanding what they are saying without distraction and avoiding absolutely the temptation to implement any suggestion the moment it is made. Turn away from the keyboard and maintain eye contact. Only once everyone is out of the room should you then go through your notes and begin implementing the agreed changes.

- **If in doubt, cut it out.**

  When viewing and evaluating our material we will usually get hunches. We must heed these gut instincts (they are usually right!). If you have a hunch that something is not quite working, either fix it or cut it out.

  Also, at this stage, we must identify and remove any extraneous material that does not serve the film and its central argument. The same is true for any repetitions. An unpleasant habit of television is to repeat information endlessly to ensure that the audience has really got it. Personally, I believe this is a waste of time and deeply patronising. We must respect our audience's intelligence and avoid repeating information as much as possible.

  Ask: if I stripped out this piece of voiceover, would the story still be well told?

  Last of all, remove anything that interferes with the pace of the film. This does not mean anything which is cut slowly, since we need fast and slow sequences, but rather anything which is over-long or hard to grasp. If needs be, find a simpler way of dealing with it.

  If upon viewing the film your attention starts to wander or you notice your fellow collaborators playing with their phones or looking out of the window, it is usually a sign that this part of your film is lacking energy and/or interest. Look to remove these sequences and join up the gaps, restructuring them in a livelier, more engaging way. Alternatively, find a livelier or more shorthand expression for the information.

- **If necessary, watch the film in two passes.**

  Viewing the whole film for the first time can be overwhelming. There is usually a lot to take in. For example, it is easy to miss an error in the story while distractedly thinking about the music.

A good solution to this is to view the film in two passes: once for story and once for sequence craft.

At times, when watching for story, I may even look away from the screen so that I am able to focus purely on the narrative delivery and story logic without becoming distracted by the sequence of pictures. If anything related to the narrative stands out, I take note.

When watching for editing style, I focus on the pictures: the order and timing of the cuts, as well as the sound design and music. Again, I take note of anything that stands out and deal with it immediately afterwards.

Sometimes, to aide this process, I will even watch the cut with the sound off so that I am focusing solely on pictures. It is remarkable how things can just spring out.

- **Do not interpret feedback literally.**

Frequently those giving feedback will make requests or suggestions that are not possible to implement. Perhaps this is because you have tried their suggestions at an earlier stage of the editing process and know they just won't work, or you know that by implementing their suggestion you will compromise something else of far greater significance.

For this reason, we must always be careful not to take feedback too literally, especially if we can see it will damage our film. Of course, there is a balance to be struck between defending a choice because it is familiar to you (and you like it) and accepting that a sequence could be improved by the proffered suggestion.

So, always ask yourself: What did they really mean when they said that? What is the desired effect they are looking for? Can you meet that requirement in a different or better way than that suggested?

I was once in an edit where the client asked for their logo to be bigger. It was already filling the screen (and in our opinion, getting in the way). So I made it 'bigger' by playing it back on a bigger screen. The client said, "That's much better," and signed it off!

Tip! If after a viewing, three people suggest one thing and three people suggest another, do not change a thing!

Most feedback we get is subjective. It can become hard to quantify the value of any given suggestion. We must avoid tinkering with our film simply to satisfy whimsical requests since each change can present new problems. If on the other hand several people make the *same* suggestion, it is more likely to be representative of the reaction of the general viewing audience.

- **It's OK to pose problems, as long as we have solutions.**
  Viewings are a two-way dialogue. We must be receptive to the input of others, and we must also be prepared to assert our own opinions, too.

  Inevitably, as we watch our film with others, we will notice things that could be improved or are not working at all. We may also disagree with some of the suggestions that others propose. This is a healthy and normal part of the viewing process, and we must have confidence in our own judgement.

  However, when we do make our voice heard and draw attention to an issue of any kind, we must be prepared to offer a solution alongside it, either an alternative idea as a counter to the suggestion or a new way of thinking about a problem.

  As editors, we are primarily problem solvers. We are there to facilitate the editing process and make it a pleasant and smooth experience for all involved. We must not be troublemakers.

This viewing process is usually repeated several times; each pass refining the content and the craft of the edit. It can be hard to know when to stop, and this is usually decided by our collaborative partners. Personally, I make it a goal to stop cutting once the value of the proposed changes becomes hard to quantify. Inevitably, we reach a point of diminishing returns, usually after about four or five viewings.

Below is a simplified extract from my viewing notes (and some thoughts from my series producer) midway through editing *Forces of Nature*[7] for the

BBC. We had cut all of the scenes and this was our third viewing. While it does not show every kind of scenario which we will likely encounter, it will give you a snapshot of the kind of things which can arise.

Pre-Title

- More variety in music track. Monotonous. Perhaps break and start again.
- Lose some time. Running at four minutes, should be more like three.

Post-Title: Sulphur Mine

- 05:25—Add extra beat out of titles into first sequence.
- 07:42—Sync levels up "its toxic." Can't hear what they're saying. Possibly subtitle.
- *Series Producer: loose sync "we have to go and do it again . . ."*
- 09:00—End music here and tighten next sequence.

Tanzania—Iron

- 15:35—VO "molten spinning core"—is the core really spinning?
- 17:12—VO repeating previous line. Cut.

Cave Dive—Water Solubility

- 22:43—Music needs to be more uplifting and wondrous here.
- 23:20—"Very dangerous"—save this sync until the second beat of this story, when story turns to danger.
- 28:10—Use shots back above water to end the diving scene.
- 29.26—*Series Producer: "any close shots of faces we can use here?"*

Ibex—Salt

- 30:40—Translations/subtitles incorrect. Italian translation needed.
- 34:04—Trim in end of music and out shot.

Life Montage

- 34:20—Music now too similar to last track. A little more driving here instead.

Japan Squid—Controlling Chemistry

- 36:30–200,000,000 Yen. How much is this in dollars?
- 39:14—Music levels too high. I can't hear sync.
- 39:40—"We've got firefly squid . . ." comes a bit out of nowhere. VO before sync to say something like "back on the boat, things are looking up"—set this up better.

Mayflies—Life's Chemistry

- 41:20—This junction needs some breathing space. Turn in is a bit hard.
- 42:00—*Series Producer: extra sequence needed here about how we get energy from our food.*
- 43:10—VO "they no longer have mouths"—should be clearer—"once they emerge from the water as adults, they no longer have mouths."
- Do we need this scene? Feels a bit out of place in our story. Possibly move earlier? Before Squid?

Notes continue . . .

Remember! Before viewing your film and making any major changes, make a duplicate copy of your master timeline sequence. It is always worth having a copy of the cut from each viewing as a reference point since, once we start working on changes, the position of each of the elements and reference points is easily lost. Retaining the earlier version also serves as a useful reminder of what was being improved and whether the improvements are a success or not!

Give your sequence copies a clear name (e.g., *"Programme title 02—Viewing Copy—Date."*)

Key Points

- The first time you view, view alone.
- Imagine an audience is watching with you.
- We are aiming for perfection. Do not let things slip by.
- Physically sit back from the keyboard.
- If in doubt, cut it out. Ask: if I stripped out this piece of voiceover would the story still be well told?
- Respect the audience's intelligence.
- If necessary, watch in two passes.
- It can be helpful to evaluate a picture sequence by watching with the sound down.
- Do not interpret feedback literally.
- Editors are problem solvers. We are there to facilitate the editing process and make it a pleasant and smooth experience for all concerned.
- In a big viewing, our allegiance is primarily to the director.

WORKING TO A FINAL DURATION

> "Story as such can only have one merit: that of making the audience want to know what happens next. And conversely it can only have one fault: that of making the audience not want to know what happens next."[8]
>
> —E. M. Forster

We should aim for our films to be as short and punchy as they can be. This does not mean that we should rush our storytelling or exclude anything that is essential to the story. Five minutes can seem like a long time for some films while, for others, an hour can pass very quickly. We must concentrate our efforts on making the clearest, most concise film possible: the one that keeps our audience most engaged.

Many documentaries, particularly those intended for television, must be finished to a specific length. An hour of BBC television, for example, must be fifty-nine minutes (with a small amount of leeway allowed on either side). Other broadcasters have their own requirements.

The first rough cut of most films is invariably longer than it needs to be. There are several reasons for this. First, there is usually so much we want to say and keep in the first pass. Equally, we often want to keep our options relatively open until such time as we can see the film as a whole. Only once we have everything distilled in our timeline are we able to evaluate and refine this content again. Second, it can be hard to judge how the narrative is working as a whole when we have been working so closely on little sections at a time.

Getting the film to its final duration is usually the last of the editor's jobs. We deal with this just before the film is picture locked. Until this point in the edit, we are busy crafting the film. We are still refining and re-cutting sequences, playing with the shape of our film and, while dealing with this, the duration is constantly changing. It would be distracting, as well as a waste of time and creative energy, to attempt to deal with duration at the same time. Once we have a film structure and scenes that are near to locked, having viewed the film a few times and made improvements, we can make the final trims and adjustments necessary to get the film to time.

Getting the Film to Length

Once we have a film that is working well, in terms of story narrative and sequence craft, we can next think about getting the film down (though occasionally up) to its intended length. I have stressed that it is best to leave final decisions about duration until near the end of the edit, but it helps to be conscious of our running time throughout the editing process.

First, we should ensure that we do not cut our scenes excessively long the first time around (as we have discussed in an earlier chapter) or we will likely have a first cut for our film that is grossly over length. Losing significant time will usually require major re-cutting and restructuring, which can be both complex and time consuming and psychologically harder as we have become more committed to the film 'as is.' Simply getting to the end of a first cut for our film will take significantly longer than it needs to.

Second, we must ensure that our film is not significantly short. I find that if the cut looks as though it will be just a minute or two short, I will think about which scenes could be extended. Is there an interesting aspect of a story that we could add or expand? (This may be something reinstated from an earlier, longer cut). If the film looks as though it will be even shorter than this, by say five or six minutes, then the director may wish to consider shooting a new scene. Finding time of this length—by expanding a little of each scene—will likely slow the film down and create problems with its overall flow.

On the whole, I find that it is much harder to add time to a film than to take it out. For this reason, we should aim for our first cut to be slightly longer than it needs to be (i.e., we should make our first pass of each scene tight and well, but without being too strict). If you have doubts about the options with which you are presented, consider leaving both in the cut until you are able to watch the film back as a whole and in a position to make a fresh and more informed judgement.

I usually find that my first cut for an hour-long television documentary is around ten minutes over length (i.e., seventy minutes). Each subsequent pass of the film reduces this in time, though the duration still fluctuates as some material is removed and new material is added in. Once the balance of the narrative is working and I have refined the sequences, I look to remove any remaining excess time, usually working closely with the director.

I will watch the film on a final pass, thinking about duration alone. While watching I keep the following in mind:

- **Look for repetition.**
  Each scene and story beat must be telling the audience something that they have not heard before. This succession of story beats, each building on the last, is taking them from the film's beginning (a place of conflict) to its end (a place of resolution) in as straight a line as possible.

  We must listen and watch for any information that is a direct repeat of something we have already been told and for any interview sync, voiceover or any pictures which we have seen or heard before. If there is actuality that is affirming something spoken elsewhere, perhaps consider losing one or the other. Occasionally a small amount of repetition is useful for reminding the audience of a significant point, though this should be kept to a minimum and, wherever possible, we should deliver the information in a new way. Generally, if we have to remind our audience of something we have already told them earlier on, then there is a structural error. Look to remove the repeat.

If we are aiming to lose a significant amount of time from our film, perhaps as much as six to ten minutes or more, we may want to consider losing an entire scene. Trimming small sections from each individual scene can cause major problems with the flow of the narrative and the rhythm of each sequence. Is a scene that is doing a very similar job to that of another scene really necessary? Do all of your scenes contribute significantly to the overall narrative? Is there a scene that is in some way disconnected or extraneous? If I took the scene out, would the film still make sense? Perhaps it may flow even better.

- **If you have big time to lose, find big cuts.**

This may sound obvious, but as we fall in love with our story and rushes and get used to seeing and hearing our film the way we have made it, it can be hard to let go of anything. As was once said to a budding author by his publisher: "You must learn to kill your darlings." It all feels important to us and it can be hard to decide what to cut. Many directors also suffer from this. A director's cut of the film (a version of the film which reflects the director's intentions) is almost always longer than the one that survives the scrutiny of the studio or television network. As a result, finding the cuts that are needed to bring our film down to time can become a major challenge.

Some filmmakers I have worked with will try to find the two or three minutes of cuts through tiny little trims here and there (of only a few seconds each) without letting go of anything significant. This method of losing time, known to some as *salami slicing*, or as I prefer to call it, *death by a thousand trims*, is a sure way to ruin the flow of any film. We may get the time out of our film eventually but we will probably add a number of bumps and collisions in the process.

Up until this point, we have patiently crafted our film with neatly timed pauses between dialogue and allowed space for our music and narrative to breathe. While the audience may not know the reasons for it, they will sense this is a film of high quality and craft. They will know the film is good. Unfortunately, however, every little trim can upset this careful balance a break the flow of our film.

Rather than disturbing the flow of a film that is working, albeit overlength, we must instead look to make a handful of large, confident cuts. In this way, the flow of the film will remain intact and we will more easily get the film down to duration.

I am always surprised how easily these cuts are forgotten once they have been made. Indeed, it can be hard to remember that they were ever there in the first place and quite what the fuss was all about.

- **Look for an economy of words.**
  Another way of losing time is to trim down the words in the film. Each statement in interview sync and voiceover should be neat and conversational. When viewing the film, look for any lines which seem verbose or perhaps, on further inspection, unnecessary. Can you find a more shorthand expression?
- **Focus on cutting dialogue, not pauses.**
  Many who are less familiar with the cutting process (not least the higher echelons of executive producers) will suggest that we lose time by cutting out pauses, or giving less room for the music to breathe. This is usually a fundamental error.

  While pauses between dialogue and space for music does not appear to contribute to the overall integrity of story in ways that are easily described or quantified, they are essential to the flow and balance of the finished film. They make a major contribution to the emotional impact of our story (the single most important aspect of our storytelling), giving the whole a sense of proportion, balance and poise. They are the punctuation marks that make the sentence work.

  For this reason, I believe that we should always defend and preserve the musical breaks and other pauses in our film and look primarily for time savings in dialogue.
- **Consider intercutting scenes.**
  A neat way of compressing time is to intercut two scenes. This can work particularly well with action-led scenes, where two things could be happening in parallel.

  When we intercut two scenes, we focus on the best and most significant aspects of each. We no longer need the setup shots, which would have originally played through each of the individual scenes, since intercutting assumes that some time and activity has occurred in between each burst. We can justifiably make credible leaps in the action and progress each story narrative more quickly.

Key Points

- We should be aiming for our films to be as short as possible.
- Think about duration last of all and once everything else is working.
- Remove any information or scene that is a repetition of something else in your film.
- If you have big time to lose, find big cuts—and avoid many smaller, fiddly cuts.
- We must always defend and preserve the musical breaks and other pauses in our film at the expense of dialogue.
- Look for more economical uses of words.
- It is much harder to add time in to a film than it is to take out. Do not be too brutal on your first pass.

REACHING PICTURE LOCK

> "Art is never finished, only abandoned."
>
> —Leonardo da Vinci[9]

We have nearly climbed the mountain. We began the edit with hours of rushes and perhaps only a few rudimentary story ideas. From these simple beginnings we have broken down and organised our material and shaped it into a clear, compelling narrative. We have crafted exciting and dynamic sequences, rich in visual style, sound design and, where needed, music. Subsequently, we have undertaken a comprehensive process of viewing, taking on board the comments of others to refine and improve the film. We have now reached *picture lock* (see figure 5.2).

While this sounds rather definitive, it is not always easy to know when to stop cutting. As a perfectionist, I always feel inclined to keep working away to make the film still better, and many directors I have worked with are inclined to do the same. However, the truth is a film cannot really ever reach perfection. We can always keep tinkering: trying out new and different things. But

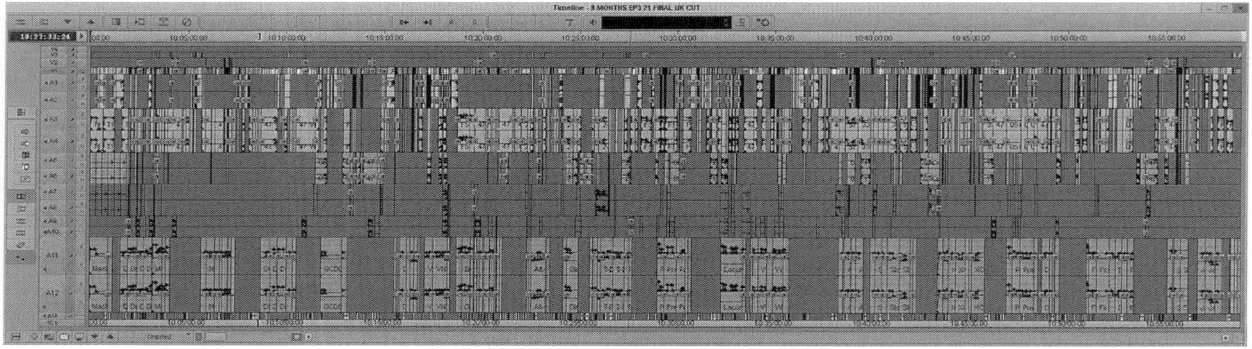

Figure 5.2 Final Sequence Timeline

Job done. The picture locked timeline ready for final post-production; audio mix, grade and then broadcast.

the plain fact is we reach a point in every film where it can become hard to tell whether what we are doing is really making the film better or actually making it worse. So we need to know when to stop.

I believe that it is best to stop cutting and declare the film finished once we have made all of the changes that *strongly* and *measurably* improve the film and have watched the film on a further pass or two to make subtle refinements. Once we have done this, it is time to put down our tools.

This process of coming to understand when the film is as good as it is ever likely to be can be greatly aided by one simple but not always readily available device. Where the editing schedule allows it, walk away from a film for a few days. Return to it for a final viewing with a fresh perspective. Then—and only if absolutely necessary—make refinements.

NOTES

1 www.brainyquote.com. Accessed 23 October 2016. www.brainyquote.com/quotes/quotes/s/stevenspie398353.html
2 Matthew Dyas. *Forces of Nature* (BBC, 2016).
3 Marina Parker, "Forgiveness." *Life and Death Row* (BBC, 2016).
4 Gabriella Oldham, *First Cut: Conversations with Film Editors* (University of California Press, Berkeley: 1995), 115.
5 www.goodreads.com. Accessed 23 October 2016. www.goodreads.com/quotes/691809-it-is-easy-to-decide-on-what-is-wrong-to
6 www.brainyquote.com. Accessed 23 October 2016. www.brainyquote.com/quotes/quotes/v/viggomorte535658.html
7 Matthew Dyas & Stephen Cooter. *Forces of Nature* (BBC, 2016).
8 John Yorke, *Into the Woods: How Stories Work and Why We Tell Them* (Penguin, London: 2015), Kindle Edition, 96.
9 www.brainyquote.com. Accessed 23 October, 2016. www.brainyquote.com/quotes/quotes/l/leonardoda380290.html

THE CUTTING ROOM RELATIONSHIP

> "Half the job is doing the job, and the other half is finding ways to get along with people and tuning yourself in to the delicacy of the situation."
>
> —Walter Murch[1]

There is one final piece of the editing jigsaw that we need to understand. It does not relate to the craft of the film in the most direct sense, though it is deeply connected to it. This is the relationship we form with our creative partners. On a professional level, we are working primarily for the director over and above the other creative contributors. It is the director who we must support (and protect) as rounds of viewings and the sometimes intemperate opinions of others threaten the balance of the film. It is the strength of the creative partnership we have with the director that is the greatest determinant of the film's ultimate quality and success.

Directors want to know you are going to serve and protect their film at all costs. Because of this, cutting the film is really only half of the editor's job. The other half is being a good companion, friend, mentor, surrogate husband/wife, as well as a trustworthy, dependable, modest and positively-inclined professional. After all, we are working with *people*, which is to say with individuals and their sensitivities, insecurities and foibles. Though it is occasionally hard to believe, these individuals have a life outside of the edit, which comes with (and sometimes brings into the suite) its own challenges. I have been an observer of all manner of life events unfolding during the edit: engagements, marriages, affairs, births, deaths, breakdowns and a great number of things in between.

Whilst editing, we will usually spend many hours each day with the director. We will probably see more of them than we do of our family or friends. In this way, working with a director for the first time can feel a bit like a shotgun wedding. We cannot always choose whom we work with or know in advance what we are getting ourselves into. We just have to hope we are compatible and that we can manage to regulate our behaviour and sometimes theirs, too.

I feel lucky that, with one exception, I have formed strong, long-lasting relationships with the directors with whom I have worked and have begun many friendships that have extended beyond a single project and beyond the cutting room itself. The exception I refer to will forever stick in my mind. It was the beginning of an eight-week edit, and I sensed early on that the director was very much on edge. On closer inspection of her rushes, I could see why: there was very little 'in the can,' and what was there was poor. We were going to struggle to get this film together. Being the experienced director she was, I'm sure she knew this. However, she was unwilling to seek help, or more crucially, admit to any weakness. I knew the director well on a social level prior to working with her, and I decided to try to use humour as a means of diffusing the otherwise difficult atmosphere surrounding our work together. On day two, in order, perhaps, to distance herself from the serious issues we were having with the film, she started shouting, "Everyone on this production is terrible! My researcher, my director of photography, everyone is hopeless! And my assistant producer is just so aggressive!" My response (foolish in retrospect) was, "What? Even more aggressive than you're being?" Needless to say, she flipped. Aiming a number of expletives in my general direction, she left the cutting room, slamming the door. I was upset about the whole event as I was not expecting such a vehement reaction to my words, which were meant to be lighthearted rather than an attack. So, I called the production manager (the person in charge of managing the team), explained what had just happened and suggested he might want to find another editor. To my relief, I was assured that none of this was out of this particular director's character and that things would work out. In the event, she did return two hours later and in an apologetic mood. We made up (there were lots of tears and hugs) and the film got finished. However, the unfortunate consequence of this rather forced resolution was that from that point onward she was archly over-polite and accepting of almost everything I suggested. I'm not sure which of her *modus operandi* I preferred!

Fortunately, most of the time, cutting room relationships, based as they are on high professional standards, work well. And, after all, we both have the same goal in mind: to make the best possible film. This is important common ground, which helps foster good relations even amongst those unlikely to go on a walking holiday together!

There are a few things to keep in mind that will help us to establish good working relationships and ensure that our collaborative partners are left with a lasting positive impression of us.

- **Ask lots of questions and listen . . . listen . . . listen . . .**
  As editors, we really need to understand what our directors want from their films. By understanding our director's vision as well as their tastes and preferences, we are better positioned to help them. We can save an enormous amount of cutting time if we know the direction in which our director would like the film to go.

  At the start of the edit, I will always ask the director: what is this film about? I want to clarify the meaning of the film in my own mind so I can keep focused on this central point throughout the edit. Before cutting a scene I will always ask: what is this scene about? I am hoping for a short, focused answer. If the director says, "Well, it's about this and this and this," then I know we have a problem. We will then discuss the scene further, refining its purpose until it expresses one clear thing. Only then will I begin cutting.
- **Take the director's ideas and make them better.**
  Once we have understood our director's vision, we can then set about making it a reality and, confident in our craft, a better reality than they thought possible. This could be as simple as making improvements to the way you structure the scene, or it could be in the quality of the picture sequence, sound and the clever use of music.

As editors, we must feel it is our duty to tease out the scene's hidden values. These may be values that the director does not even know exist.

This is where the spark in the director–editor relationship lies. Directors love to have their voice heard and feelings respected, while they also like to be surprised by something new and see their vision bettered.

- **Do not just be a yes person.**

Working with the director does not mean doing everything he or she says. As editors, we are *expert* collaborators with our own knowledge and experience. We are there to listen, understand and improve ideas. Part of this is to give our advice, make suggestions and help shape our films.

If you feel strongly that an idea is not working, then say so. However, we should be careful to present solutions along with problems, not just say, "Hey, this doesn't work, but I don't know why or how to fix it."

Remember, no idea is an intrinsically bad idea, so do not be afraid to have an opinion. Opinions are good. John Cleese brilliantly said, "It's self-evident that if we can't take the risk of saying or doing something wrong, our creativity goes right out the window. . . . The essence of creativity is not the possession of some special talent, it is much more the ability to play."[2]

- **Create a barrier between the shoot and the edit.**

As the editor, we can only see what is inside the rushes frame. This is all that matters, since this is all the audience will ever see.

Most directors will arrive in the edit carrying some degree of baggage from the shoot. They will have opinions and feelings towards their rushes based on how they were feeling on the day of the shoot, what sort of pressures they were under or even the sort of lunch they had. These opinions are worth avoiding. We must resist adopting our director's appraisal of their rushes until we have had a chance to view them for ourselves.

We should try to see and evaluate the material for what it really is, for what is *inside* the frame and not be influenced by what may have occurred *outside* of it. The director might say, "Oh we must use that great shot of the lion in the game reserve. We spent three hours up a tree to get it." However, if in reality the shot is out of focus, poorly framed and the lion is so far away that we can hardly see it, then the shot is clearly not fit for the cut. We must see what the director has really got from the shoot and be honest about it (while still being respectful).

One of the great ways we can add value to the film is by providing a fresh—and relatively objective—pair of eyes.

Tip! When watching new rushes or assembling a first cut of any scene, try to work alone. This way, you can form your own opinions without any premature input or back seat involvement.

- **Approach the task with humility but not diffidence.**
  Life is not fair, and we cannot always get our own way. This is also true of filmmaking, which is after all, collaborative.

  We must be careful not take any reasoned critique of our film personally. Almost everything in filmmaking is subjective, and there are rarely any clear-cut right or wrong decisions. Everything derives from a point of view. As a result, what people will have to say about our edit can vary enormously. One person might love it whilst another might hate it. They are both entitled to their opinions and neither is categorically right or wrong. What is most important to remember is that criticism is rarely personal, so learn to take it on the chin. This is definitely something that comes with practice.

  I remember working with a director who clicked his fingers where he wanted me to make an edit! I could hardly believe it. I wanted to scream at him, though thankfully I did not. I had to breathe hard, turn around slowly and say, "Look, I value your input, but let me have a go cutting this first. When I'm finished, we'll watch it together, and if you don't like what I've done, I'll gladly change it."

  One unfortunate truth about (but important measure of the success of) editing is that very few non-editors will ever notice the cutting. That is, unless it is really bad. So make sure you leave a lasting impression on those you work with through the quality of your collaboration and the service you provide.

  Ultimately we are all working for what serves the film and our audience best.

- **Ensure you maintain personal integrity.**
  We must always be a good friend and partner to our director. We must ensure that they feel safe and confident in our company. Part of this is to have a highly developed sense of personal integrity. We must keep all conversations in the cutting room private and avoid speaking ill of anyone who is not present. Should you engage in gossip, the person with whom you are temporarily joined at the hip will know that you may do the same to them under different circumstances.
- **Know your rushes really well.**
  We must study and learn our rushes completely so that we are able to make the most of them. Rushes are laborious, complicated and expensive to acquire, and so we must respect them. Take your time to view and organise your rushes at the start of the edit and, in the process, commit them to memory.
- **Never claim to be an expert.**
  Claiming expertise (particularly if you don't have it) is dangerous. I believe that the moment we make such claims, we close our minds to learning and experimentation. We must always remain judicious and open to learning new ideas.

  Sometimes, when reflecting on a suggestion someone has made, I will think to myself, "Oh that'll never work." I have learnt to resist the temptation to say and even to think this. By not wishing to appear stubborn and giving their idea a go (even as a quick rough test), I am gratified by how well this is received and often surprised at how wrong I am sometimes proven to be. I have learnt some great tricks in this wholly unexpected way.
- **When you're working, work.**
  When we sit down to start editing, it takes time to get into a flow: into the 'zone' in which our ideas fly and our work rate accelerates. If we want to be productive, then we need to ensure that we get into this zone and stay there as soon and for as long as we can, and to do that we need to avoid distractions.

  There are a few ways to do this. First, put your phone out of reach and close laptop lids. I admit I am sometimes guilty of not doing this. It can be hard—but essential—to ignore them.

Second, plan each day in advance. I make a list of tasks I need to achieve each day and I cross them off as I go. I do the same for my week. This way I know I will hit the necessary deadlines and keep on schedule.

Third, follow your instincts. Keep moving forward and making decisions. There is no great benefit in endless deliberation. What's the worst that could happen? If you make a mistake, you just have to go back and change it again. Besides, mistakes are good! They are great! They help us learn, improve and discover.

We should aim to develop a positive attitude towards making mistakes.

If you are still struggling to make a decision, do something else and come back. Get up and walk around the block if necessary. The answer will usually come unbidden.

- **Have a life outside of the edit.**
  Finally, I love my job but I also want to have a life. I want to see my wife and children—as well as the wider world. Having a life outside the edit is extremely important for our mental health as well as the creative process. The richness of our life outside the edit feeds in to the edit itself. As John Le Carre said, "A desk is a dangerous place from which to view the world."[3] Personally, I find travelling a particularly effective source of relaxation, learning and inspiration. It allows me much needed time to reflect and frees me from my daily habits, feeding my curiosity for other people and cultures, and allowing me to return to work with fresh perspective. Even on a day-to-day level, I do not believe in burning the midnight oil (though, of course, many filmmakers do enjoy this), and I like to have good meals as well as a proper night's sleep.

  Answering e-mail during the day, making phone calls and enjoying protracted chats with the cleaner eat in to edit time, and this ultimately eats in to our free time. Keep focused and keep distractions to a minimum.

Key Points

- Editing is only half of the job, the other half is getting on with people.
- Ask lots of questions.
- Take the director's ideas and make them better.
- Don't just be a yes person. Debate fosters the creative process.

- No idea is a bad idea.
- Focus only on what is in the frame.
- Criticism is rarely personal, so learn to take it on the chin.
- Know your rushes really well.
- Never stop learning and experimenting.
- When you're working, work. Go with your instincts and keep moving forward!
- Develop a positive attitude towards making mistakes.
- Have a life outside of editing.

NOTES

1 www.azquotes.com. Accessed 23 October, 2016. www.azquotes.com/author/10566-Walter_Murch

2 Warren Bennis, *On Becoming a Leader* (New York: Basic Books, 2009), 89.

3 www.brainyquote.com. Accessed 23 October, 2016. www.brainyquote.com/quotes/quotes/j/johnlecarr143875.html

WORKFLOW SUMMARY

We have now covered all of the processes and systems involved in editing a documentary.

We have discussed basic organisational skills, narrative structure and the practicalities of editing a picture sequence, including the function of sound design and music. We have also explored the methods by which we can further improve our film and the essential interpersonal skills one requires to be successful. These are the primary functions of the film editor's job.

I have one penultimate and important point to emphasise. Thus far I have explained the process of editing a picture sequence in the following order: pictures first, then sound design and finally music. To be clear: I chose to set out matters in this way in the hope that by doing so, I would provide a clear and logical view of the mechanics of all of the steps in the editing process. This was for expositional purposes. Though there are instances where this order of working is appropriate, in reality, I find it is generally the case that the whole editing process works best if these stages are followed in the *reverse* order (i.e., music, then rudimentary sound design and finally pictures).

The reason for this is simple. Since sound determines so much of our sequences' shape and flow (and the majority of our sequences' timing comes from the audio footprint), it is wise to get the audio broadly working first and then build the pictures on this framework. We can then work with all of the elements together to refine and improve them further, once we have this structure in place.

With this in mind and as a quick summary, I now set out the working method that I use when editing a new scene from the beginning to end:

1 **First, I organise and watch the rushes.**
I begin the edit by organising my rushes into individual sequences by scene. Once I have some understanding of the narrative line through the film, I then choose a scene to cut first. This is usually something relatively straightforward. I watch the rushes for that scene. I make selections from interviews, actuality, pieces to camera and all other spoken material (with the director if possible), as well as selecting the best of all B-roll.

2 **Next, I establish a structure for the scene.**
I make a new sequence. In that sequence, I block out the dialogue that I have just selected, placing it in an order that is clear and dramatic. I focus on selecting the emotion-rich statements from my contributors in preference to anything excessively expositional. Where needed (and working with the director, if available) I use voiceover to bridge gaps and explain expositional elements of the story. This is now my sync and black assembly for the scene.

I play the assembly back to ensure that it makes clear sense. I remove any material that is repetitive or long-winded and clarify the words where necessary (ensuring the language is as short, simple and conversational as possible). I also try to ensure at this stage that interview and voiceover reveal information step by step and, insofar as possible, in bite-sized chunks with each thought linking to the next.

I am also careful to ensure that this assembly is running at a sensible length, so as not to waste precious edit time cutting material that will likely hit the floor before picture lock. For example, if the final duration of the film is to be sixty minutes and I have twelve primary scenes to cut, each one will be around five minutes. Of course they will each vary a bit, but I know for instance that if my assembly is ten minutes long, then it is probably too long (especially since pictures, music and sound design will open out the sequence further still once it is cut together). If the sequence is too long, I look for appropriate cuts.

3 **I decide, at least initially, where I am likely to need music.**

I establish which parts of the scene will benefit from music. I am looking for emotional hooks in the story to find the right points at which to start and end the music before the next narrative step in the scene begins. Once I have decided this, I will often source the music. I audition tracks against the sync and black assembly in order to get a feel for what is going to work. Once I have found the right track, I lay it into my sync and black sequence timeline.

I then pace out the interview sync, actuality and voiceover around the music, giving breathing space and punctuation where needed. I also cut up and reposition the music as needed to hit the right points of the dialogue.

Initially, I do not spend much time making the timing of the audio perfect, since once I start cutting pictures, the timing of things will probably change again. I just want to know that it's all going to hang together before I start getting into details.

4 **I build some basic sound design.**

I usually start by searching for some general atmospheric sound effects that fit each part of the scene. This could be say, wind or rain, whatever can run under the scene as a general bed. After I have found these, I search for a few more specific sounds that add richness and punctuation (based on my understanding of the pictures I have to support the scene). I place these down into the sequence in the relevant spots.

Now I am increasingly certain how I will cut the pictures, and I am building up a mental picture of how the sequences will work.

5 **Next, I open the assembly sequence that contains my rushes selections for the scene.**

I skim through my selections again and re-familiarise myself with the material. I am looking for the first shot to jump out at me, knowing that this is the shot with which I can begin to cut the sequence. Often this is something close-up, unusual or intriguing; though, if looking for something spectacular, it could be a wide shot. In any event, something that will capture the audience's interest.

Once I have identified the shot, I copy it into the front of my sync and black assembly. From here, I continue to build my sequence of shots, going with whatever catches my eye whilst also thinking about where the narrative needs to go next and building up an impression of the scene as a whole. I trim and adjust each shot as I go in order to work in rhythm with the sound design and music and, where needed, the dialogue.

I will also adjust the music and sound design where necessary to acknowledge significant rhythms and movements in the pictures. I will also source extra sound effects to match up with the visuals where helpful.

6 **I repeat this process.**

Once I have finished cutting a sequence, I begin to cut the next sequence. I ensure that I change the pace and mood of each sequence so that there is always a contrast between each section of my scene. I want to keep the audience engaged and guessing all the way through.

By the end of this process, I will have cut my scene.

7 **I watch everything back.**

Once I have a rough cut for my scene, I watch it back once or twice and make some instinctive adjustments based on my first impressions.

Ideally, I will watch the first cut of each scene with the director. This is the first opportunity to really begin our collaboration and from here on we will work more closely together. After watching the cut, we discuss what we like and what we don't; what we think is working and what is not.

The changes that come about from this first viewing will generally involve clarifying information, removing repetition, adjusting the order of pictures or the timing of music and making small cuts.

8 **I repeat this process for each of the scenes until I have a first rough cut of my film.**

At first, I cut each individual scene in its own timeline so that I have space to play and move elements around freely and without fear of knocking something out of place elsewhere in the edit. Once I have completed a version of the scene, I copy it back to the master edit timeline. After I cut each subsequent new scene, I migrate it back into the master edit timeline, building up a complete first rough cut for the film.

9 I watch the whole film back.

Once I have an initial cut of the whole film, I set about watching it so that I can improve it further. Again, I will watch with the director so that we can discuss our reactions and make a plan to improve the film even more.

In this viewing, I reappraise each scene in the context of the whole. I remind myself of the film's central argument and assess whether it is remaining on message. I am interested in ensuring that each scene contributes to a logical progression of this central argument from beginning to end.

Since I have cut each scene in relative isolation, I am particularly interested in the junctions between scenes. These are the areas that usually require detailed attention and some finesse. Their efficacy can only really be judged by watching the film and understanding its rhythm as a whole.

Watching the film as a whole allows me to understand its overall pacing, where it needs quickening up, where it needs breathing space, where repetition needs excising or where gaps in story logic need support (or removing all together).

Whilst broadly I advocate considering sound before pictures when cutting a sequence, there are instances where we may still wish to think of the pictures first. I find this visual approach particularly useful when I have a large amount of rushes to work with and a multitude of possible sequence configurations. If I connect a few shots in the timeline first, it helps me get a grip of the sequence order and how I might play things in order to tell the best possible story. I will shift these around (aside from the audio structure) adding and remove shots until I feel I have a good working order (without finessing the cut points between shots too much at this stage). Next, if I feel the sequence requires music, I will source this and lay it into the edit and then trim the shots around the music (as well as any dialogue) and adjust further as needed until I have a working sequence. Last of all, I will refine the more detailed points of music and sound effect levels and give the sequence an overall polish.

A further advantage of prioritising pictures over sound at this early stage is that it helps us to focus on the picture sequences' ability to tell their own story (as, ideally, they always should insofar as the rushes allow). The alternative—allowing a particular set of words to dictate the pace—might well skew the whole sequence and create a less than smooth visual story. In any case, written words in the form of voiceover and interview sync can often change multiple times during the edit, so we should always ensure that the picture sequences can hold their own.

Key Point

- While a good film feels whole and cohesive, it is really made up of lots of smaller blocks linked together.

CONCLUSION

> "Film editing is now something almost everyone can do at a simple level and enjoy it, but to take it to a higher level requires the same dedication and persistence that any art form does."
>
> —Walter Murch[1]

While editing does require a reasonable slice of natural talent, I believe that, for the most part, our editorial skills develop with time, practice and patience. I found that to be particularly true in the early stages of my career, and I believe it still. We must practice all we can.

In order to do this most effectively, to begin with at least, we must take every editing job that we can, no matter how trivial it may at first seem. The only way to learn and improve our editing is by applying the skills we have learnt to the practical needs of a defined project and getting the feedback of others. If you are a relative beginner, then at first these projects may be low-paid and may have to be fitted around other work and competing demands on one's time. Live with this, if you can. Find a way to survive and focus on the valuable experience these early opportunities will bring. I took this idea rather to an extreme when I began, working in an edit facility as a junior technician for six months without taking a day off. When I wasn't contracted to work, I was hiding in an edit suite, practising on my own side-projects. I took this as being part of the 'apprenticeship,' and it worked. I was a freelance editor cutting prime-time television by the time I was twenty-two. Some of my friends were still spending their day in their pyjamas. While I do not necessarily recommend this extreme level of commitment, I do believe that hard work is the key and that there is no shortcut to success.

We must also watch as much television and film as we can. I say *film* in the truest sense: cinema as well as documentary. It is through watching the work of others that we can gain inspiration as well as learn new ideas and techniques. All of this will feed in to our own craft. Further, by watching the work of others, we can keep up with the latest trends in filmmaking (and at least understand them, even if we do not wish to copy them ourselves). I find that cinema in particular helps me to discover new and different qualities in filmmaking, as well as dramatic ideas for my documentary projects. So much of what is practiced in cinema can be applied to television documentary making.

I believe, contrary to some, that we must put all of our eggs in one basket if we are to be successful editors. We must throw ourselves into it with all the commitment and energy we can muster. Editing is always challenging and requires intense focus and dedication in order to make progress. The rewards are extraordinary, and they come to those who persist. Editing documentary is a wonderful privilege, and I feel grateful to be where I am today.

If you have cut for a long time, then keep challenging yourself with new and varied projects. This will stretch and continually sharpen your skills. If we cut the same kind of film again and again, we risk regressing since we learn nothing new and become complacent in the knowledge we already have. If you find yourself saying, "This is so easy. I have done it so many times before," or worse, "This is so boring, I can hardly bear to do it again," then you are cutting the wrong film. If I am honest, I should confess that have been in this situation several times myself, and to my knowledge there is just one solution: seek out new challenges and seize new opportunities.

Go where the learning curve is steepest and the expectations are high. This is the only way truly to master the craft and realise one's personal best.

Finally, remember that rules are made to be broken. Whilst I believe we should first learn the rules and how to apply them, as I hope this book has gone some way to explain, once we have begun to master our craft we should feel free to discard them and, by experimenting, discover our own methods and techniques, our own individual voice.

The documentaries of tomorrow will not look like the documentaries of today, and it is experimentation together with a positive attitude towards mistakes and short-term failure which will make them so. I have only to look at my early editing efforts at making skateboarding films to realise just how true this is. I recently watched my first film—a fifteen-minute video ambiguously titled *Sticker Foot* which I edited more than fifteen years ago—and was delighted and embarrassed in equal measure. I took that as a good sign: my early instincts were sound enough, but my skills have progressed enormously in the intervening years.

I would like to think that in another fifteen years I will look back and feel exactly the same about the work I am doing today.

NOTE

1 Michael Wohl, "Interview: Walter Murch." Accessed 23 October, 2016. www.peachpit.com/articles/article.aspx?p=23895

GLOSSARY

180° rule—a cinematography guideline that states that two characters in a scene should maintain the same left/right relationship to one another.

2.5 D—a technique of using still images where each layer can be to cut out and separately manipulated to create movement and perspective, simulating the appearance of 3D. See also *rostrum* and *Ken Burns effect*.

4k—see *UHD*.

A

AAF (advanced authoring format)—a professional file interchange format designed for the post-production industry. AAF allows the cross-platform exchange of both audio and video, abstracting the creative decisions and preserving the references made at source. See also *OMFI* and *XML*.

actuality—a term used in documentary to describe the coverage of real-life events, places and people – often where the subjects are seemingly unaware of the camera's presence.

aerial shot—a shot taken from an airborne device, such as a helicopter or drone. See also *drone shot*.

American Cinema Editors (ACE)—an honorary society of film editors founded in 1950.

anamorphic—the technique of shooting a widescreen picture onto a non-widescreen recording medium. The image is effectively stretched on playback to fit the new aspect ratio. See also *aspect ratio*.

angle (AKA camera angle)—the viewpoint from which the shot is depicted.

animation—the technique of creating the illusion of motion from individual still frames.

archive—film footage, usually of a historical event, brought into the edit from an outside source. It is usually taken from other films or library sources that license its use. See also *stock footage*.

artefact—a visual defect in an image caused by the malfunction or limitations of camera equipment. See also *dropout*.

aspect ratio—the ratio of the width to the height of an image.

assembly—the first unpolished edit of a sequence or scene. See also *rough cut*.

asset—see *file*.

assistant director—see *assistant producer*.

assistant editor—assistant editors are responsible for providing all required logistical assistance to the editor(s). This may include importing new rushes media, making play-outs, and providing other departments with technical information relating to the edit.

assistant producer—the assistant producer will aide the director in all areas of production and post-production of the documentary, from organising filming locations and setting up interview contributors, to arranging logistics and maintaining order on location. In essence, they will fulfill the role of an *assistant director* though, due to the small size of the average documentary crew, may take on significant other responsibilities.

Aston—see *title caption*.

audio mix—the process by which the film's final audio is mastered, usually once the edit is complete. This will include balancing audio levels, adding further sound effects and cleaning up dialogue, as well as determining the panoramic positioning of the sound and adding effects, such as reverb. See also *reverb*.

auteur—a filmmaker, generally a director, who is closely involved in all aspects of the filmmaking process, such as writing, directing, producing and editing.

automatic dialogue replacement (ADR)—the re-recording of dialogue by actors, presenters or other contributors in a sound studio during post-production. This is usually performed to playback of the edited picture in order to match lip movements on screen. Though not commonplace in documentary, when adopted, ADR is used to replace poor quality location sound such as in instances where there is a high level of background noise or to change the delivery of a line. ADR can also be used to insert new lines of dialogue conceived during editing.

axis of action—in continuity editing, the Axis of Action is an imaginary line that passes through the two main actors of a scene, defining the spatial relations between them. When cutting, the camera is not supposed to cross this axis, as it would reverse those spatial relations and potentially disorientate the audience. See also *180° Rule* and *continuity editing*.

B

backlighting—lighting for a shot emanating from behind the subject, causing them to appear as a silhouette.

B camera—a second camera crew, often needed for complicated action sequences or stunts. See also *Second Unit*.

bin a digital container which holds one or more files related to the edit. They work in a similar way to folders, which are commonplace in all computer operating systems.

BITC (burnt in timecode)—an on-screen readable version of the timecode of a clip or sequence. BITC is often used when creating exports of edited sequences for use by other creative contributors to the edit such as composers who rely on accurate references to allow them properly to effect their work.

blocking out—the initial arrangement of spoken rushes materials to structure a sequence or scene using interview clips, actuality and pieces to camera. These sometimes feature voiceover in between to bridge the gaps. At this stage, the scene does not contain any structured picture sequences or music and will have black gaps between the spoken elements. Scenes are blocked out prior to their first assembly. See also *assembly*.

bluescreen—a process whereby interview contributors or other subjects work in front of an evenly lit blue background. The background is then replaced in post production, allowing other footage or computer-generated images to form the background imagery. Similar to *greenscreen*. See also *chroma key*.

boom microphone (AKA boom)—a microphone attached to the end of a long pole. The boom is extended above the contributor who is speaking, outside of the frame. Once in the edit, we often find our rushes will have split audio with boom on one channel and camera on-board audio on another. In these instances, we are usually well advised to use the boom—which generally provides clearer, richer sound.

British Academy of Film and Television Arts (BAFTA)—an independent charity that supports, develops and promotes the art forms of the moving image. As well as hosting a year-round programme of events, BAFTA has a coveted annual award ceremony that recognises excellence in many disciplines including editing.

B-roll—the supporting shots necessary to edit a sequence. These shots can cover a wide number of scenarios, such as: shots around an event picking up details from within the story and the setup of the location, actuality sequences covering live events such as demos or interactions between people, cutaway shots. See also *actuality*, *cutaways* and *general views*.

budget—the money available to produce the film, usually once commissioned and until final completion and broadcast. The costs will include such things as development time, wages of crew and other contributors, equipment hire costs and all post-production expenses, including the editor. Also see *schedule*.

buzz track—see *wild track*.

C

CGI (computer generated imagery)—the use of computer graphics to create or enhance a shot within a film.

channel controller—a senior television executive who is broadly responsible for the network's output.

chroma key—a digital technique that allows for specific colour elements to be replaced with different picture elements. See also *bluescreen*.

cinema verité—a naturalistic style of documentary making in which no directorial control is exerted. Translated literally as *cinema truth*. Films of this genre strive to observe without the audience being aware of the camera's presence and without artificial additions in post-production, such as non-diegetic music, sound effects or voiceover narration. Also see *diegetic sound* and *non-diegetic sound*, *sound effects* and *voiceover*.

cinematographer—see *director of photography*.

clip—a short segment excerpted from a film.

close-up shot (CU)—a feature or part of the subject takes up most of the frame, revealing much detail.

cold open—a short segment of a TV show's action before the title sequence or opening credits are shown. Also see *teaser* and *trailer*.

colour correction (AKA grading, colour timing)—the computer-based process of mastering a film's final pictures, usually once picture lock has been reached. The primary aims of the process are to match colours from shot to shot and camera to camera, as well as giving the scenes a visual style where required. The job is performed by a colourist or colour timer (US). See also *colourist* and *picture lock*.

colourist—the image artist who is responsible for colour correcting the finished film.

commercial music—music produced by a mainstream artist and available through a commercial record label.

commissioning editor—a television executive tasked with deciding which programmes a channel will make and managing that channel's overall programme making budget. Commissioning editors frequently take an executive role in the editing of a film, viewing the film and providing notes where necessary to ensure that the finished film matches the brief. See also *executive producer*.

composer—an individual or group who compose or produce music specially tailored to a film.

compositing—the process of combining visual elements from separate sources into single images (or sequences of images), often to create the illusion that these elements are parts of the same scene.

conform—the technical process of restoring a low-resolution clip or clips to their full quality original-source resolution. The process of conforming will usually take place at the end of the offline edit and before the online edit and grade. See also *Offline Edit*, *Online Edit* and *Grade*.

continuity editing—*continuity editing* refers to a style of editing that maintains a sense of continuous space and time between shots when in fact each were shot out of sequence. This style of editing is very smooth and closely simulates the way in which we usually encounter the physical world.

co-producer—a production company or broadcaster who contributes to the making of a film or series of films, primarily undertaken by another production company or broadcaster. The contribution of the co-producer will usually be financial, contributing to the programme's budget, as well as editorial, having a creative say in how the film is to be made. See *broadcaster* and *production company*.

crosscut (AKA intercut, parallel cut)—two separate sequences and sets of rushes are interwoven. Two separate events are unfolding in parallel action to suggest that the sequences are taking place simultaneously.

crossfade—see *dissolve*.

cut (AKA edit)—the point in a film where one shot instantaneously changes to another. See also *dissolve* and *transition*.

cutaway—a shot designed to cover an undesired picture edit. On their most basic level, this cutaway could be a presenter's facial expressions in response to an interview answer or their hand gestures. See also *B-roll*.

D

depth of field—the distance between the foreground and background elements of a shot giving a focused image.

dialogue editor—a sound engineer who specialises in editing dialogue.

diegetic sound—any sound which is represented as an original source from within the film's world. This can be on or off screen and can consist of dialogue (such as interviews, discussions, interactions or arguments), natural sound (captured in the field) and incidental music (represented as coming from instruments within the story space). See also *non-diegetic sound*.

director—The principal creative individual who guides the making of a documentary. The director usually controls the artistic direction of the film (including its narrative) and manages the required creative talent.

director of photography (DoP)—the chief member of the camera crew who is responsible for the artistic and technical decisions relating to recording a scene in the manner desired by the director.

digital imaging technician (DIT)—a person who provides on-set quality control, image manipulation and technical assistance to the camera department. They may also assist the editor by labelling and ingesting rushes. See also *assistant editor* and *ingest*.

digitise—the process of converting camera rushes from tape (either analogue or digital) into file based media ready to be edited. The term has largely fallen in to disuse with the arrival of file-based image capturing that (already existing in a file-based format) does not require digitisation. See also *ingest*.

director's cut—a version of a film that reflects the director's original intentions.

dissolve—the editing technique of gradually transitioning from one image to another. See also *cut* and *transition*.

documentary—a non-fiction narrative that provides a journalistic record of an event, person or place.

drone shot—photography that utilises a remote-controlled unmanned vehicle to capture high-quality aerial footage. It is generally considered easier and cheaper for many documentary makers to use than the more traditional employment of a helicopter and large film crew.

dropout—a momentary loss of data in an audio or video file either on tape or disk. Dropout can result in momentary audio glitches or pixilation. See also *artefact*.

dub—see *audio mix*.

dubbing mixer (AKA re-recording mixer)—an audio engineer responsible for mixing all of the sound elements (such as dialogue, music, sound effects and voiceover) to create the finished film. See also *foley* and *sound design*.

Dutch Tilt ('on the Dutch')—a shot where the camera is set at an angle so that the horizon is not parallel with the bottom of the frame.

E

editor—the editor works with footage gathered by the director, making selections and combining these shots along with other elements into sequences that ultimately constitute the finished film. The editor's job is both technical and creative: working with images, dialogue, graphics, music, sound effects and other elements to create a compelling and meaningful experience for the audience. The editor is the last person in the filmmaking assembly line and so is the ultimate determinant of what the audience will see in terms of both content and context. The editor is the chief creative partner of the Director. See also *director*.

EDL (edit decision list)—a file used in the post-production process of film editing. An EDL contains a systematic index of reel names and timecode data indicating where each clip can be obtained in order to conform the final edited sequence. In modern editing, EDLs are less frequently used and have been replaced with more sophisticated interchange formats such as XML. See also *AAF, offline edit, OMFI, timecode* and *XML*.

effects—filters created in the edit to change attributes of either picture or sound. These can be obvious, such as inverting the luma (light) of an image to create a negative-like appearance, or less obtrusive such as flipping an image horizontally in the frame. See also *flip* and *luma*.

episodic—a film which juxtaposes story events which have no, or only casual, narrative relations.

establishing shot—a shot that captures the environment or context in which the scene and characters are set. This establisher is usually an extreme wide shot. See also *extreme wide shot*.

executive producer (EP)—A person who helps manage the more business related processes of making a film. They are not usually involved in the technical aspects of the filmmaking process, although they will view the edit and give notes to ensure that the film meets the broadcaster's overall expectations. Typically, an executive producer handles legal issues relating to the film and manages the dialogue between more senior executive stakeholders, such as commissioning editors. See also *commissioning editor, line producer* and *series producer*.

export—the transferring of data from the edit software to another file-based format. This can be a number of different kinds of file for different purposes, such as a single video file for creative partners to view or a multi-track audio file for an audio engineer.

exposition—contextual information necessary to the progression of the storyline.

extreme close-up (ECU)—a very tight shot which shows extreme detail. It is often used to show intense facial expressions as it is too close to show general reactions or emotion.

extreme wide shot (EWS)—a shot that captures the environment or context in which the scene and characters are set from a distanced perspective. The purpose of this shot is to show the audience where the action is taking place. In documentary, this shot is often referred to as a *long shot*.

eye trace—the direction our eyes are naturally taken following action around the frame.

F

fade—a gradual transition from an image to complete blackness (fade out), or vice versa (fade in). See also *dissolve* and *transition*.

field—a field is one of the many still images that are displayed sequentially to create the impression of motion on the screen. Two fields comprise one video frame. See also *interlace*.

file—a stored piece of information within the edit project

final cut—the final edited version of a film. *Final Cut* is also the name of a popular edit software. See also *picture lock*.

fine cut—a polished yet unfinished version of the edited film. See also *assembly* and *rough cut*.

flashback—a scene that breaks the chronology of the main narrative by depicting events that happened in the past. See also *flash-forward*.

flash-cutting—a sequence edited with many quick short shots.

flash-forward—a scene that breaks the chronology of the main narrative by depicting events which happen in the future. See also *flashback*.

flash frame—a very short shot, often just a frame in duration, that appears in a sequence of images. Flash frames are usually unintended either due to an editing mistake or equipment fault.

flip/flop—the reversal of an image across either its vertical (flip) or horizontal axis (flop).

focus—the sharpness of an image.

folder—a digital container that holds one or more files related to the edit. See also *bin*.

foley—the addition of recorded sound effects after the shooting of a film. See also *sound design*.

foley artist—an audio technician who creates foley sound effects. See also *foley*.

frame—an individual still image of the many that compose the moving picture. A frame can also refer to the two-dimensional space in which the moving picture exists.

frame rate (AKA frames per second, FPS)—freeze frame (AKA freeze)—the frequency at which frames in the moving image are displayed. Broadcast television in the UK has a frame rate of 25 frames per second, while in the US the standard is 29.97 frames per second.

freeze frame—a single motionless image extracted from a moving image. See also *still*.

G

goof—see *out-take*.

grade—see *colour correction*.

graphics—the application of computer generated imagery. In documentary television, the term *graphics* refers to simple two-dimensional illustrations such as maps or intricate titles created outside of the edit software. See also *animation*, *compositing* and *visual effects*.

greenscreen—see *bluescreen*.

guide commentary—see *voiceover*.

H

high angle shot—a shot where the camera looks down on the subject from up high. High angle shots can make the subject appear small and vulnerable.

high definition (HD, HDTV)—a system for storing, displaying and transmitting moving images primarily at a resolution of 1920 × 1080, though in some instances 1280 × 720. See also *NTSC*, *PAL*, *SECAM*, *standard definition* and *UHD*.

I

incidental music—see *diegetic sound*.

independent documentary (AKA Indie)—a documentary not produced by a major studio.

ingest—the importing of digital camera assets into the edit software environment ready for the editor to cut. See also *digitise*.

intercut—see *crosscut*.

insert—a small programme package which forms part of a longer film. Inserts are particularly common in television programmes that are shot 'as live.' These films are mainly based in a studio environment and punctuated by small films (inserts) that take the audience outside of the studio space to add variety and dynamism to the programme. *Insert* can also refer to a cutaway shot. See also *cutaway*.

interlace—an image recording and transmission method in which the lines of the image are displayed alternately in two interwoven lines. Interlacing has the effect of doubling the perceived frame rate of the moving image without consuming extra bandwidth, giving a smooth, even motion. Interlacing has gradually been phased out in most broadcast environments with the rise of high-definition file-based recording, being replaced with progressive imaging. Also see *field* and *progressive*.

J

jib shot—a smooth camera movement usually moving up or down, created by placing the camera on the arm of a mechanical crane.

judder—an artefact introduced when images sampled at one frame rate are converted to another. This is particularly noticeable when images are slowed down, thus duplicating the original frames, creating a noticeable jerkiness in the motion of the shot. See also *artefact*.

jump cut—a cut between two shots from the same setup and framing next to each other, creating a noticeable jump in the action. While not always desired or intentional, jump cuts can be used to deliberate effect to give a feeling of quick-fire, disjointed activity.

K

Ken Burns effect—a type of panning and zooming effect created from still images. The name derives from extensive use of the technique by documentarian Ken Burns. See also *rostrum*.

Kuleshov effect—an experiment designed by Lev Kuleshov in which a shot of an expressionless face was cut in alternation with three other shots: a plate of soup, a scantily-clad woman and a child in a coffin. The film was shown to an audience who believed the expression was different each time, that of hunger, desire and grief respectively. In truth, the expression was precisely the same each time. The experiment revealed a human need to identify meaning in the materials we encounter.

L

Law of Two and a Half—a theory of sound design proposed by film editor and sound designer Walter Murch, which states that our brains are able to consciously track only about two and a half individual sound 'layers' at any one time.

letterboxing (AKA letterboxed, letterbox)—the practice of shrinking a film shot in a widescreen aspect ratio (such as 16:9) to a standard-width video format (4:3) just enough so that its entire width appears on-screen without changing the original film's aspect ratio and thus leaving black areas above and below the image. Letterboxing is designed to give audiences who are only able to view the film in a standard-width video format the advantage of seeing the film as originally intended without interfering with their shot composition. The disadvantage is that the entire image must be shrunk, which makes viewing on smaller TVs more difficult.

library music (AKA production music)—music produced by a record label specifically for use in television and film. This music is produced and catalogued to fit a wide variety of different film production needs and is not written specifically for the film in question.

line producer—a producer who is responsible for managing every person and issue during the making of a film. In documentary, line producers are usually only present on larger-scale productions. See also *executive producer*.

list film—see *episodic*.

locator—see *marker*.

long shot—see *extreme wide shot*.

looping—see *automatic dialogue replacement*.

low angle shot—a shot that is positioned anywhere below the eye line. The psychological effect of the shot is to make the character or object look big and powerful.

luminance—the intensity of light emitted from an image.

LUT (look-up table)—the difference in balance needed to colour correct a rushes shot from its original camera source to its finished look. Rushes are often shot with relatively low contrast and colour levels, enabling the colourist latitude to manipulate the images in post-production. This discrepancy between the raw rushes shot and the final corrected shot is its LUT. See also *colour correction*.

M

marker—a way to attach comments to an edit sequence timeline, either for yourself or other editors to read. They appear on a track just like any clip in the sequence and appear as small coloured dots.

master shot—a single shot, usually taken from long range which contains all of the key action for a scene. Master shots are commonly used to cover live events as they ensure that there is adequate coverage of the key action. In addition, closer shots can be photographed and subsequently edited together into a single sequence to make the finished programme.

meta-data—a set of data that describes and gives information about other data. In documentary filmmaking, we receive rushes with some meta-data embedded in the clip, such as its timecode, and often more specific details such the camera used. We can also add meta-data to clips in the edit bin. This information could include the type of shot, lighting conditions, etc. Meta-data is useful for navigating within our project to locate shots, as well as assembling our sequences. See also *timecode*.

mid shot—a shot that captures the subject in more detail than a wide shot, whilst still showing enough for the audience to feel they are seeing the whole subject. This shot is an approximation of how you would see a person 'in the flesh' if you were having a conversation with them.

montage—a film editing technique where rushes from a number of different sources, places and times are cut together into a single sequence. Montage can be used for a number of purposes, such as building a sense of time passing or an accumulated sense of story journey. See also *crosscut*.

motion blur—the streaking effect of rapidly-moving objects in a frame.

Motion Picture Editors Guild (MPEG)—a professional union representing picture, sound, music, assistant, animation, technical directors, librarians and apprentice motion picture editors.

N

non-diegetic sound—any sound recognised as coming from outside the space of the story event. This can consist of: voiceover narration, sound effects and pre-recorded music. See also *diegetic sound*.

non-linear editing—the computer-assisted editing of a film, which is the dominant tool of today. Prior to non-linear editing, films were assembled either in a linear sequence between tapes (known as *tape to tape editing*) or with physical celluloid film.

NTSC (National Television System Committee)—the standard television broadcasting system used in the US, Canada and Japan. The term *NTSC* has largely been phased out with the rise of HD and UHD, which tend to refer to frame rates in more general terms rather than technical standards set by regions of the planet. See also *frame rate*, *PAL* and *SECAM*.

O

offline edit—the principal stage of editing where rushes are assembled into the finished film. In the early days of non-linear editing when storage costs were high and bandwidth was limited, the offline editor would work with low-resolution, heavily compressed media files to assemble the film. Once complete, the finished programme sequence would be moved to a more sophisticated and expensive *Online Edit* to master the film at full resolution. Today it is increasingly common for the offline editor to work with full-resolution rushes. See also *audio mix, colour correction, conform* and *online edit*.

off-speed—see *slow motion*.

OMFI (open media framework interchange)—a file format that aids the exchange of digital media across applications. While the format can carry both audio and video, OMFIs are primarily used in broadcast to transfer audio from an edited sequence to the final audio mix. The primary benefit of an OMFI is its ability to preserve the sequential structure and referencing of the audio media from the source. While OMFI has been the industry standard for around two-decades, it has largely been replaced with *AAF*. See also *AAF* and *audio mix*.

online edit (AKA online)—a technical process performed in the final stage of the documentary post-production. The function of the online edit is to adjust final title captions and ensure that the images in the film meet the broadcaster's technical standards. The online editor's job is predominantly to add technical improvements to the raw footage that the editor has assembled in the offline. See also *offline edit* and *title caption*.

out-take—a shot, sequence or scene not included in the final film, usually because of an on-camera mistake made by the cast or crew. See also *goof*.

over-the shoulder shot—a shot taken from the perspective of the close back of one person facing towards another. This shot helps to establish the position of each person, as if looking at one person from the other's point of view.

P

PAL (phase alternating line)—a standard encoding system for broadcast standard definition television in the UK and much of Europe. See also *high definition, NTSC, SECAM* and *standard definition*.

pan—the action of rotating the camera about its vertical axis. See also tilt.

pan and scan—the technique of resizing and reshaping an image from one format frame size to fit another. In the edit, it is particularly common to pan and scan archive footage of square proportions to fit a widescreen frame. See also *letterboxing*.

parallel narrative—a storytelling mode where multiple characters tell their own story with some common thread between them. Each thread is explored separately and individually though their own scenes, which are then intercut to provide variety, counterpoint and contrast. See also *episodic* and *three-act structure*.

pickup—footage shot after the principle photography of a film is complete. Pickups usually arise out of an editing need; when a new shot is needed to bridge a story gap. Pickups are usually small and relatively minor.

picture in picture—an editing effect where two separate video images are displayed within the frame simultaneously.

picture lock—the final sequence of the film, once all changes and amendments are complete. Once picture locked, the film is ready for final picture grading and audio mixing. See *audio mix* and *colour correction*.

pixilation—the display of a digital image where the individual pixels are apparent to the naked eye of the viewer. See also *artefact* and *dropout*.

point of view (POV)—a camera angle that shows what the subject is looking at from a first-person perspective. It gives the audience a sense of standing in their shoes.

post-production—work performed on a film after filming has taken place. Post-production usually involves editing and can involve colour correction, audio mixing and visual effects. See also *audio mix*, *colour correction*, *pre-production*, *production* and *visual effects*.

pre-production—the planning and arrangements made before the start of filming. In documentary, this generally includes the early research, script editing, setting up of contributors and location scouting. See also *production*.

presenter—the person (often famous and/or well respected) who introduces the items in a programme: either on-screen, in voiceover or both. See also *voiceover*.

previsualization (AKA previz)—an early stage of visual effect creation where we are able to see the first wireframe models of a shot. Previsualization allows the creative team to experiment with different staging and art direction options (such as lighting, camera placement and movement) before committing to the more expensive and time consuming process of rendering the effect in detail.

producer—in British television, a producer handles many of the editorial and creative aspects of the film's post-production. This will include working with the editor to structure the film and write the script. In most instances, the director who shot the film will also produce the film, taking it through post-production to completion. In the US and in other disciplines, a producer will supervise the many organisational aspects of the film's production, such as budget and staff. This managerial role is defined in UK documentary as a production manager. See also production manager.

production—the phase of filmmaking during which the film is shot. Production can also refer to the filmmaking process as a whole. See also pre-production and post-production.

production company—the organisation which is associated with the making of a movie.

production co-ordinator—a member of the production team responsible for practical matters relating to the film, such as hiring equipment, finding accommodation for the cast and crew and ensuring the smooth operation of the post-production team. The production co-ordinator works primarily to the production manager and director. See also director and production manager.

production manager (PM)—a member of the production team who supervises the film's budget, hires the crew and ensures that all departments are doing their respective jobs within the parameters of the budget. See also producer and production co-ordinator.

proxy—a low-bandwidth duplicate of an original rushes media file. Proxies are created for the purpose of offline editing and generally adopted when the bandwidth of the original rushes clip is prohibitively large or too complex for the edit software to work with. See also offline editing.

pull back—a shot where the camera physically moves away or zooms out from the subject to reveal the full context of the scene.

Q

QC (quality control)—the technical assessment of a film made by an operator (though some software solutions now exist) once the final master file or tape has been created and before broadcast. Quality control is designed to catch technical errors in the film, such as high luminance, flash frames or title captions outside the safe area. Virtually all films and television programmes require quality control. See also *flash frame*, *luminance* and *safe area*.

R

reaction shot—a shot which shows a subject's reaction to the contents of the preceding shot.

render—the process of calculating effects in an editing programme to create a composite full-motion version that can play back in real time.

re-recording mixer—see *dubbing mixer*.

researcher—an assistant to the director whose responsibilities include developing the programme idea as well as fact-checking scripts and helping on location.

reverb (AKA reverberation)—an audio effect which prolongs a sound. Reverb can be used to change the perceived size and dynamics of the space in which the sound is projected.

reverse shot—a shot taken at a 180° angle from the preceding shot. In dialogue scenes, reverse-shots are usually edited together by alternating between the two subject's points of view, often over their shoulders. See also *over-the-shoulder shot*.

room tone—the 'silence' recorded at the location of an interview. Room tone allows the editor to smooth the gaps between dialogue edits and ensure that it remains consistent and clean. See also *wild track*.

rostrum—a move in the form of a zoom, tilt, pan, rotation or any perspective shift applied to a still image. See also *Ken Burns effect*.

rough cut—the first unpolished edit of a sequence or scene. The rough cut is the first stage in which the film begins to resemble its final product. See also *assembly* and *fine cut*.

running order—the order of the scenes in a film.

rushes—specially shot camera footage.

S

safe area—the area of the picture that can be guaranteed to be seen on a television screen. Domestic television screens will usually crop a small portion of the outside edge of the recorded image. The use of safe areas ensures that the most important parts of the picture, such as titles and other visual information, can be seen by viewers.

scene—a continuous story block set in a single location or following a particular person or theme.

scene card—a visual method for helping to structure a film. Scene cards are physical cards, and on each card we summarise an individual scene of the film. We can then shuffle these around to find the clearest, most logical and dramatic order to place the scenes in the film. See also *running order*.

schedule—the allotted time to create the documentary film. The schedule is usually broken down in to the key stages of production such as initial script development, production and post-production with targets at each stage, to ensure the film is completed on time and to budget.

score—the original music written to accompany a film.

script—the written version of the film that details the story, setting and dialogue. A documentary script consists of transcribed dialogue and, where needed, voiceover A script will also include a visual treatment for each scene. See also *Shooting Script* and *Transcription*.

SECAM (*Sequential Couleur avec Mémoire*)—a standard encoding system for broadcast standard definition television in France, the Middle East, much of Eastern Europe and parts of Africa. See also *NTSC*, *PAL*, *high definition* and *standard definition*.

second unit—a small camera crew responsible for filming scenes of less importance. See also *B camera*.

sequence—a series of shots that have been edited together to form a story package. Sequences are usually designed to tell their own stories and by way of their arrangement have an apparent beginning, middle and end. See also *montage*.

series—a collection of films put together in episodes, usually linked by a common theme or thesis.

series producer—the individual who oversees the production of a documentary series. The series producer's job is primarily managerial, looking after the team of directors and producers, while they will also have an editorial say on the film's production and ensure that there is continuity and cohesion across each episode. See also *director*, *executive producer* and *producer*.

setup—the positioning of the lights and camera for a specific shot.

shoot—the recording of images onto a camera.

shooting ratio—the difference between the total number of hours of rushes and the amount used in the final film. A film with a shooting ratio of 2:1 would have shot twice as much footage as was used in the film.

shooting script—a script conceived during the early stages of production before the film has been shot. See also *script*.

shot—a continuous uninterrupted series of frames. A film is made of multiple shots put together in sequence.

slow motion (AKA slow-mo, off-speed)—a shot that shows pictures moving at a slower speed than normal. This can be achieved two ways, either by shooting the pictures at a high frame rate on location, known as shooting *off-speed*, or by slowing down the shots during the edit. This latter method is less preferable, since it will produce judder as frames are duplicated to slow down the shot. See also *artefact*.

sound design—the process of sourcing, selecting and manipulating or generating audio elements to create a desired effect or mood.

sound designer—the chief audio engineer responsible for designing and creating the audio components of a film. See also *dubbing mixer*.

sound effect—see *spot effect*.

split-screen—the display of two separate images side by side within the frame. See also *picture in picture*.

split-track—the separation of audio channels to isolate a particular group of sounds. Split-track exports are commonly used while editing to provide a composer with reference visuals from which they can compose. In this instance, the music component of the edited sequence is split onto a separate audio channel of the export (such as the left) from the rest of the mix (on the right), allowing the composer to turn off the music channel at their discretion and recompose to pictures which can be fed back to the edit. See also *Export*.

spot effect—sounds added artificially during post-production. See also *audio mix*, *diegetic sound*, *non-diegetic sound* and *sound design*.

source music—see *diegetic sound*.

standard definition—a system for storing, displaying and transmitting moving images at a resolution of 720 × 576 (in the UK PAL system) and 640 × 480 (in the US NTSC system). Standard definition pictures are significantly lower in resolution than high definition pictures. See also *high definition*, *NTSC*, *PAL*, *SECAM* and *UHD*.

steadicam shot—a smooth camera shot achieved by attaching the camera to a body-mounted mechanical harness.

still—a single static image. See also *freeze frame*.

sting—a short arresting shot or sequence of shots, usually accompanied by sound effects or a short musical phrase, designed as a form of punctuation between scenes or to format a series of programmes.

stock footage—footage brought in from an outside source, usually intended to match and supplement present-day rushes. This may be for reasons of simplicity, budget or time.

storyboard– a sequence of images demonstrating the planned shots for a film production.

subtitles—captions that are superimposed over a film which translate or describe dialogue.

sync and black assembly—the first spine of a scene consisting of interview sync, actuality and voiceover in between. It is a structure made up of spoken elements (much like a basic radio programme), and the only visual element comprises the interview clips and actuality, with empty black spaces in between. See also *assembly*.

sync pull—a concise sequence of clips that contain the most useful spoken parts from an interview or actuality sequence.

synopsis—a brief summary of the plot and characters of a film. A synopsis will usually be written early during the pre-production of a film and prior to the shoot. See also *Treatment*.

T

take—a single continuous recorded version of a particular shot, usually where there is some form of choreographed action or dialogue taking place.

teaser—a short trailer that gives a sneak look at what the film will be like. Trailers are intended to peak an audience's anticipation. See also *trailer*.

temp track—guide music used in a film as a placeholder until it is replaced with a final score, usually that of a composer. See also *composer* and *library music*.

three-act structure—a filmic story structure based around the principle of conflict and resolution. These films are dividend into three parts, or acts: the initial setup of the story and its conflict, the attempts to resolve that conflict and the resolution of that conflict. See also *episodic* and *parallel narrative*.

three-point edit—an editing technique used to insert a clip by setting three edit points: usually an in *or* out point of the source clip, and then in *and* out points in the timeline into which the clip will be inserted.

tilt—the action of rotating a camera either up or down. See also *pan*.

timecode—the internal clock data from the camera itself. It is a twenty-four hour clock based on a number format as 00:00:00:00 (hours:minutes:seconds:frames). For example, 03:01:05:17 would be three hours, one minute, five seconds and seventeen frames. Timecode generally ensures that each frame has its own unique reference, creating a systematic way of identifying the data for each clip and the syncing of materials from different sources.

time lapse—a shooting technique whereby the frequency at which frames are captured is much lower than its playback rate. This creates a form of animation through which we are able to show a process at a speed that would otherwise take a long time to occur. It is the opposite effect to a slow motion clip. See also *slow motion*.

timeline—a graphical depiction of the audio and video tracks sequenced one next to the other in the edit.

title caption—text generated in the edit which appears on-screen in the programme. This text could be (though is not limited to) captions for interview contributors, locations and other expositional information relating to the narrative.

title safe—see *safe area.*

tracking shot—a shot where the camera physically moves alongside the action.

trailer—an advertisement that contains extracts from the film. In television, these short trailers will run between longer scheduled programmes in order to raise audience awareness and stimulate anticipation ahead of the film's broadcast.

transcript—a written version of interviews and other dialogue taken from rushes. Transcripts are a useful time-saving device during the edit, as you do not have to watch through your entire interview in real-time to locate the best parts; instead one is able to skim a paper document.

transition—the editing technique of combining scenes or shots. See also *cut* and *dissolve.*

treatment—a written proposal for a film that summarises the narrative, its characters and each of the major scenes. It is a longer version of a synopsis. See also *synopsis.*

two shot—a shot which fits two people comfortably into the frame, usually side by side. This kind of shot is often used in interviews and is a natural way to introduce two people, establishing the relationship between them.

U

UHD (ultra high-definition)—a system for storing, displaying and transmitting moving images at a resolution four times greater than high definition and above. UHD 4K carries a resolution of 3840 × 2160 and UHD 8K a resolution of 7680 × 4320 pixels. See also *4K, NTSC, PAL, SECAM* and *standard definition.*

V

visual effects—the process by which imagery is created or manipulated during post-production, outside the context of a live action shot. See also *animation, compositing* and *graphics.*

voice of God—a third-person form of narration where the voiceover artist is disembodied and omnipresent, exuding absolute mastery and knowledge and clearly outside the spatial and temporal boundaries of the world the film depicts. See also *voiceover* and *voiceover artist*.

voiceover (AKA VO, Guide Commentary)—a piece of narration within a film where the voiceover artist is not present on-screen. See also *voice of God* and *voiceover artist*.

voiceover artist—the unseen person who does the speaking necessary to create a voiceover.

W

whip pan—a panning movement fast enough to give a blurred image.

wide shot—a shot in which the subject takes up the full frame with their head almost at the top of the frame and their feet at the bottom.

wild track—the recording of ambient sound from location. It is used in the edit to supplement the sound design of the film and in some instances replace the on-camera audio track. See also *room tone* and *sound design*.

wipe—a type of editing transition where one image replaces another by travelling from one side of the frame to the other and delimited by a border. See also *dissolve*, *fade* and *transition*.

working title—the temporary name by which a film is known while it is being made prior to the agreement of its final title.

X

XML (extensible markup language)—a file format that allows the easy interchange of documents between different software packages. XMLs are commonly used in editing for transferring clips and sequences of clips between different creative departments, preserving their source attributes and configuration between them.

Z

zoom shot—a shot in which the focal length of the camera alters either by increasing to magnifying objects (zoom in), or decreasing (zoom out) to widen the angle.

INDEX